CONVERSATIONS WITH MY AGENT

and

SET UP, JOKE, SET UP, JOKE

CONVERSATIONS WITH MY AGENT

and

SET UP, JOKE, SET UP, JOKE

ROB LONG

B L O O M S B U R Y

LONDON · NEW DELHI · NEW YORK · SYDNEY

First published in this format in Great Britain in 2014

Conversations with My Agent was first published in 1996 by Faber and Faber Limited.
Set Up, Joke, Set Up, Joke was first published in 2005 by Bloomsbury Publishing Plc.

Bloomsbury Publishing Plc
50 Bedford Square
London
WC1B 3DP

www.bloomsbury.com

Bloomsbury is a trademark of Bloomsbury Publishing Plc

Bloomsbury Publishing, London, New Delhi, New York and Sydney

A CIP catalogue record for this book is available from the British Library

ISBN 978 1 4088 5582 9

10 9 8 7 6 5 4 3 2 1

Typeset by Hewer Text UK Ltd, Edinburgh

Printed and bound in Great Britain by CPI Group (UK) Ltd, Croydon CR0 4YY

To my parents

This book is half true.

(And so is the one right after it.)

To the reader:

The first book in this two-book compilation, *Conversations with My Agent*, was published in 1996. That should depress me, I suppose – that was a long time ago, and I was a young man then – but on the other hand, in those days writing a book was pretty much the only way to tell a personal story. If I were to start today, I'd probably fritter all of this material away in a series of Tweets or blog posts or status updates or some other form of non-remunerative writing. That's Rule One of being a professional writer: *never* write *anything* for free.

About ten years later, I published the second book, *Set Up, Joke, Set Up, Joke*. It's essentially the same story, just darker and older and slightly more impressionistic. That's Rule Two of being a professional writer: if you're going to tell the same story twice, make sure you punch it up.

Now, ten years after the second book was published, they're both being published together. My plan is to split them up again in ten years and begin the cycle again, creating the illusion of productivity but in fact doing as little writing as possible.

And that's Rule Three.

Contents

Conversations with My Agent   1

Set Up, Joke, Set Up, Joke   171

Acknowledgements   367

CONVERSATIONS
WITH MY AGENT

BOTTOMS UP

Fade in: Spring 1993

I am a co-executive producer of the long-running, phenomenally successful television series *Cheers*. My writing partner, Dan Staley, and I have risen rapidly through the staff-writing ranks since 1990, when we drove on to the Paramount Studios lot in my decrepit rust-heap of a ten-year-old Subaru (bought in New Hampshire for $800; 72,340 miles on the odometer; strange, acrid/sweet smell wafting from the front end during left turns) and began our careers in television. I am a know-it-all twenty-seven-year-old and, from my tiny mountaintop, two years working on *Cheers* meant a lifetime. A career. *Cheers*, the IBM of television shows.

Last December, Ted Danson, star of the show, meal-ticket for hundreds (including me), the man who portrayed Sam Malone – rogue bartender, ladies' man, athlete – decides, 'What the hell, time to move on.'

So I do what you do when you work in Hollywood and something bad happens. I call my agent. An hour or two later, my agent calls back.

CUT TO:

INT. LUCILLE BALL BUILDING, PARAMOUNT STUDIOS – DAY

MY AGENT (*over phone*)   What do you want?

ME   You called me.

MY AGENT   I did?

Pause.

5

SFX: papers rattling.

Oh yeah. Listen, the show's not coming back.

ME   I know.

MY AGENT   I know you know. I was just *reiterating* for convenience. Listen, you and Dan are in a good position right now. There's a lot of heat on [*my agent mentions a famous Hollywood actor*] to do a series with you guys at the helm. There's just one fly in the ointment, but otherwise, you guys should take the meeting.

ME   What's the fly in the ointment?

MY AGENT   What are you talking about?

ME   You said that there's a fly in the ointment.

MY AGENT   There's no fly in the ointment.

ME   But you just said –

MY AGENT   The fly in the ointment is that they need a script by the end of the month.

ME   It's the nineteenth.

MY AGENT   I think your obsession with dates is unhealthy.

ME   Hmmmmm.

MY AGENT   This is grownup time, boys. It's a cold world out there. *Cheers* is *fini*. Think it over.

SFX: click, dial tone.

CUT TO:

A few months later, the script is unwritten, the famous Hollywood actor's interest in us and television is history, and we are contemplating signing a 'development deal' with a large studio. Another conversation with my agent – this one in person.

CUT TO:

EXT. PATIO, ORSO'S RESTAURANT – DAY

MY AGENT   Good news. You've got a pilot commitment from the network.

ME   Wow. Great! What does that mean?

MY AGENT   Nothing.

ME   So why is it good news?

Beat. Rolling eyes in my direction. A 'Why-do-I have-to-put-up-with-this' take to the waiter.

MY AGENT   It's good news because it means you're a player. It means that when you approach the studio for an overall deal, you have something to bring to the party. You can bargain from a position of strength.

ME   Great! Does that mean more money?

MY AGENT   Definitely not. You're in a very weak position.

ME   But I thought you said –

MY AGENT   Look, it's not 1989, okay? There's no development money around. It's 19-fucking–93. Everything's different. I mean, my God, there's no Berlin Wall anymore. Do you want to turn back the clock? Is that it?

ME   But I thought you said –

MY AGENT   Things are tough. What I said was, *Things are tough.*

CUT TO:

A development deal is one of those entertainment industry creations that, when described, sound suspiciously like goofing off. Essentially, the studio agrees to pay a writer a minimum sum, over two years, in the hope that the writer, once the novelty of being paid good money – sometimes, great money – to do absolutely nothing but sit and think wears off, will become so thoroughly disgusted with a workday that begins at eleven in the morning and ends roughly after lunch that he just decides, 'What the hell, I may as well create a hit television show.'

The reason these deals last two years is that it takes at least one year for the writer to become tired of moseying into the office at eleven and skulking out at one-thirty. Or so I'm told. My personal mission, over the next two years, is to test that particular old wives' tale.

The development deal was signed in March 1993 and would take effect on 1 June. Signed, of course, is a not quite accurate term. No piece of paper was actually produced, you see; no contract drawn up. In Hollywood, written – that is to say, legally binding contracts are thought vulgar. In fact, just asking for a written contract is apt to bring out the latent Mafiosi in Industry denizens. 'I'm giving you my word,' their pained expressions seem to say. 'What? You don't *trust* me?'

And besides, the actual document – thirty pages long, perhaps, and cast in language sadistically designed to render generally accepted accounting phrases like 'profit', 'loss' and 'guarantee' into 'numerically impossible', 'insurmountable' and 'yeah, *right*' – is a sheaf of papers that will be tied up in dense, expensive legal wrangling for the duration of the two-year term of the deal itself. And since almost all of the wrangling centers around what the colorful phrasemakers who run things in this town like to call 'the back end' (i.e. syndication money, overseas sales, reruns, spin-offs, video games, toys, whatever), and since any 'back end' money is way, way, way in the fuzzy distance, there's no particular rush to settle the issues once and for all, certainly not for the lawyers, who have second houses to buy and children's tuition to pay for. So the 'back end' just sits there, waiting. The two schools of thought among writers are, one, 'No matter what, *don't let the studio screw you in the back end*'; and two, 'Hey, you may not have a back end at all, so tell the studio, *if you pay me a lot of money now, I'll let you screw me in the back end.*'

So one settles for a 'deal memo' – one sheet of paper that lists the key elements of the deal: money, title, office requirements, parking (I'm serious) and a secretary. In short, the five pillars of happiness for the 818, 213 and 310 telephone area codes.

In fact, the only problem with a development deal is that almost everyone in Hollywood has one. That kind of mitigates its prestige. There is even a sardonic term for it, 'development hell', which refers to the endless round of meetings and adjustments that the studio or the network (or, worst-case scenario, the studio *and* the network) demand of one's original script or idea. Since they've got you for two years, they reckon, they may as well stretch every decision out exactly that long. Thus follows one of the Industry's most immutable rules: time constraints – due to star availability, network time slots, opening dates, whatever – always work in the writer's favor. The less time you have, the less meddlesome the studio and networks can be. Sadly, the reverse is also true.

At the final wrap party for the eleventh and last season of *Cheers*, I was staring blankly into the distance, drink in hand, listening to the band, Los Lobos, play. It was a quiet, reflective moment. I thought about the last few months of the show, the camaraderie, the friendships, the emotion of saying goodbye. And I also thought about the gifts. The crystal beer mugs; the gold pins; the signed Hirschfeld etchings; the director's chairs. And I thought about the parties; not just this one, but the penultimate show party. The bottles of Cristal; the Cohiba Esplendidos; the grilled shrimp; the Beluga. And the media attention. The interviews; the profiles; the constant refrain, in every article, in every interview: '. . . It's the writing, really. It's all in the writing . . .' The actors, who by that time had certainly earned the right (by Hollywood standards, at least) to be cranky and inflexible and insane, were unflappably charming and professional – no diva scenes, no trailer wars. And I realized that not once during my tenure on the show, not once, did the network or the studio say, 'No, you can't do that.' Oh, occasionally they would call and ask us, pretty please, not to say 'up your ass' or 'she's a bitch', and we would always comply. But mostly we were left alone. Nobody thought too much about us. *Cheers* just was.

My thoughts were interrupted by the approach of a studio executive, who also had a drink in his hand. A big drink. And not his first.

'Thinking about the good times?' he asked.

I nodded.

'Think all you want. They're over. You and your partner are just development schmucks now.'

He laughed merrily, clapped me on the back and hustled over to the bar.

Uh oh.

A few days later I got a call from a publicity person. She wanted to know whether I would be attending the party in Boston on 20 May (yes, this would be the third party) to celebrate the broadcast of the final episode. I'm from Boston, you see, and in the show's previous visits – to shoot location footage or bits of exterior scenes – I've always been trotted out by the publicity people as the local boy, available, as they say in the trade, for interviews. That no one, to date, had yet taken them up on the offer made no difference. The publicity person wanted to know if I was going, and would I be available for interviews.

I thought about this: a round trip, first-class ticket; a suite at the Ritz; a generous expense account with which to take all my pals from Boston to dinner. Everything like it was on my previous visits with the show. *Yes*, I thought. *Yes*, I said. *Yes, yes.*

She must have heard me ordering room service in my thoughts.

'This will all be at your own expense, of course. I just wanted to know if you were planning to be there anyway, to visit your parents or something. You could drop by the party, maybe do an interview, whatever. Let me know.'

Click, dial tone.

Uh oh.

10

I spent the first week of May fly-fishing in northern California, and the last three weeks traveling in Hong Kong and Vietnam. On 20 May, the date of the last *Cheers* broadcast, I was in a bar in Halong Bay, in northern Vietnam, drinking Vietnamese beer and eating boiled crab. I went there at my own expense, of course, and did no interviews. I returned home to a different planet. I landed at LAX, headed through customs and was quickly shuttled to the 'guy-in-development' line.

Going out to dinner in Los Angeles, so simple two months before, now became slightly harder. Before, one simply asked a production secretary to call up the restaurant and book a table for seven o'clock. (People eat early in Los Angeles.) No two-days-in-advance; no 'I'll-see-what-I-can-do'; just a crisp, 'No problem. We'll see you at seven o'clock.'

Restaurants always ask for a telephone number to 'confirm your reservation', or so they say. What they really want to do is check up on you, to make sure that you are who you say you are. Otherwise, any old grubby film student can call the Ivy, say, and book a table for Mr Eisner, show up and politely explain, after being seated, that Mr Eisner was unaccountably detained. I know this for a fact – I was once a grubby film student. The important thing, when giving your number, is to use the right three-digit exchange: Paramount is 956, Disney 560, Tri-Star 280, and the others – well, I don't know the others. Ask my production secretary. When I get one. When I get into production.

The point is, when you've got an office and you're in production, you get a table. Otherwise it's, 'We can fit you in at five-forty-five or nine-thirty.'

It's now the beginning of July. My partner and I are beginning the process of developing our own series. We are having dinner with our agent next week. The conversation went something like this:

CUT TO:

INT. MY HOUSE – DAY

MY AGENT (*over phone*)   Let's have dinner. We need to talk.

ME   But we *are* talking.

MY AGENT   I mean in person. I mean in *reality*.

ME   Oh.

MY AGENT   This is development, okay? I'll be in your face until you're in production.

Uh oh.

ME   Um . . . okay. Dinner sounds fine. How about Morton's at eight?

MY AGENT   Good.

ME   I'll call and make the reservation.

MY AGENT   No, *I'll* call and make the reservation. You won't get one.

ME   Wow.

MY AGENT   That's life.

ME   I know. I'm just remembering a time when I could easily get a table, when I was an important person.

MY AGENT   I've got some news for you, sweetheart. You were *never* an important person. The *show* was important. The *show* got the table. You were just some guy.

ME   Wow.

MY AGENT   You want to be important? Create a show of your own. Get a hit on the air. Then you'll be important.

ME   Wow.

MY AGENT   And the only way you get a show on the air is to do a little work. That means showing up before eleven and staying past two. See you at Morton's.

SFX: Click, dial tone.

Uh oh. Uh oh. Uh oh.

FADE OUT.

FLASHBACK

Fade in: September 1988

I drove into Los Angeles for the first time on Labor Day 1988 – the hottest day of the year, air yellowed by smog and ozone, rattling into town from Las Vegas in an eight-year-old Subaru station wagon, my back sticking to the seat – and wanted nothing less than to fall in love with the city at once. I had driven clear across the country – six days of heat and highway – heading for film school at UCLA. I was twenty-three and still young enough to think that one's first glimpse of a city would create a lasting and meaningful impression.

What I glimpsed, coming over the hill on the 10 Freeway, was downtown Los Angeles. Downtown is where banks, investment houses, big accountancies, consultancies, oil company headquarters and other adult-run and managed concerns make their offices. Downtown has nothing to do with the Industry, except in a vaguely peripheral way. In the six years I have lived in Los Angeles, not counting that first passing through, I have been to downtown Los Angeles precisely five times.

Later that week, after I had moved into a small room in a large house in Brentwood, I learned a bit about Los Angeles geography and its complicated class system: Pasadena and San Marino are on the east side of downtown, and have an old money, old line, aristocratic bearing due to the large numbers of East Coast millionaires that moved west in the first half of the century for – get this – the clean, dry air; Hollywood, high above Sunset Boulevard on the hills, is a maze of zigzaggy roads and treacherous turns – deadly to those who enjoy a generous cocktail hour – with nutty, rambling houses peopled by Industry types, rock-star types, foreign types and drug-dealer types; moving south and west, West Hollywood is the center of the gay universe, its surrounding areas the young industry assistant and production assistant ghetto, where all the young aspirants to agent/executive/producerhood live; then Beverly Hills (enough said); then Bel Air (shhh); then across the great divide, the 405 Freeway, heading into the Haute West Side – Brentwood, Pacific Palisades and, where I now reside, Santa Monica – places rich and cool, sophisticated, beach-centered, casual, child-friendly and Industry-heavy with actors, lawyers, television writers, top-line agents, studio executives and doctors. Over the hill is the Valley, which, no matter how big the houses get or how rich the inhabitants, remains utterly and always 'the Valley'.

People who live across the great divide, the 405 Freeway, maintain that the air is smogless (smog, presumably, respectfully clinging to the airspace above the cheaper, less fashionable parts of town) and that the temperature is ten degrees cooler. People who live across the great divide rarely, if ever, venture beyond the border at night. They eat 'in the neighbourhood', which, while it often entails a fifteen- or twenty-minute drive, generously encompasses the Brentwood/Palisades/Santa Monica area as it ruthlessly excludes all points east of the 405. It is not uncommon to see two studio chiefs and a network president or two, all shopping at the Gelson's supermarket in the Palisades on a Saturday, all with children in tow, out of their slick suits and into sweat-pants and T-shirts, all the ruthlessness and power drained from their bodies in the face of four children, three of whom each want a different kind of cereal and one of whom has to go to the bathroom, *Right now, Daddy! Right now!*

So it wasn't my first glimpse of the city that made me think, 'Okay, I can live here.' It was the rich hustle and bustle of Gelson's, the huge tower of perfect oranges and emerald green lettuces, the dazzling six kinds of apples and pears from Washington state (each in its own Styrofoam valise) and the short Mexican man, standing at a huge orange press, ready to squeeze a gallon of fresh orange juice for the asking. (In general, of course, it is the ubiquitous short Mexican man who makes Los Angeles livable in at all: he squeezes the juice, tends the garden, washes and parks the car and clears your table at the restaurant, pretending not to hear you while you complain, 'the illegal immigrants are ruining this city!')

A few days later, I started film school.

CUT TO:

INT. UCLA CLASSROOM – DAY

I file in with two dozen other writer-ish looking folk, all in the Master of Fine Arts (a master's degree! for writing movies!) Screenwriting Program in the School of Theater, Film and Television (notice what comes last?) at UCLA. We take our seats.

The head of the program, a bearded, elfin-looking guy in pressed jeans and a white shirt, greets us.

HEAD OF PROGRAM   *(passing out sheets)*

I'm passing out a list of the scripts I've written, and the subsequent events that led to me getting cheated out of screen credit. The important thing, though, isn't the list of scripts I wrote, but the book I wrote on scriptwriting, which will be the text for this class, and which is available at all of the big bookstores for $22.95. Okay? Buy the book. Class dismissed.

Between now and the middle of December (roughly three and a half months) there are only nine class meetings scheduled, of which this one, lasting all of ten minutes, is the first.

DISSOLVE TO:

INT. UCLA CLASSROOM – DAY

I have been in film school several months. What I have learned is: the first ten pages of a screenplay are important; the teachers in the

19

program who aren't writing movies are writing books about writing movies; two classes a week, an hour and a half apiece, leaves me plenty of free time; and, at this rate, I will never get my MFA.

In this particular class, we are required to present the first ten pages of our current scripts. I have just presented mine.

CLASSMATE #1   I like it.

CLASSMATE #2   Yeah. I like it too.

CLASSMATE #1   But isn't there too much dialogue? I mean, all that talking and talking and talking.

ME   Yeah, I guess it's kind of talky.

CLASSMATE #2   You know what it is? It's *television*. That's what it is.

It takes me quite a long time to realize that this was meant as an insult.

CUT TO:

The truth is, I knew I was writing television all along. But they don't have any television classes at film school. They have classes *about* television ('Mass Media in the Age of Reagan: Plugged In and Tuned Out' and 'Video Texts: MTV, Madonna and Strategies of Discourse'), but they don't have any classes about how to *do* television.

And again, the truth is, I had wanted to do television all along. Dan Staley and I met as Yale undergraduates. We wrote two plays together, mounted two successful productions and had made a rough pact to eventually try our hands at Hollywood. Our timing was a bit off: I am two years younger and so was finishing up my final years at Yale while he was beginning a very promising career in advertising, but other than that we were on track.

Two years before, in my final year in college, we took a stab at sitcom writing. Someone told us (most stories about early failures begin with the words, 'Someone told me . . .') that we needed to write an episode of a then-popular show, *Newhart*, get it to someone in the business, and we'd be flown out to LA and never look back. So we wrote a *Newhart* script, called a 'spec' script for two reasons: one, it's short for 'speculative'; and two, because 'spec' also describes the importance of the authors in the landscape of Hollywood. We polished up the script, sent it to a friend of a friend of a friend – a big-time, old-line TV-writing veteran – and we waited for the messenger to bring us the plane tickets to take us away.

What we got back, instead, was our script. Covered in notes and pencil marks, and, appended to it, this note:

CUT TO:

INSERT SHOT: NOTE ON SCRIPT

Rob's trembling fingers clutch the note. It reads:

> *This is the worst spec script I've ever read in fifteen years of reading these things. You've made the main character totally unlikable!!! There's no moment at the end!!! Terrible. Just terrible.*

CUT TO:

INSERT SHOT: THE SCRIPT

Rob's whitened fingers flip through the pages of the script. He stops at a bit of dialogue; next to it this penciled note:

> *no no no No No NO NO NO!*

CUT TO:

So off I went to film school, to discover, if possible, what we had done wrong. And what I learned was this: for all the hype and fantasy that centers around 'breaking into the business', the simple truth is – for television writing anyway – the more businesslike the approach, the more success it will garner.

The way to do it is simple: write a couple of specs (by that time, Dan and I had our *Newhart* and a *Murphy Brown*), send them to a bunch of agents and wait.

21

Simpler, of course, in one way; much harder in another. The waiting part is easy, though nerve-racking and infuriating. Getting the names of various agents is also trouble-free: a matter of calling up the Writers' Guild and asking for the 'agency department'. It's the writing of the specs that's tricky. It has always amazed me how many people who are trying to break into the business declare, 'Oh, I *know* my stuff is funny – that's not what I'm worried about – it's that I don't know anyone who knows anyone.'

Not so fast, amigo.

CUT TO:

INT. MY (STUDENT) PLACE – DAY

I have identified three agents who specialize in television writers. My writing partner, 3,000 miles away in New York, has decided to trust me in this particular phase of our career.

I am folding up a letter.

CUT TO:

INSERT SHOT: LETTER

My confident fingers hold up the letter for a final inspection. It reads:

Dear [name of agent]
My writing partner, Dan Staley, and I have written two spec scripts for television – a Newhart *and a* Murphy Brown. *We are currently seeking representation.*

Dan and I met as Yale undergraduates and have been writing together ever since. I am an MFA student at the School of Theater, Film and Television at UCLA. Dan is a Clio Award-winning copywriter based in New York.

Would you be interested in reading our work?
I look forward to hearing from you soon.
Sincerely

I sign the letter with a flourish, seal it in an envelope, am about to affix a stamp and then I think better of it. I'll hand-deliver each letter today, right now. My day is free, after all. I do have a class, but that is several weeks away.

CUT TO:

INT. MY (STUDENT) PLACE – DAY

Later that afternoon. I am trying to decide which book to take to the beach, Barbara Tuchman's A Distant Mirror *or Paul Johnson's* Modern Times. (*In my film-school idleness, I have decided to catch up on my serious reading.*)

SFX: phone rings.

I answer it.

ME   Hello?

FEMALE VOICE   Is this Rob Long or Dan Staley?

My heart goes into systolic/diastolic reverse.

ME   This is Rob.

FEMALE VOICE   Hi, this is [*she gives her name*]. I work for [*she gives the name of one of the agents I sent my letter to – a major agent at a big agency*] and we got your letter today, which was strange because it didn't even have a stamp on it – anyway, [*she mentions the agent again*] wants to read your specs.

ME   (*quavery voice, trying to sound cool*)

Great. Super. I'll send them.

FEMALE VOICE   Don't. I'll have a messenger pick them up this afternoon. Okay?

ME   O–

SFX: click, dial tone.

I rush outside with the scripts and sit on the lawn, waiting for the messenger to pick up my future.

23

CUT TO:

INT. MY (STUDENT) PLACE – DAY

The next day. I am giddy with excitement. A big agent is reading our specs. Maybe he's reading them right now and chuckling to himself. Maybe he's going to call to ask me to lunch. Maybe he's assembling a huge team of agents to woo us with promises and flattery.

I get a grip. I think, 'This is Thursday. He's going to wait until the weekend to read the specs, love them and start our careers. So the smart, prudent, careful thing to do is call Dan in New York, tell him to quit his job today, now, fly out here ready to meet this guy Monday morning, Tuesday at the latest.'

I pick up the phone to call Dan.

SFX: doorbell.

I hang up the phone without dialing, cross to the door, open it.

The agency messenger is there. With a package roughly the size of two television scripts. I sign for it. Tear it open right there at the open front door. Our scripts come tumbling out.

With a note.

CUT TO:

INSERT SHOT: NOTE

Trembling fingers. Again. The note reads:

> *Dear Dan and Rob*
> *Thank you very much for the opportunity to read your work. Although the writing has many fine points, I do not feel it is strong enough for me to give you the 100 per cent enthusiasm that you deserve and that this industry requires.*
> *Sincerely*

And below that, the agent's name, typed.

No signature.

And below the typed name:

DICTATED BUT NOT READ

Yikes.

CUT TO:

Soon, after the initial sting wears off, I recover my composure. A friend from film school recommends a sure-fire recovery technique: compile a comprehensive enemies list, placing that agent's name and the name of his assistant at the very top, and swear a solemn vow to one day, one way, wreak a terrible and bloody revenge. I find this suggestion immensely useful, and a good deal cheaper than a huge bottle of bourbon.

One down, two to go. Both of the remaining agents have our scripts. I dig a deep trench, fortify it with ammunition and pointed sticks, and wait.

And, it turns out, wait.

I wait four weeks. Unable to wait any longer, I call Agent #2.

CUT TO:

INT. MY (STUDENT) PLACE – DAY

I am in my pyjamas, on the phone. It is 11 a.m. Since the messengered rejection note, I have let myself fall into some bad habits. I explain who I am to the agent's assistant, memorizing her name for possible future inclusion in my enemies list.

A pause. Suddenly the agent breaks into the conversation.

AGENT'S VOICE   I know why you're calling and I know what you want, but I've been very sick and I just haven't read the material yet, okay? I haven't read it. I've been sick, and I'm building a new house and that's just madness – *Don't ever build a house! Just don't do it!* – and so, no I haven't read them, but yes, I am going to and what was your name again just so I have it?

ME   It's Rob L–

25

AGENT'S VOICE   Oh. Here it is in front of me.

SFX: click, dial tone.

CUT TO:

In the end, of course, that agent's voice became *my* agent's voice. We signed the agency papers in early December 1989. By the middle of January 1990, we were preparing for our first meeting with the then-producers of *Cheers*. From there to a staff writing job on the show, and three years later we were co-executive producers.

It seems fast in retrospect – and it seemed fast then, too – but the lucky break and the fast climb also followed a certain logic: we kept our heads down and wrote our specs; we approached agents methodically; we made the right choice and signed with a no-bullshit, straight-talking agent without a trace of the schmoozer; and we were very, very, very lucky.

My film school career was truncated, of course, which disturbed my mother ('You may need a graduate degree to fall back on.') But, oddly, *didn't* disturb the head of the graduate writing program ('Go! Get out of here! This is a trade school and you've found your trade! Now, git!')

The moment I withdrew from the screenwriting program, I also withdrew from the posture that my time in Los Angeles was a dilettante's adventure. Eighteen months before, I had moved to a new city 3,000 miles from home, to break into a notoriously closed and clannish business. What comforted me when the jitters came, when the what-am-I-doing-here's crept up, was a stack of law school applications by my bedside. Small comfort, I know; and yet there is nothing more wasteful or pathetic than trying to get invited to a party that simply won't have you – and I was terrified that a year or two would tick by, then a third, then a fourth, and still this elusive business would elude me. I'm a fold-your-tent person, a proponent of the strategic surrender and the cutting of losses. By this time, Dan had a thriving career in advertising – he'd won a

26

Clio and a One Show award – and I, on the other hand, had an eight year-old Subaru burning oil every time it idled.

I comforted myself with denial and self-delusion. I told myself that this was a phase, a lark, a quick shot and then grow-up time. It's impossible to fail at something to which you've applied the most desultory and disingenuous effort. The only way to avoid frostbite and altitude sickness is not to try to climb the mountain in the first place. Leaving UCLA, I went immediately from 'student' – a nice, respectable status – to 'aspirant', or, worse, 'wannabe'. Had I thought about it at the time, *really* thought about it, right now I'd be a third-year associate at a large New York law firm, wondering if the senior partner thinks my neckties are too flashy.

FADE OUT.

DEVELOPMENT, HEAVEN AND HELL

Fade in: Summer 1993

Comedy writers have a long-running debate, one that lasts through bottles of wine and into the early morning hours. It is known as the Mickey Mouse Question, and it goes like this. Mickey Mouse is not a funny character. He neither tells jokes nor does anything funny, he has no point of view, no real character, and his girlfriend is an uptight bore. Bugs Bunny, on the other hand, is a brilliantly inventive comic genius, sharp-witted, physically agile, a fearless wise-guy who thinks nothing of donning a dress, producing an anvil out of thin air, kissing his enemy on the lips and, in the face of death and torture, calling out a cheery, 'What's up, Doc?' Bugs is much funnier than Mickey, no contest. Why, then, is Mickey the billionaire movie star? People don't seem to be able to get their fill of that little rat, him with his squeaky voice and gee-whiz attitude. Mickey is completely inoffensive, involved in a long-term, caring relationship, optimistic. Bugs is the opposite: he's a wild man with a raging carrot-dependency, big with the exploding props and the verbal abuse, and one of these days he's going to go over the edge. Mickey never will. He and his girlfriend will spend their days in inoffensive, unfunny bliss. But it is Bugs who makes us laugh, and isn't that, after all, enough?

Creating a television sit-com means choosing between Mickey and Bugs, between a universe of likable, not terribly funny people and a universe of vaguely disturbing, very funny people. Networks tend, on the whole, not to like funny characters very much. If they had their choice, every sit-com would be a family or group of

Mickeys, with maybe a Bugs living next door. Writers, unfortunately, on the whole prefer a big group of Bugses with a Mickey around to say things like, 'What's going on here? Are you all out of your minds?'

The networks like things likable. The writer likes things funny. Sometimes – rarely – these two forces mesh and create a funny, likable show. Sometimes – usually – the network gets its way and another show hits the airwaves set in the Village of the Happy People, where characters learn things and share and hug and make everyone sick. And sometimes – with roughly the frequency of Halley's Comet – something slips through the sticky machine and comes out both funny, likable, sharp and new. *Seinfeld*, say. Or *Cheers*.

Cheers had only one guiding principle: be funny. When in doubt, be funny. Don't go too long without a laugh. The underlying philosophy of this attitude is a kind of humility: the audience, more or less, was as intelligent as we were. They had roughly the same sense of humor, had roughly the same level of cultural awareness, were as loath to be preached to as we were. As difficult as it is for a cultural élitist – a writer! an educated person! – to admit, we were no smarter than our audience. And this, I think, is what ensnared the intellectuals into the *Cheers* trap – and make no mistake, *Cheers* was an officially approved show for highbrows and smarty-pants. We lured them into the tent with intellectual references, a few Kierkegaard jokes, a pun here or there, but what kept them watching was what kept the rest of the audience watching: we did a show about a bunch of people who hung out in a bar, a guy who chases women, another guy who talks all the time, and another guy who drinks beer after beer after beer with remorseless, unmitigated monotony.

This is what Dan and I were after; something funny, something new, something Bugs-like. Since we were then – sadly, no longer – in our twenties, it made sense to create a show about people we might know, about friends we might have and about experiences we might remember.

It was the height of the 'Generation X' obsession, and though we were technically members of that benighted demographic, we knew no one with a goatee, no slacker, no plaid shirt in a bad band. The people we knew who were between twenty and thirty all had jobs and bills and unfulfilled longings. The Gen-Xers on television and in movies all seemed like they were written by middle-aged people trying desperately to be hip. They reminded us of old Bob Hope skits, when he would don a hippie wig and love beads and prance around shouting 'Groovy, baby!'

CUT TO:

INT. OUR OFFICE – DAY

SFX: phone rings.

MY AGENT (*over phone*)   How's development?

ME   It's okay. We have an idea for a show.

MY AGENT   Which is?

ME   I think we'd rather wait and clarify it a bit before we tell it.

MY AGENT   Are you familiar with the term 'passive aggressive'? That's what I think you're being right now.

ME   It's just that –

MY AGENT   I'm not just an agent, you know. I'm a *resource*.

ME   I know, but –

MY AGENT   Every other client I have tells me their ideas. Not you two. You two have some kind of an insane secrets club. Okay, fine.

ME   Look, it's not much of an idea. It's about five guys in their twenties who share an apartment.

MY AGENT   I love it. Gen X, right?

ME   Well, not –

MY AGENT   Grunge, hanging around, environmentalism, but with an edge. I love it.

ME   Actually, we're going for something slightly more realistic.

MY AGENT   Like that MTV thing?

ME   Realer.

MY AGENT   Realer? How realer? I mean, on that MTV thing, they show kids *in the bathroom*. How much realer do you want to get?

ME   We want to do a show about what it's really like to get out of college and face the world and be broke and struggle in your job and worry about the future. We don't want to do something bubblegum nice and we don't want to do something self-consciously Generation X-y. That's just hype and media nonsense. Most people in their twenties are working at jobs, paying off student loans, just trying to face an uncertain future.

MY AGENT   News flash: that ain't funny.

ME   It could be.

MY AGENT   What's it going to be like?

ME   What do you mean, what's it going to be like? It's not going to be like anything. It's going to be like us. It's going to be like our friends.

A long pause.

It's going to be a cross between *Taxi* and *Bosom Buddies*.

MY AGENT   Oh. Oh! OH! I get it! I love it! Put in a 'nice guy' character. And make sure the rest of them are all likable.

FADE OUT.

STUDIO FIREPOWER

Fade in: September 1993

Henry Kissinger, the Mike Ovitz of diplomats, once defended Richard Nixon by saying that no matter how paranoid a person becomes, it must be remembered that 'even paranoids have real enemies'.

In Hollywood, of course, paranoid behavior is so prevalent, so hysterical and, in the end, so justified that it hardly needs defending. The cringing, wheedling, red-eyed panic-meister who works in the front office of a big studio is not paranoid for nothing. The reason he chain-smokes and sweats up the sheets and sees enemies around every corner plotting his departure is simple to understand: he indeed has enemies, they are in fact around every corner, and he's right, they want him out.

If he's a valuable employer, if he's respected among his peers, the trade paper *Variety* will proclaim the next day that he 'ankled' – left of his own accord, negotiated his own severance package, in general, behaved like a gentleman. If not, he will be described as 'axed' – studio security was called, he was escorted off the lot. In a genteel town like this one, of course, people are rarely axed. Mostly they ankle. But there is no shame in being axed, or ankling when everyone knows it was really an axing. The only shame lies in the severance package, or lack of it. Ideally, after a spectacularly unsuccessful two or three years of studio-chiefing, with an after-tax loss in the hundreds and millions of dollars, after a slew of bad-to-mediocre pictures, including one or two high-profile outright bombs, a decent studio executive should expect to be axed (though reported as ankled in the trades) with a hefty multi-million-dollar settlement. Otherwise, people might say he didn't know how to do his job.

Sad to say, the television side of the business is tougher. TV is the smarter, savvier, plain-faced little sister to the feature film's glamorous, popular, slutty lap dancer. The older girl is a wild time. She's sexy and great looking, but she's a heavy spender and a little bit stupid. The younger girl wears glasses, can read a financial statement and is Daddy's favorite. Daddy, in this tortured analogy, represents the moneybags financiers – your Bronfmans, your Redstones, your Allens – who can spot a money tree a mile away. And money isn't growing on a feature film that cost him $60 million to make and $15 million to promote. It's growing on a tree called *Baywatch* or *Home Improvements* or *Friends*. What is the Information Superhighway, after all, but better and faster TV? And what could be more primitive, more backward, more *Luddite* than turning out the lights and making shadows on a screen?

Who do *you* want to take to dinner? Don't for a minute think that the younger, plainer, smarter sister wouldn't trade it all – her smarts, her self-respect, her money – for one chance at glamour and sex. Most TV writers actually aspire to work in features for less money and almost no power. And ordinarily smart money men running smart companies (think Seagram, and the Japanese before them, and Crédit Lyonnais before *them*, and Coca-Cola before *them*, and TransAmerica before *them*) trip over themselves to get into a business in which employees actually compete to spend money. Their money. And when these movies don't do well at the box office – or, more realistically, do well the first weekend after multi-millions are spent on bus cards and billboards and radio spots and TV commercials and the *next* weekend sees a 30 per cent drop-off – well, what's the excuse? We didn't spend *enough*. We dropped only $15 million for promotion. We should have dumped $20, $30, hell – $50 million. And you'll have to pay me more next time, by the way. And I want a piece of the *un*adjusted gross from dollar one. We're partners in success. In failure, go fuck yourself.

She's a bitch, the feature business.

Little old me, all I want is a couple of shows on the air. After that, I promise to take my sack of money home.

CUT TO:

INT. OUR OFFICE – DAY

SFX: phone rings.

MY AGENT (*voice-over*)   I have good news and bad news.

ME   What's the bad news?

MY AGENT   Don't you want to hear the good news first?

ME   No, actually. I'd like to hear the bad news.

MY AGENT   That's not healthy. You should want to hear the good news.

ME   Okay, okay. What's the good news?

MY AGENT   Sure you want to hear?

ME (*slowly*)   Yes.

MY AGENT   The good news is that I've finally managed to shake off this horrible cold.

ME   Uh huh. And what's the bad news?

MY AGENT   It's not actually that bad. [*My agent mentions the name of an important executive at our studio*] is out!

ME   What?

MY AGENT   He's out. Gone.

ME   Ankled or axed?

MY AGENT   What?

ME   You know . . . like in *Variety?* Is he ankling or has he been axed?

MY AGENT   What the hell are you talking about? What kind of crap is that – ankled or axed? He's been *fired*, okay? *He's out!*

ME   Hmmm.

MY AGENT   I don't think you understand the problem here. The man who was most responsible for bringing you to this studio, the man you have an *important relationship* with, is no longer there. You are under very different auspices, my friend. It behoves you to establish favored-nation status with his replacement.

ME   Who is his replacement?

MY AGENT   Let me call you back.

SFX: click, dial tone.

CUT TO:

I know my agent is serious when I hear that strange, elaborate, nutty diction. I am worried. This industry runs on relationships, it is true. If the guys in the front office like you, you get extra perks: a shower in your office, say, or aggressive support when dealing with the television networks. But when someone new comes in, he or she brings in a new team, to whom you are nothing but a figure on a spreadsheet, an unproductive asset burning up overhead expenses.

The studio, though it has agreed to pay you a minimum sum over two years, nevertheless expects you to earn that money. And when a new guy comes in, his first priority is to solidify his power base by a), firing a lot of underlings and hiring news ones; and b), making trouble for people like me who have deals that pre-date his administration.

CUT TO:

INT. OUR OFFICE – DAY (MOMENTS LATER)

INTERCUT WITH:

INT. MY AGENT'S OFFICE – DAY

MY AGENT   (*into phone*)

I know who the new person is at your studio.

ME   Who is it?

My agent mentions someone I've never heard of. This isn't hard, as I've really never heard of most people who work in this business.

Who's that?

MY AGENT   Excuse me? *Hellooo?* Are you in this business?

ME   Sorry. I've never heard of the guy.

MY AGENT   It doesn't matter. What matters is that *I* know who he is.

ME   And do you?

MY AGENT   You're darn right I know him. *We have a relationship.* I told you this was good news.

CUT TO:

Armed with this good news, Dan and I are ready to approach our newly installed studio bosses with a television series idea. We are ready to 'pitch'. The way it works is this. The studio pays us to think up an idea. We pitch the idea to the studio development people. If they like it, we then go to a television network (for us, one network in particular; we have a *relationship* with that one, you see). If the network likes it, we write the first, or pilot, script. If they like the script, we cast and shoot the pilot. If they like the pilot, we're on the air. If we're on the air, we get to order hugely expensive lunches from hugely expensive restaurants and no one from studio accounting calls us.

It never works that way. It works this way. The studio isn't really sure about the idea, but goes along with it out of fear. The network demands changes. In one frenzied, short-tempered week, a pilot is shot. By the time the prime-time schedule is announced, sometime in May, you no longer care that the network is not selecting your show for its fall schedule.

All that matters, really, is survival. Maybe your little show will be picked up by the network for its mid-season schedule, as a replacement for one of the shows that the network currently professes absolute confidence in. Maybe you will sell your show to another network. Or, maybe, you just take a few months off and come back fresh for mid-season, or next season, or something. You have failed, but in that inexorable, peculiar, nerve-racking Hollywood way, you have failed upwards.

It is the latter scenario, I am certain, that is in my personal Tarot cards, and I am anxious to be on my journey. Dan and I are preparing our pitch to the studio.

CUT TO:

INT. OUR OFFICE – DAY

INTERCUT WITH:

EXT. MY AGENT IN A LEXUS, DRIVING ALONG SUNSET BOULEVARD – DAY

MY AGENT   I'm going over Coldwater Canyon, so this could get scratchy.

ME   Okay.

MY AGENT   [*Inaudible*] . . .

ME   What?

MY AGENT   [*Inaudible*] . . . idea?

ME   What?

MY AGENT   [*Inaudible*] . . . your pitch for Chrissakes . . . don't . . . [*inaudible*] . . . around, you know?

ME   I can't understand you. Your signal is breaking up. Why do you insist on having important conversations on that damn thing when you're going over the hill? I'll be in the office all day. Call me when you get to a real phone.

I am about to hang up when the static suddenly clears.

MY AGENT   You don't have to get so huffy.

ME   Well, I –

MY AGENT   None of my other clients yells at me, you know.

ME   I'm sorry.

MY AGENT (*in a tiny voice*)   I have feelings too, you know.

ME   I'm sorry.

MY AGENT   Forget it! It never happened. You have a bad, out-of-control temper. You fly into demonic rages. *Okay.*

ME   But –

MY AGENT   You're under a lot of stress. Everyone at the studio is new, you don't know anyone in the development office, the studio is cutting back on their half-hour comedy production and I'm sure you've heard the big rumors.

ME   What rumors?

MY AGENT   You haven't heard?

ME   No. What's going on?

MY AGENT   Brace yourself. [*Inaudible*] . . . in New York tomorrow. Which means [*inaudible*] . . . a tiny window of opportunity. [*Inaudible*] . . . does not look good.

SFX: static, crackle, then nothing.

CUT TO:

Later that day I discover what the rumor is. The first thing I learn is that it is not a rumor; it is the truth. Several bidders are attempting to buy the studio where I work. I learn this at lunch with a bunch of other writers. A discussion of the various possibilities, and the future of our business, ensues.

CUT TO:

EXT. PATIO, COLUMBIA BAR & GRILL – DAY

The Columbia Bar & Grill – or 'C. Bag', as we used to call it – is no longer in business – or, as a friend of mine puts it, 'no longer in the business of feeding people in the Business'. Its demise was a shock to most of us. Tucked in on the corner of Sunset and Gower, it was the TV industry's daytime commissary. On the ground floor of the Sunset-Gower Studios, up the street from Paramount, a ten-minute drive from Burbank – going out to lunch to C. Bag was almost like not going out at all, because everyone you were avoiding was there, eating a scallop-and-arugula salad, and making the international sign for 'I'll call you': left hand in a fist pressed against the cheek, right index finger pointing at the designated callee.

Writers in development go out to lunch. Writers in production order in. Writers in development tend to eat together, providing all the perks of being in production (the laughs, the gossip, the bitter complaining) without the ghastly drawbacks (the hours, the actors, the network executives).

Today, we are talking about the latest takeover attempt of our studio.

WRITER #1 It's going to be the phone company, boys. The phone company is going to own our asses by Thanksgiving. I read it today in the 'Calendar' section of the *Times*.

WRITER #3 Which *Times?*

WRITER #1 LA.

WRITER #3 That's your problem right there. In the *New York Times*, it's very clearly going to be a consortium of cable companies.

WRITER #2 No way. That shopping network thing. That's what the *Journal* says.

WRITER #3 You read the *Wall Street Journal?*

WRITER #2 No. A guy on CNBC was talking about the article.

44

WRITER #3   I'm telling you: a big cable company.

ME   I don't get it. Why would anyone want to own a giant studio? How many companies have lost their shirts in this business?

WRITER #1   You're forgetting: studios have valuable assets.

ME   Such as?

WRITER #1   Um . . .

WRITER #2   Such as us! We're assets!

ME   We are?

WRITER #3   He's right! We are! Well, not *us personally*, but the shows we create and work on make millions and millions.

ME   So some guy is willing to spend $8 *billion* for *us?*

WRITER #2   Essentially.

ME   Boy. Wait till he finds out how long we take for lunch.

WRITER #4   You guys are missing the point. We as writers are under siege. The sanctity of the written word is being diminished every day. With interactive television, the art of storytelling will gradually fade away. And virtual reality will eliminate the need for any kind of writerly activity. It's scary. We're the last practitioners of our art form. We're the last artists of the written word. As keepers of the ancient troubadour's art, we should be more vigilant about the growing corporatism and coarsening of what is, in fact, the most profoundly humanistic activity ever – man's highest achievement.

ME   What's your new show about again?

WRITER #4   A little black boy who's adopted by an old lady with superpowers. And who knows? With all this upheaval, I may never see a dime of syndication money.

WRITER #2   Jesus, really?

WRITER #4   *Really.*

CUT TO:

Later that day, it's time for the pitch. My agent drops by the office before the meeting, in what is billed as a casual 'I-was-on-the-lot-for-other-business-thought-I'd-drop-by' drop-by, but is, in fact, an 'I'm-coming-to-the-pitch-with-you-whether-you-like-it-or-not' drop-by.

Our agent comes to meetings with us. At first we thought this was standard operating procedure, until an older, wiser, more experienced writer took us aside and said, 'You know, having your agent come to meetings and pitches makes you look like the two biggest *wusses* in town.'

So we're trying to wean ourselves from agent-in-towism. Today, though, is not the day to make our stand. This is our first meeting with the new management of the studio – new, that is, for now; the buy-out still hasn't taken place, so there's a *new* new management somewhere in the wings – and it's important that we get them enthusiastically behind our sit-com idea.

CUT TO:

EXT. STUDIO LOT – DAY

We walk with our agent across the lot to the administration building.

MY AGENT   Be very up, okay? Really sell. Put your brain in come-and-get-me mode. Don't just sit there like you do in my office. Come alive.

ME   I'm not going to hop around the room and humiliate myself.

MY AGENT   Who's telling you to do that? Did I say do that? I never said, 'Hop around the room.' I said, 'Be active. Move around the room,' is what I said.

ME   Okay.

MY AGENT   But hopping can be effective, since you brought it up. It gets their attention.

ME   Shouldn't the fact that they're paying us a lot of money to come up with ideas be enough? Shouldn't simple business acumen be enough of a motivator? They've paid us to do a job and we've done it. Why should we have to sell ourselves? We're already bought.

My agent grabs my arm and pulls me away from the administration building door.

MY AGENT   Let's reschedule. You're in no mood to pitch and you're babbling, besides.

CUT TO:

So we reschedule. The pitch meeting is set for next week. The studio takeover battle continues to rage. The stock has hit a high of $80 per share. Whoever wins, it is clear that there will be sweeping changes at the top.

CUT TO:

INT. OUR OFFICE – DAY

SFX: phone rings.

I answer.

INTERCUT WITH:

INT. MY AGENT'S OFFICE – DAY

SFX: CNBC Financial News on television in background.

MY AGENT   It's 'good news, bad news' time. I'll give you the bad first, because you're so pessimistic. The development guy at your studio is out.

ME   Wow.

MY AGENT   He was an idiot, anyway. It's actually good that he's out. But it means that your pitch meeting is postponed until his replacement is settled.

47

ME   Who's the replacement?

MY AGENT   What does it matter? You don't know anyone anyway. But actually, he's a writer – a *former* writer, I should say – so you may know him. Did the pilot about the black kid and the old lady who can fly and read minds. It was a cute show. The network just didn't buy it, though. It was too *edgy*, you know?

ME   So what's the good news?

MY AGENT   The good news is that your studio's stock just hit $80 per share.

ME   Why is that good news?

MY AGENT   It's good news if you bought at $25.

ME   Yeah, but I didn't.

MY AGENT   Yeah, but I *did*.

FADE OUT.

SECRET AGENT

Fade in: October 1993

In Vietnam, in the summer, the heat can get so intense that in the city markets, the caged monkeys slowly go bonkers. Their tiny brains, genetically designed for a leafy, jungle climate, quite literally cook in the hot city sun. As they turn alternatively catatonic and mad, the monkeys begin to attack each other with tremendous violence. The few that manage to survive their time in the cages can then look forward to the relative peace and tranquillity of being eaten for dinner.

Los Angeles in October is a bit like that, except for the smell. October is the month of heatwaves and smog alerts and hellish, apocalyptic canyon fires. The Santa Ana winds – hot, dry, desert winds that whip through the city for days on end – work their October magic. The final box-office figures for the summer movies come rolling in, and with them the ritual movie-studio firings and resignations and 'seeking other creative venues' memos: something like, 'It is with great regret that I accept the resignation of Hapless Studio Executive. In his eighteen months with our studio, Hapless has made invaluable contributions and will be missed. We wish him great success as he seeks other creative venues. Signed, Triumphant Ruthless Shark.'

Just as the tension eases on the feature-film side of the studio lot, it heats up considerably on the television side. About the third week in September, the television networks première their fall schedules, in what must rate as one of the finest displays of corporate incompetence in the world. By the end of October most of them have failed, and the ones that had been touted as surefire hits – pegged by Madison Avenue advertising agencies and network bosses as absolutely-no-doubt-about-it-go-ahead-and-spend-the-money-hits – well, those are dead by 1 October.

Happily, we're not on the air. For the first time in our short careers, the fall television schedules are an abstraction and we view them with a certain uninterested gaze.

It's a curious attitude switch: with a show on the air, you become a tireless handicapper – 'If they move *The Nanny* to Wednesday, and shift us to Monday, we get the football lead-in, which is our demo . . . look at our numbers in Minneapolis!' – and an even more desperate excuse-monger – 'Of *course* we dropped six points. We were up against live hurricane coverage in Dallas, and they don't promote us, and our lead-in is weak, and the numbers are wrong!'

Without, as they say in Texas, 'a dog in the fight', the whole business seems like an interesting chess game. Kind of like semi-retirement.

Sadly, it's a short-lived retirement. By mid-October, we've pitched our series idea to the studio and are polishing up the concept before we take it to the network, billed in a way guaranteed to create really rotten karma: 'the guys who ran *Cheers* have an idea for a new show!'

CUT TO:

INT. OUR OFFICE – DAY

We're sitting in the large room of our bungalow on the lot. On the wall, a blank greaseboard, save for one word written in large green letters: 'Characters??'

SFX: phone rings.

INTERCUT WITH:

EXT. LAX AIRPORT – DAY

My agent races through the terminal, on a cellular phone.

MY AGENT   How's the thinking coming along?

ME   Fine, I guess. A little slow, maybe.

MY AGENT   Slow? Slow? Who cares how long it takes? Listen, don't let them rush you. You're creative. You need time. Your idea is solid, and terrific, and funny, and you shouldn't worry about some studio geek's idea of a schedule, okay? *Okay?*

ME   Okay.

MY AGENT   I'm going to be out of town for a week or so.

ME   Oh. Okay. What if we go to the network before you get back?

MY AGENT   Won't happen.

ME   How do you know?

MY AGENT   Because I'm going to be *out of town*. They know that. You know that. We'll all start talking again when I get back. *Okay?*

ME   Okay. Fine. Maybe I'll get out of town for a week or so, too.

MY AGENT   Forget about it. You should be thinking about what you're going to do if the network passes on your idea. I mean, let's be honest here: it's a flimsy premise and a longshot at best.

ME   Wha –

MY AGENT   No time to talk, tiger. They're boarding.

SFX: static

FLIGHT ATTENDANT (*offscreen*)   We'd like to board our First Class passengers to the Big Island of Hawaii –

SFX: static, click

53

CUT TO:

Perhaps it isn't the smoggy air, or the 90 per cent humidity, or the blood-boiling temperatures that drives those monkeys to madness and violence. Perhaps they all have agents.

So I sit in my office, drinking from a tiny bottle of French mineral water, thinking about the future. The newspaper and the trade papers have been read, lunch has been ordered and eaten, so my plan is to do a quick bit of thinking about the future, and then home by three or so. Another phone call, this one, happily, not from my agent, but from a friend of mine from film school. This friend now works for a rival agent at an extremely aggressive, extremely cut-throat young agency.

CUT TO:

INT. OUR OFFICE – DAY

INTERCUT WITH:

INT. MY FRIEND'S BOSS'S OFFICE – DAY

My friend is on the speaker phone. His boss is staring at him while he's talking to me, all the while fiddling with two steel balls.

MY FRIEND   How's it going?

ME   Fine. As a matter of fact –

MY FRIEND   Look, I'll cut to the chase here. I know you're busy. Are you happy with your agent?

ME   That's an awfully complicated question.

MY FRIEND   Because I'll be honest with you, my boss would really like to sign you and Dan. I mean, really. Really, really, really. How about breakfast tomorrow at nine. No, ten. Ten. The Four Seasons at ten. Okay?

ME   Um . . .

MY FRIEND   C'mon! You guys have a big future! The whole town is talking about your new series idea! Personally, I *love* it.

54

I mean *love*, like I'm *in love with it.*

I glance up at the greaseboard. Beneath 'Characters??' is scrawled: 'Story??'

ME   What, specifically, do you love about it?

MY FRIEND   The milieu.

ME   The milieu. Hmmmm.

MY FRIEND   C'mon! Have breakfast! [*In a low voice*] It'll really raise my stock around here . . . okay? Be a pal . . .

ME   Well, you see –

MY FRIEND   Perfect. See you there.

This time no click, no dial tone. Instead, I hear my friend shouting to his secretary to get the head of one of the networks on the line.

Maris, get me Jeff Sagan–

SFX: now I hear the click, now the dial tone.

CUT TO:

My friend has done this purposely to impress me. He wants me to know that he calls people like Jeff Sagansky – then the head of CBS – on the telephone. What he doesn't realize is that to me, and to almost every other writer in television, talking to network presidents on the telephone more often than not comes under the category of Grim Duty, not Bit of Sunshine in a Dark World.

But because I am weak and easily pushed around, I arrive at the Four Seasons promptly at ten, convinced that I'm about to meet with an agent I have no intention of signing with, and to eat a breakfast I have no intention of paying for.

To be honest, a part of me is curious. And an even bigger part of me is willing to entertain the possibility of switching agents. The fellow I'm about to meet is a dynamic powerhouse. He's famous for his excellent client list – as is my agent – and for his ability to get the very best deal for his clients – as is my agent. He's also deferential, quiet and a good listener. My agent falls somewhat short on those particular points.

The Four Seasons Hotel in Beverly Hills is the only place in town to have a private meal that is nonetheless seen and noted by everyone in town. It's the home of the breakfast meeting. If my agent were not in town, I would have insisted that we meet somewhere else. Meeting another agent for breakfast at the Four Seasons is as discreet as, well, meeting another woman for breakfast at the Four Seasons. It implies a certain willingness to go public, an indifferent attitude.

CUT TO:

INT. FOUR SEASONS HOTEL – DAY

I walk in, give my name to the hostess, grab a copy of Variety *from the stack by the phone and, in a flash, I'm ushered to my friend's table, beneath one of the brightest lights in the place.*

The table is one of three that is raised on a small platform. It is the center table, flanked by two enormous flowerpots. It is impossible not to notice us. It is impossible not to know what is going on: two men in suits plying another man in jeans and a polo shirt with orange juice and coffee. Suddenly, as I ascend the platform and take my place under the searchlight, I know what it feels like to cheat on one's spouse. Except in this case, the best I'm going to get out of the bargain is breakfast.

Handshakes all round. Some brief, insincere flattery. Coffee is poured. I order the 'Alternative Cuisine' breakfast, which is, essentially, a bowl of cereal and a fat-free muffin. It will cost this agent and his agency roughly $17.

My friend says nothing. He stares at me robotically throughout the following.

AGENT I hear you're not happy with your agent?

ME Well, that's not entirely true.

AGENT   Of course it isn't. But you're not sure you're getting the best career advice, right?

ME   Well, maybe.

AGENT   Of course, well maybe. Let me be totally honest with you. You're not. No well. No maybe. Even if I wasn't interested in signing you – which I am [*laughs*] – even if I wasn't even in the agency business – which I am [*laughs again*] – I'd tell you to look elsewhere. I would. Really. I'm not even lying to you.

I look over at my friend, who is busily spreading pear butter on a carrot muffin. He spreads the pear butter thickly, and with great intensity, on one half of the muffin, then on the other. Then he places both halves on his bread plate. Then his boss, the agent, picks up a half and takes a big bite.

[*Mouth full*] Let me tell you something about myself. I have no life. I have no wife. I have no girlfriend. I go home at eleven, sometimes twelve o'clock, and I'm up by six. What do I do with my time? What do I do? *I serve my clients. That's what I do.* I'm not an agent agent. It's not my job. *It's my state of being.* Okay?

He pops the other half into his mouth and chews at me. I'm very frightened. All of a sudden I realize that of our little breakfast party, this agent is the youngest one present. I am twenty-eight years old, and I'm having breakfast with a man who is younger than me, has his muffins buttered and dressed by an underling, who has no life and is proud of it, and who, if he gets his way, will be calling me at least once a week. No, I think to myself, I'd rather stick with the devil I know. I'll take the quick shifts of opinion, the endless vacations, the indifference, the sometimes incoherent conversations. My agent may be irritating, but compared to the man who's buying me breakfast, I have it easy.

CUT TO:

Later, back at the office, the agent calls. I am sitting in my office with a few other writers, and when my secretary tells me who is on the phone, I suddenly have the urge to pick up the phone and whisper urgently, 'Darling, I told you never to call me here . . .'

CUT TO:

INT. OUR OFFICE – DAY

The agent calls. I put him on speakerphone.

AGENT   (*offscreen*)

How'd I do? Are we in bed together?

> *An unfortunate turn of phrase, but very common in Hollywood. Sexual metaphors are rampant in business discussions, mostly due to the high probability that one party is about to be screwed.*

ME   You know what? Breakfast was great and I liked what you had to say, but to tell you the truth, I'm happy where I am. Thanks.

A long silence.

AGENT   Okay. Fine. You're making a big, dumb mistake. A huge career-killing mistake. But I respect you for it. I respect your loyalty. Give me a call if you change your mind.

ME   I will. Thanks.

But before I could say goodbye:

AGENT   Noreen, get me Warren Littlefie–

SFX: click, dial tone.

CUT TO:

The great thing about flattery is how flattering it is. Just knowing that someone as young and shark-like as that agent wants to sign us is a tremendous energy boost. We work feverishly for several more days, convinced, beyond all reason, that the series idea we have yet to announce, involving characters we have yet to settle on, following a story we have yet to conceive, is nevertheless the talk of the town.

We are hot, we tell each other. We are sought after, we say. Our profile is rising. Our days as 'the guys who run *Cheers*' are over; we're 'industry professionals' now. Players. And if it took a little disloyalty to find that out, well, it's a small price to pay.

CUT TO:

INT. OUR OFFICE – DAY

MY AGENT   Hi. Back again.

ME   How was your vacation?

MY AGENT   Wonderful. And how was *your* week?

ME   (*Guilty, acting cool*)

What? What do you mean? What does that mean?

MY AGENT   Nothing. Just a question.

Somebody told. Somebody saw us eating at the altar in the Four Seasons. I'm dead. Dead.

You sound nervous.

ME   Well . . . I'm a little . . . tired.

MY AGENT   From what?

ME   (*defensive, hysterical*)

From thinking, okay? From thinking about the new show! What if nobody wants it?

MY AGENT   What are you talking about? Everyone loves the concept.

ME   What?

MY AGENT   I called the network driving back from the airport yesterday. Gave them a 'heads up'. They *love* the milieu. By the way, is the messenger there?

59

ME   What messenger?

My secretary tells me that the messenger is indeed there, as if by cue, with a large envelope. I open up the envelope and a document tumbles out, spiked by red plastic tabs, indicating the places for me to sign and initial.

The guy just got here. What's this?

MY AGENT   Sign and give it back to him to bring back to me.

ME   What is it?

MY AGENT   Oh, it's the standard agency renewal contract. You know, what you signed when I took you on as a client? When you were a starving film student? When I took a chance on you and staked my reputation on you? Remember? It expires officially next month, but I thought, hell, why not get a jump on things. So sign. *Now.*

I sign.

Let's meet. Catch up. Talk. Whatever.

ME   Okay. Breakfast?

MY AGENT   No. Dinner. Nothing gets accomplished over breakfast. Right?

ME   Right.

MY AGENT *(cheery)*   Right. See you tonight.

ME   Tonight? I can't –

MY AGENT   Great!

ME   But –

MY AGENT   Jason, get me Jeffrey Katz–

SFX: click, dial tone.

FADE OUT.

60

HIPE

Fade in: January 1994

The main reason that television sit-coms are so bad is that too many educated people are involved in creating them. The television development process works like this: writer comes up with idea; writer pitches idea to studio; studio 'gives notes' – that is, suggestions for changes and additions; writer and studio then go to network to pitch idea; network then either has no interest or does, in which case it 'gives notes'; writer and studio come back to network with refined idea, incorporating network notes; network then either has interest, and 'green lights' the project, in which case writer begins writing script, or network loses interest and tries, instead, to interest writer in a show that the head of the network came up with about a talking dog who can only be heard by a mildly retarded little girl.

The intensity of the network's enthusiasm depends upon the pitch. And the pitch, foolishly enough, depends upon the writer.

The dirty little secret of the entertainment industry is that everyone in it is a salesman. A nicely dressed salesman, sure, but beneath the Armani and the Revos flutter-beats the heart of a sample-case-lugging, family-neglecting, wife-cheating, just-trying-to-catch-a-dime salesman. Think Willy Loman with a cell phone.

Out here, we call it a 'pitch'. Anywhere else, they'd call it what it really is: 'a sales call'.

CUT TO:

Begin Flashback Sequence

INT. NETWORK COMMISSARY – DAY

Early morning. For some reason, my partner and I have been enlisted by the studio (and our agent) to pitch a Cheers *spin-off. It's a long, long shot, as everyone (except us) knows, but the current studio head is a legendary salesman, and has a compulsive need to sell TV shows twenty-four hours a day.*

The news that Cheers *would not return for a twelfth season was still fresh. The studio and our agent had cajoled us into coming up with a quasi-spin-off idea for one of the cast members (no, not Kelsey Grammer of* Frasier, *sad to say) who had shown only the barest glimmer of desultory interest in the series. But, good boys, we think up a series idea and head to the network.*

It is our first pitch. It is, truth be told, our first meeting with anyone from the network. Although we have been writing and producing Cheers *for two years, we're still very new to the business, still the 'boys'.*

The studio executive arrives late. He hustles in.

STUDIO EXEC   Ready?

MY AGENT   Of course they're ready! Of course!

We head up to the network president's office.

STUDIO EXEC   What are we pitching, again?

ME   Um . . . Cheers spin-off.

STUDIO EXEC   We are? Great, great.

We stride down the hall to the door.

Top-line me.

He keeps charging down the hall. Stops at the president's door.

ME   You don't know what the show is about? You didn't read the material we sent over?

64

STUDIO EXEC   Nope.

ME   Um . . . okay, the show is about –

STUDIO EXEC   Too late!

He hustles into the office, and is glad-handing the gathering like a City councilman up for re-election. The office is packed: me, my partner, my agent, the studio executive, the network president, the network vice-president, the network's other vice-president, the network head of 'current comedy' and someone else whom I still cannot identify with any certainty.

We've got the funniest goddamn idea I've ever heard in *my life! In my whole fucking life!* And I'll be totally honest with you guys – right here, right now – if you don't want it, you're fucking nuts, *fucking nuts!* – But fine, okay, I've got two other buyers who *cannot wait to get into business with these two guys!*

Dramatic pause. He nods at my partner, Dan.

Rob –

He nods at me.

– and Dan – They *know how to do a television show.*

Another pause. I do not know it yet, but for years to come, the network president will get me and my partner mixed up.

Hit it.

And I begin to pitch our idea. My agent, for the first time, is silent. In one feverish thirty-minute blast, my partner and I outline the characters, the story of the first episode, and sketch out a few more possible story ideas. The studio executive laughs the loudest, nudges the network president a few times, as if to say, 'See? aren't my boys good?' and generally behaves like a nervous host.

But his eyes are glassy and out-of-focus. His laughter, while loud, is sometimes strangely out of sync with the pitch.

We finish to general laughter. A pause.

(*slowly, with passion*)   This is a show about *people with dreams* . . .

DISSOLVE TO:

INT. NETWORK OFFICES HALLWAY – LATER

The pitch has gone well. My knees are still wobbly. I didn't realize how nervous I was until I stood up from the couch and felt cold sweat patches on the backs of my knees and saw the twisted shreds of the note pages in my hands.

ME   How'd we do?

STUDIO EXEC   We made a sale, kiddo.

ME   Great!

STUDIO EXEC   What's the show about, again?

CUT TO:

A few weeks later, the show and the pilot faded away. The star lost interest, we were tied up wrapping the last few episodes of *Cheers*, the heat on the idea steamed away and evaporated.

CUT TO:

INT. OUR OFFICE – DAY

SFX: phone rings.

MY AGENT   The pilot went away.

ME   What?

MY AGENT   Your pilot. It *went away.*

ME   Went away where?

MY AGENT   Who knows where. It just up and went.

ME   Well, can we send somebody after it to grab it and bring it back?

MY AGENT   What are you talking about?

ME   What are *you* talking about?

MY AGENT   I'm talking about the show you pitched. Since the actor passed on it, it's a dead project. The good news is that the studio guy loved the idea. I mean he *loved* it.

ME   What, specifically, did he love about it?

MY AGENT   The milieu.

ME   He loved the milieu?

MY AGENT   He *freaked* for the milieu.

ME   Yeah, but it's a dead issue. It was a waste of time.

MY AGENT   How so?

ME   Well, we didn't sell the pilot. We went there to sell a series and we didn't sell it.

MY AGENT   Is that what you think? That you went there to sell a series?

ME   Didn't we?

MY AGENT   Of course not. You're never selling the series. You're never selling the pilot. You're never selling the idea.

ME   Then what *are* we selling?

MY AGENT   *Yourselves*, shitbird! You're selling yourselves. You're saying, 'Hey, we're players in the big game. Get in business with us!'

ME   And this means . . . what, exactly?

MY AGENT   It means four things. It means the network likes you, which means the studio likes you. It means one day, one way you'll have a show on the air. And it means that I am a very, very good agent.

ME   (*counting*)

That's three things.

MY AGENT   My being a good agent counts as two things.

ME   But –

MY AGENT   Goodbye! And *you're welcome* . . .

CUT TO:

END FLASHBACK SEQUENCE

Nine months later, we pitched our second series to the network. By this time, we were grizzled veterans. The studio executive had left (ankled, axed, whatever) a few months before, but his replacement drove the same make and model car (Mercedes SE something), walked the same wearying walk into the network commissary, turned on the same I'm-dancing-as-fast-as-I-can charm the minute we hit the room. The only real difference came at the end of the pitch, while we were walking down the hall. I asked him how we did. Instead of a cheerful, 'We made a sale, kiddo!' came a bleaker, more realistic, 'How the hell should I know? This fucking business is *crazy.*'

As it turned out, we made a sale, kiddo. We now had a pilot script in development. Which means everyone pitches in to turn a fairly simple idea and a fairly humorous little script into a perfect vehicle for Mickey Mouse.

People in this business love their souped-up vocabulary: we 'green-light' things, and dump things in 'turnaround' and 'negative pick-up' and 'pitch' and make 'pre-emptive strikes'. And we love our creative talk too: we like lots of 'character conflict' and 'story integrity' and 'deeply humanistic values'. So when the studio and network executives give notes to a writer, the language can be dizzying.

CUT TO:

INT. NETWORK EXEC'S OFFICE – DAY

Our first note session.

NETWORK EXEC #1   Can we platform some of the characters in a slightly better way?

NETWORK EXEC #2   Can one of them cry? Or be quirky?

NETWORK EXEC #1   I *love* quirky.

NETWORK EXEC #3   These characters should love each other. And we should see them loving each other.

NETWORK EXEC #2   A quirky love.

NETWORK EXEC #1   I *love* a quirky love.

NETWORK EXEC #4   Don't worry so much about the jokes.

NETWORK EXEC #1   It doesn't have to be funny. It'd be great if it was funny, but it doesn't have to be funny.

NETWORK EXEC #4   Make it humorous.

NETWORK EXEC #2   Or quirky.

NETWORK EXEC #1   Think about it this way. If *Cheers* was a place 'everybody knows your name', then your show should be a place where . . . ?

NETWORK EXEC #2   Where . . . what?

NETWORK EXEC #1   Do you see the problem?

CUT TO:

We don't see the problem, but we say we do, make a few scribbles and get to work on the script.

CUT TO:

INT. MY BEDROOM – 7.30 A.M.

SFX: phone rings.

I struggle to the phone, answer it.

ME   Hello?

SFX: Mariachi music over phone.

MY AGENT   Hi!

ME   Yeah, hi.

MY AGENT   Did I wake you?

ME   Not yet.

69

MY AGENT   Here's the thing. They want the script soon. They want it Friday.

ME   (*wide awake*)

Friday? This Friday?

MY AGENT   Actually, *last* Friday.

ME   Impossible.

MY AGENT   Of course it's impossible. What are you? A time-traveler?

ME   No. I mean this Friday is impossible. And next Friday is impossible too. We need two weeks, at least. Tell them two weeks.

MY AGENT   I can't do that. Number one, I'm on vacation. I'm calling you from Cozumel. And b), I already told them they could have it Friday.

ME   What?

MY AGENT   I gotta go. We're all going snorkeling before they start the lunch buffet.

CUT TO:

This is an example of what I call the 'Hollywood Inversion Principle of Economics'. The HIPE, as it will come to be known, postulates that every commonly understood, standard business practice of the outside world has its counterpart in the entertainment industry. Only it's backwards. In the outside world, for instance, a corporation's financial health is determined by, among other things, its annual net profit statement; in Hollywood, as the HIPE predicts, it is determined by the *gross* profit statement. The difference should be clear even to people like me, who bluffed their way through one low-level economics course. Gross profit is meaningless. After the payroll is met, and taxes paid, and the producer gets his 20 per cent, and the actors their 15 per cent, and the director his 16.7 per cent, and the budget overruns are paid for, and the prints and advertising . . . Well, you can start to see why the Japanese tried so recently to sell Columbia and Universal studios back to the gypsies who sold it to them in the first place.

What no one realizes – or, more accurately, no one except those *selling a studio or assisting in the selling of a studio* realizes – is that the economics of film production are designed to make individuals very rich. Shareholders are entirely out of the picture. Many of them, for some reason, are dizzied by the HIPE. The near-term return on any investment – feature film, TV show, CD-ROM thing – is entirely spoken for by the savvy participants. The studio – and its hapless, sorry-they-ever-heard-of-Herb-Allen owners – must play the long, long game, hoping that the copyright value of a *Forrest Gump* or a *Batman Forever* pays off. Or that the television show that they deficit-finance at a couple of hundred thousand dollars a throw will, eventually, pay off in re-runs. There's an awful lot of hoping in this business.

Another example of HIPE is the sheer number of agents, studio executives, network programmers, attorneys and assorted assistants-to and associates-of who are completely at the mercy of the timetable of the lazy, good-for-nothing, shiftless writer. In the outside world, lawyers and executives are the 'go slow' guys, the bottlenecks in neckties. 'Don't do anything until we hear from the lawyers,' they say. 'I want my team of executives to take a look at this,' we hear.

In Hollywood, though, everything can happen in an instant except the one thing that can't – the writing. All the Mike Ovitzes and the Barry Dillers in the world can't change this essential bedrock truth: writers like to sleep late, they like to read the newspaper slowly, they like to have long lunches and they hate to write.

CUT TO:

INT. OUR OFFICE – DAY

I am watching cartoons on the TV that the studio foolishly provided. I press the 'mute' button on the remote control.

71

SFX: phone rings.

STUDIO EXEC Hi.

ME Hi.

Pause. Bugs Bunny and Daffy Duck are fighting over whether it's rabbit season or duck season.

STUDIO EXEC How's it going? Are you having fun?

ME No.

Pause. Bugs has produced a calendar and is wearing a dress.

STUDIO EXEC So we're thinking . . . what? . . . Script on Friday, say? Around Friday? Morning?

ME I don't think so.

Pause. Daffy has a gun.

STUDIO EXEC Gee, we really need that script.

ME We're working on it, okay? They don't appear by magic, you know. We're making adjustments, we're trimming, we're tweaking. STOP NAGGING US!

I click off the 'mute' button and hang up. But maybe I'm too slow, and maybe the sound from the TV comes up before the receiver goes down, and maybe right before he hears a dial tone, the studio executive hears Bugs Bunny screaming, 'Oh, Mr Fudd, you're sooo handsome!'

I've surprised myself: a few months ago, I wouldn't have dreamed of refusing a studio request. I have indeed graduated from 'one of the boys who runs Cheers'. I am now, 'Jesus Christ, what happened to him? He used to be so nice.'

CUT TO:

There's nothing to do but go to lunch, which poses a conundrum. Wherever we go, we're bound by the dictates of karmic bad luck to run into our studio executive. How, in good conscience, can we claim to be both feverishly toiling on our script *and* lingering over a radicchio and braised scallop salad? We solve this problem by bringing along an empty notebook and an old, inkless pen. If caught, we'll wave the executive away with a frown as our pen scratches across the paper leaving no mark. We reflect happily that this technique will also serve to establish our lunches, especially the expensive ones, as working lunches and therefore fully tax-deductible.

CUT TO:

INT. OUR OFFICE – DAY

4 p.m. I am smoking a cigar and finishing a small whiskey from a bottle I keep around the office for emergencies.

SFX: phone rings.

MY AGENT   I hear you yelled at a studio exec.

ME   I didn't yell.

MY AGENT   I didn't say you did.

ME   Yes, you did.

MY AGENT   You're getting defensive.

ME   Yeah, but –

MY AGENT   What is this? A 'gotcha' conversation? Are we playing 'gotcha'? Well, fine, but I can play with the best of them, okay?

Pause. I pour myself another Scotch.

ME   Okay, okay. I yelled.

MY AGENT   Good for you. Bust his chops a little. If they push and you roll, then the next time they just push harder. You want me to call him and scream a little?

ME   No, no. You're on vacation. I can handle this.

MY AGENT   Because it's no trouble.

ME   Really. No.

Pause.

MY AGENT   Please?

ME   If you really want to.

MY AGENT   It's raining down here and I'm going out of my tree.

CUT TO:

Begin Montage

1 *A clock – hands spinning around the face, time passing*

2 *A spinach and poached salmon salad – disappearing in time-lapse photography*

3 *A computer screen – disappearing in time-lapse photography*

4 *Another salad*

5 *A cigar, burning*

6 *The clock – spinning . . .*

7 *An HP LaserJet printer – spitting out pages*

End Montage

DISSOLVE TO:

INT. OUR OFFICE – DAY

SFX: phone rings

INTERCUT WITH:

INT. MY AGENT'S OFFICE – DAY

Our script is lying open on our agent's desk.

MY AGENT   I love it. It's hysterical. It's brilliant. It's perfect.

ME   I'm glad to hear it.

MY AGENT   Besides, you'll punch it up.

ME   What?

MY AGENT   It's a first draft. First drafts are first drafts. The studio will have notes. The network will have notes. *I* have notes.

ME   I thought you said it was perfect.

MY AGENT   *Nothing* is perfect.

ME   But you said –

MY AGENT   What? 'Gotcha' again?

ME   Well, what should we do? Should we send it to the studio now?

MY AGENT   Don't you want to hear my notes?

ME   Not really.

Pause

MY AGENT   You're being passive-aggressive.

ME   I'm sorry. I'm trying to be aggressive-aggressive.

MY AGENT   Funny. Look, it's reality time, okay? Everyone is going to have notes. They're all going to want changes. Some changes you make. Some you fight.

ME   Uh huh.

MY AGENT   Mine you make.

ME   And theirs?

MY AGENT   You make theirs too.

ME   Whose do I fight?

MY AGENT   How the hell should I know? I don't have a crystal ball.

ME   But if I roll over every time they push, don't they just push harder next time?

MY AGENT   Yeah. And next time you just roll harder. It's like that Frank Sinatra song, 'I Did it Their Way'.

ME   That's not –

MY AGENT   I don't want to have this conversation.

CUT TO:

The next day, I read in *Variety* that super-agent Swifty Lazar has died. I never met Swifty, but I always admired his big, black spectacles. Perched on his bald head, which itself was perched on his tiny, round frame, the glasses made him look like a huge, jovial insect. Lazar's nickname was Swifty, but people who knew him well always called him Irving – another example of HIPE: having a nickname that's used only by people who don't know you.

Throughout the following days, Lazar's friends and clients (and, astonishingly, these groups intersected) took out advertisements in the trades to eulogize their friend, and to advertise their grief, and also, I suppose, to make it clear that they are all now seeking representation. I wonder if I will ever be in the position to eulogize my agent in the pages of *Variety*. Lazar died well into his eighties. My agent is fairly young. I am reaching for the bottle of whiskey when the phone rings.

It's the network. They have some notes. I keep the bottle handy.

FADE OUT.

EYE CANDY

Fade in: February/March 1994

Americans have their own version of the traditional English–Irish joke – that is, a joke that takes as its premise the intellectual inferiority of a different and unsuspecting nationality. Here in the United States, we have the Polish joke, and one of the more popular examples in Hollywood goes as follows. Did you hear about the Polish actress who came to Hollywood? She slept with a writer. The idea being that anyone who sleeps with a Hollywood writer in the hope of advancing her (or his – this is a multicultural, pansexual community, after all) career has gravely, gravely misapprehended the situation.

For the most part, of course, this is an accurate assumption. Being a writer is a little bit like being a shepherd: it's quaint, people envy the solitude, but everyone knows the real money is in synthetic fibers.

In the television business, the reverse is true. Writers have a great deal of power when compared to their colleagues in the feature–film business. More often than not, the television writer is what Industry contracts define as a hyphenate: a writer-producer, say, or a writer-director. This explains why some of the best, most affecting and artful comedy and drama in the United States today can be found on television. It also explains why so much on TV is such shit.

Power is not precisely accurate. Onerous and Humiliating Duties is a better term. For though the feature-film writer is cut off from the process of casting, shooting, scoring and editing, he is usually too busy relaxing in Hawaii to care. The television hyphenate, though technically in charge of the entire production, must simper and beg and bootlick throughout the process.

The money trail, as always, tells the true story. A writer allies with a studio and together they approach a network with a proposed television show. The network is playing a short-term strategy: it makes its money by selling prime-time advertising space to national advertisers. It merely rents – or licenses, to use the Industry term – the show for two broadcasts, one first run and one rerun. After it runs an episode of a series twice, that episode reverts to the original owners, the studio, who are playing a long-term strategy. They need to assemble five years' worth of a series (usually 100 episodes or so) in order to license them in bulk to the hundreds of affiliate and independent television stations all over the country who need programming for the off-hours and non-prime-time spots on their schedules. The goal, then, is to *get on the air at all costs*. If the network puts your show on their schedule and the show lasts four years (or 100 episodes, whichever comes first), then the future is written on a million check stubs. A thousand roses bloom on your ranch in Montecito.

This system – a kind of nutty 'lend-lease' – is fast disappearing. For years, the networks were prohibited from owning the 'back-end' rights to the television shows they broadcast. The Financial Interest and Syndication Rules – what we jauntily call 'Fin-Syn' – were essentially anti-trust rules designed to keep the networks from acquiring too much control over the nation's airwaves. With the advent of cable, and a corresponding decline in network viewer share, the rules were dropped.

In the meantime, though, the major studios had grown a pretty healthy money tree in TV show reruns. But to build up enough episodes for syndication (remember: magic number 100), they need access to the airwaves. Why, though, would a network, now unshackled from Fin-Syn restrictions and in the

100 per cent-ownership TV production business, buy a show from an outside supplier? Why make someone else rich?

To protect themselves from being shut out of the big game, the big studios have been slowly getting into the network-ownership business. That, along with the cable channels, has trebled the number of TV-show buyers. Good news for the writer in the near term: more buyers, more money, more places to sell a series; bad news for the long term: fewer independent stations buying reruns, a syndication glut, constant shuffling and tumult.

If at this point the reader is thoroughly confused, the reader must not, under any circumstances, quit his day job. If, perversely, the reader readily grasps the above concepts, the reader is encouraged to come to Hollywood to seek his fortune. If the reader is thoroughly confused, but is nonetheless intent on coming to Hollywood to seek his fortune, the reader is not a reader, he is a writer.

The writer's part in this pageant is crucial: he has to do all the work. He has to think up the show and sell the pilot and cast the episode and rewrite the script and edit the picture and, if lucky, produce the series that airs on the network that some mogul, after consultation with Herb Allen, wants to buy. He has to do this while surrounded by people – studio guys, agent guys, network guys – whose job, essentially, is to *watch* him do his job.

CUT TO:

INT. OUR OFFICE – DAY

SFX: phone rings.

MY AGENT   Are you excited?

ME   About what?

MY AGENT   Always so dour. Always immediately negative. Why is that, I wonder? I meant about your pilot. Are you excited about your pilot?

ME I guess. It's a lot of work, though.

MY AGENT Of course it's a lot of work. That's the problem with your generation. No work ethic. I'll be at lunch until four or so. Try to cheer up. Before I go, I just had a brainstorm for your cast: Hugh Grant.

NB: This was way, way before Hugh Grant's rise, fall and rise again.

ME Hugh Grant?

MY AGENT You know the guy. From *The Wedding Funeral?*

ME I don't think he'll do a series. He's a movie star now. And besides, isn't he English?

MY AGENT Why don't you ever see the good in people?

DISSOLVE TO:

INT. OUR OFFICE – LATER

We are in the midst of casting our pilot. Dan and I are attempting to create an ensemble of young, comically nimble actors. The network, meddlesome as always, wants us to create an ensemble of young, comically nimble actors who look terrific in bathing suits.

SFX: phone rings.

INTERCUT WITH:

INT. RANGE ROVER – DAY

The network executive is driving along San Vicente Boulevard.

NETWORK EXEC Are you excited?

ME About what?

NETWORK EXEC (*laughing*)

You writers! Always so sarcastic.

A long pause.

Here's why I'm calling. I'm wondering if you've looked at [*mentions the name of a young actor*] for your show.

ME   Yeah, we looked at him.

NETWORK EXEC   Isn't he terrific? Isn't he the funniest? Don't you just want to eat him up?

Another long pause.

ME   To tell you the truth, he didn't really impress us.

NETWORK EXEC   I'm sorry?

ME   He had trouble pronouncing certain words.

NETWORK EXEC   Which words?

ME   Small words. Easy words. Words, frankly, that ordinarily don't give people trouble.

NETWORK EXEC   Well, we like him a lot over here. A lot. And we'd like to see him in a series. Very much. He may not be a rocket scientist, but he's got a great look.

ME   But he's clinically illiterate.

NETWORK EXEC   And you can't work around that? Okay, okay. You don't like him. How about Hugh Grant?

See note above.

ME   Is he available?

NETWORK EXEC   Of course not. He's a movie star. I just meant a Hugh Grant type. You know, English. They pronounce everything so beautifully over there. And I know what a stickler you are about that.

DISSOLVE TO:

INT. OUR OFFICE. CONFERENCE ROOM – DAY

Later that day we see 137 young actors and actresses. They all clutch their 'sides' – theater lingo for Xeroxed excerpts of the script – in white-knuckled panic. Some have worried the few stapled pages into a

*twisted twig-looking thing; others have methodically shredded each
page (hence the term 'Method acting'). Many of them have difficulty
reading the words aloud. Some stumble over syntax. Others manage to
get the set-up and the punch-line reversed, imbuing our simple,
straightforward script with a dreamy, surreal Luis Buñuel quality.
Mostly, though, as products of the American education system, they
answer the question: Why are the Japanese ahead of us?*

Begin Montage

I. An OLDER ACTRESS *– here to read for a supporting role – the
neighbor character to our main characters, five young men who share
an apartment. It isn't a big part – a few pages, at most – but she
attacks her sides with gusto.*

A few moments after her audition:

OLDER ACTRESS Can I say something? This writing is *deft*. It's
highly deft writing. That you two could write a show about a
woman who lives next to five young men . . . What can I say?
It's something special.

2. A YOUNG ACTOR *– in full grunge. He flips through the sides
quickly, runs his dirty fingers through his greasy hair, coughs, sniffs,
then:*

YOUNG ACTOR I'm gonna improv a lotta this shit, okay?

3. A YOUNG ACTRESS *– starts to read, stops, tears welling in her
eyes.*

YOUNG ACTRESS (*sobbing*)

You don't want *me!* You want somebody a *lot thinner.*

4. An OLDER ACTRESS *– here to read for the neighbor character.
She reads a bit, stops, glares at us.*

OLDER ACTRESS A woman would never say that in a million
years. You're going to change it, right?

5. SUCCESSFUL YOUNG ACTOR – *here because the network loves him and he knows it.*

SUCCESSFUL YOUNG ACTOR   My agent is begging me not to do half-hour. He thinks I'm more of a feature actor, y'know? But I read the script and fell in love with it, and thought, 'Hey, maybe I *can* collaborate with these guys.' Sorry that I can't audition. You know, formally. It diminishes me in the marketplace.

End Montage

CUT TO:

Casting, sadly, is everything. The network reserves the right to veto any casting choice, which they exercise on an informal basis – glaring at the actor, loudly suggesting replacements, stubbornly refusing to laugh at anything he does during run-throughs – or in a more formal way – simply demanding that he be fired before they order an episode or, worse, referring to the whole enterprise as 'casting contingent'.

The most unbearable part of the process is that the network is often, even mostly, right. Their casting choices are difficult to swallow precisely because they are so on-target. After all, unburdened by any serious work or responsibilities – like, say, writing the damn thing – they are free to toss around actors' names and watch lots of demo tapes. So when we troop in a motley caravan to the network's offices, bringing with us the actors we've chosen for each part – actually, *two* or more actors per role – for network casting approval, it's one of those rare moments when the network actually has something valuable to contribute.

It's galling on a biblical scale.

But it's much, much worse for the actors. By the time we drag them to the network, they've auditioned for the role no less than three times – twice for us, once for the studio – each time waiting in the waiting room with another actor who looks similar, acts similar, and who they just can't help thinking is a notch or two better-looking.

At the final network casting session, facing a grim and humorless battery of studio and network executives – sometimes a dozen or so – they often crack and deliver their lines (for the fifth time) in a totally new, totally unfunny way. It's called 'unwinding at the network.'

CUT TO:

INT. OUR OFFICE – DAY

SFX: phone rings.

MY AGENT (*offscreen*) Are you excited?

ME About what?

MY AGENT I forgot. You're playing cool. Okay, I can swing with that. I just got off the phone with the network.

ME Oh.

MY AGENT They're concerned.

ME About what?

MY AGENT They think you're going too . . . characterish . . . with your casting.

ME What?

MY AGENT They think you're casting ugly people.

ME We're trying to cast good actors who can do comedy.

MY AGENT And?

ME And what?

MY AGENT And who look good in their underpants.

ME How should I know if they look good in their underpants? Let me make this very clear: I am not going to ask someone to

86

take off their trousers just so I can see if they look good in their underpants.

MY AGENT So you *are* casting ugly people.

ME We are trying to cast funny actors.

MY AGENT Could you please tell me what's so funny about six guys who look like the Elephant Man?

ME What?

MY AGENT Maybe you don't understand the power structure here. The network likes young, good-looking people. America likes young, good-looking people. That's how you get on the air. That's how you stay on the air. If you've got some sicko thing for circus freaks, fine. But not on network television. My God, not after dinner. People want to see someone like Hugh Grant being funny. Why don't you cast someone like Hugh Grant?

ME I'd love to. If you can figure out a way for us to somehow come up with six young, great-looking, funny, nimble actors who can pronounce the word 'patio', then sign me up. Until then, we're stuck with thalidomide babies and bearded ladies.

CUT TO:

Unexpectedly, ten of the 168 actors we have auditioned are both talented and suitably winsome. This enables us to go to the network with ten choices for six parts, allowing the various network executives to audition each actor one more time and participate in the final decision. We could – indeed, we are legally entitled to – simply make our choices and cast our pilot as we see fit. That is, of course, the bold choice. But why be bold when one can be on the air for four years (or 100 episodes, whichever comes first), at which point the future is written in an aimless, rich adulthood punctuated by ungrateful children?

CUT TO:

INT. MY CAR – DAY

We're driving away from the network after our final casting meeting. Remarkably, we've all agreed on our casting choices without rancor.

SFX: car phone chirps.

INTERCUT TO:

INT. MY AGENT'S CAR – DAY

My agent is a few cars back, heading south on the 101 Freeway.

MY AGENT   Are you disappointed?

ME   By what?

MY AGENT   No Hugh Grant.

ME   I never expected to have him in the show.

MY AGENT   Always the pessimist. Always the dark side of life.

ME   What are you talking about? He doesn't do series television. He was never available. He's a movie actor.

MY AGENT   Did it ever occur to you that he may have money trouble and may be in no position to turn you down? Did it ever occur to you that he may not know he's not supposed to be interested in television? Maybe he's ill or mentally imbalanced and that's something you could take advantage of.

How remarkably prescient my agent seems.

ME   He . . . is . . . not . . . available.

MY AGENT   Maybe in a few years, then.

ME   What?

MY AGENT   He does a few bad movies, makes some bad career moves, and before you know it, he's ready to do a series.

ME   Hugh Grant?

MY AGENT   He's so good-looking that they'll probably let you cast your precious circus freaks, just for variety.

ME (*sighing*)   Great.

MY AGENT   But see him in his underpants first. You don't want to be surprised.

FADE OUT.

TESTING TIMES

Fade in: April/May 1994

One of the more common misperceptions of Hollywood is that it is rife with stories of overnight success. Nothing happens overnight, especially in this business. Every success, no matter how seemingly effortless, was coaxed and cajoled and, finally, extracted with tongs.

Night owls, flipping through the dozens of late-night television offerings, can sometimes spot a young Meg Ryan, say, on a really bad rerun of a really bad sit-com, *Charles in Charge*, in a really bad role. (Sample dialogue: 'Oh, forget about *them*, Charles. Why don't just you and me have a little *party*!') Allan Folsom, the highly successful novelist (*The Day After Tomorrow*) and highly paid screenwriter (the movie rights for *The Day After Tomorrow* sold for a sum in the six-to-seven-figure range) still counts two or three episodes of the very stinky *épater les bourgeois* TV show *Hart to Hart* in his corpus. (And he doesn't mention them in his very brief book-flap biography, either.) As a wise old friend once told me, 'At some point in your career, sooner or later, you're forced to sit down at a table and eat a very, very big shit sandwich.'

It's the least one should expect from an industry whose lingo is so evocatively violent. We 'shoot' things and 'wrap' things and 'cut' things – both 'rough cuts' and the more grim 'final cut' – we 'pitch' things and let options 'expire'. The verbs are so active it's hard to believe that most of these things occur when people are sitting alone in their cars.

Exactly one year after they called 'wrap' on the last episode of *Cheers*, they called 'wrap' on the pilot episode of our series. The intervening months had been a long, slow fuse leading up to this particular stick of dynamite. From pitch, to notes, to script, to casting – the process is designed to drain your will and ebb your strength. Along the way, though, some surprises. Our cast, for instance. They were bright and young and very funny, of course, but they also treated us like . . . well, like we were the bosses and we knew what we were doing. Which we were, but we didn't.

The cast of *Cheers*, as professional and pleasant as they were, knew that we were just 'the boys' – caretakers of a larger enterprise. They suffered our authority; they didn't seek it out. But our cast, well, for one thing, they were *our* cast – we hired them, argued for them at the network, believed in them. And throughout the production week, after every run-through of the show, we would go back to our office and rewrite jokes, sometimes whole scenes, to better tailor our show to their talents.

A TV sit-com is filmed as if it were a stage play: in one night, in front of an audience, cameras zooming all over the place. The days leading up to 'shoot night' are pretty much all the same: the actors get to the studio around nine in the morning, rehearse and sometime in the early afternoon they perform a run-through of the script for the producers (us), who then make notes, head back to their office, rewrite the script and messenger it out that night to all the actors, who tear greedily through each page, noting which actors have lost lines in the rewrite, which have gained them, and who then show up the next morning to rehearse the new material for the afternoon run-through . . . you can see where this is going. You do this for as many days as you can. It is nerve-shattering to the actors.

CUT TO:

94

INT. SOUNDSTAGE – DAY

Early morning. The actors have gathered around the table to read that day's rewrite. Although it's not usual for a producer to attend the morning reading, I do because a), I'm a control freak; and b), I've been awake since 4 a.m. anyway, keyed up and nervous.

A member of our cast raises his hand.

CAST MEMBER #1   Does anyone mind if I take a second to read over the script? I didn't get one last night.

ME   You didn't?

Another cast member raises his hand.

CAST MEMBER #2   I didn't either.

CAST MEMBER #3   Me neither.

The whole cast mumbles: 'Me neither's'and 'I didn't's'.

ME   No one got a script? I guess the messenger service screwed up.

CAST MEMBER #1   I thought I was fired.

ME   What?

CAST MEMBER #1   I thought I was fired. I thought I gave such a bad performance at run-through that you guys fired me. And that's why I didn't get a script.

ME   That's the silliest thing I've ever heard.

CAST MEMBER #2   I thought I was fired too.

CAST MEMBER #3   Me too.

The rest of the cast mumbles 'Me too's' and 'I was sure I was fired's'.

ME (*attempting to lighten the mood*)   Hey, if we fire you, we'll send you a basket of those little muffins.

CAST MEMBER #1 (*deadly serious*)   Oh. Okay. That's good to know.

ME   I was joking. We're not firing anyone. We love you guys.

You're terrific.

CAST MEMBER #1   Then why do you look so angry and pale at the run-throughs?

ME   Me?

CAST MEMBER #2   Yeah, you.

ME   That's me being *happy*. You should see me being *unhappy*. I'm just nervous, I guess.

CAST MEMBER #1   I don't know what you're nervous about. It's our asses they blame if it doesn't work.

Which is unfortunately untrue.

CUT TO:

We shoot the pilot a few days later. The audience laughs. People seem to like the show. We quickly assemble the footage and hustle it over to the network.

May is National Broadcast Network Fall Schedule Assembly Month. The networks assemble the final versions of all of the pilots they've ordered and begin to put together a fall television schedule. Of the roughly one dozen pilots they order throughout the year, four or so get scheduled.

What we do during this time is what we do most of the time: we wait by the phone. The only people who call are agents, trying to angle a foot in the door to get their clients a job, should the network order our show and should we be looking to hire a writing staff. In retrospect, it's a perfect time to get out of town. Hollywood Rule of Thumb: when waiting, it's best to be waiting in Hawaii.

CUT TO:

INT. OUR OFFICE – DAY

SFX: phone rings.

INTERCUT TO:

96

INT. ANOTHER AGENT'S OFFICE – DAY

He is pacing his office, talking into a speakerphone. He occasionally consults an index card, on which his assistant has printed my name.

AGENT   I hear you've got a hot show! Congratulations!

ME   Well, thanks, but you know, we've just delivered it to the network. They haven't bought it yet.

AGENT   Just a formality! I hear they love it! I love it!

ME   Thanks.

AGENT   Do you know who else loves it?

ME   Who?

The agent mentions the name of one of his clients.

Tell him thanks.

AGENT   Tell him yourself! I'll set up a meeting!

ME   Well, you know, it's a little early to be thinking about hiring a staff. The network hasn't bought the show.

AGENT   They will! They love it! I love it!

ME   Thanks. Again.

AGENT   Why don't I send you some of his spec scripts! They're great!

ME   *(warily)* Okay. But we're really not reading right now.

AGENT   I know! I know! But these are great!

ME   Okay. But just those. Don't inundate us.

AGENT   I won't! I won't! I swear to God! I'll just send the one spec!

SMASH CUT TO:

A MESSENGER'S CLIPBOARD

My hand in frame, signing for a package.

PULL BACK:

A HUGE STACK OF SCRIPTS

I make my way through the pile.

CUT TO:

INSERT SHOT:

An agency's cover letter. It reads:

> *Dear Rob*
>
> *As per our discussion, please find enclosed spec scripts for the following writers . . .*

A list of seventeen names follows, each with a short description.

MY FINGER RUNS DOWN THE LIST

I stop at a few descriptions:

> *Young, hip, dripping with smarts.*

and:

> *Funny to the point of hemorrhaging.*

and:

> *Meet him and fall in love.*

and:

> *Fox loves him. Won't you?*

CUT TO:

This scene is repeated roughly as many times as there are literary agencies in the Los Angeles area. For five consecutive days, the phone rings non-stop. Soon, my entire office is filled with piles of spec scripts. I consider this a bad omen. If dozens of agents call you to tell you that your pilot is on the short list or a sure thing, two things are certain: you are not on the short list and you are not a sure thing.

The studio – or, as the romantics who run things like to say, the supplier – has meanwhile decided to market-test the episode with a focus group. The network, of course, will test the episode for itself, in much the same way, but the studio wants to have its own set of data. So we troop over the hill to Burbank, to what the romantics who run things like to call a testing facility, and sit behind a two-way mirror to watch thirty-two demographically precise, audience-representative Americans in T-shirts watch our show, answer questions about it and collect $25. As they file into the room, one particularly clever young man – I shall call him Butthead – points to the mirror and asks the group leader, 'Hey. Is somebody back there, like, watching us watch TV?' The group leader smiles and shakes his head, 'Oh, no,' he says, 'no one is back there. No one is watching you. Please take your seat.' Butthead shrugs and sits. A woman turns to the mirror and begins examining her teeth.

Actually, *I* am behind the mirror. Me, and about a dozen or so people from the studio. We are watching Butthead and the Tooth Lady and thirty of her peers watch what it has taken us nine months and $1 million to produce. As they watch, they manipulate a small dial attached to each chair: they twist it clockwise if they like what they see and anticlockwise if they don't. A computer records their responses, collates them and turns the data into a line graph – or, more precisely, a two-line graph: one line measures the men's response, the other measures the women's response. The graph is superimposed on a tape of the show, which is playing on our side of the mirror. I am watching, essentially, an electrocardiogram of my career.

CUT TO:

INT. TESTING FACILITY – NIGHT

We're gathered in an airless, windowless, pizza-reeking room, watching a TV monitor scroll out information. A studio research guy is making notes, cocking his head to one side, looking mysterious.

99

ME   What does all this mean?

STUDIO GUY   It means that women love the show. Men like the
show.

ME   What does *that* mean?

STUDIO GUY   It means you're on the air. And in a good time
slot.

ME   What?

STUDIO GUY   (*grinning*)

With numbers like these, the network can't say no.

DISSOLVE TO:

INT. OUR OFFICE – DAY

*We are overjoyed. We throw caution to the wind. We begin reading
spec scripts. We begin meeting writers. We begin hearing rumors.*

SFX: phone rings.

INTERCUT WITH:

INT. REGENCY HOTEL – DAY

*My agent is in a suite, on the phone. Other members of the agency are
in the background, on different phones. They are in New York for the
traditional fall schedule announcements.*

MY AGENT   What do you hear?

ME   We're on the air. And in a good time slot.

MY AGENT   Who told you that?

ME   The studio guy. The research guy.

MY AGENT   Because of the *testing*? Don't tell me you're listening
to that crap?

ME (*small voice*)   But he said . . .

MY AGENT   I hear not so good things. I hear you're a long shot.

ME (*small voice*)   But women love us.

MY AGENT   (*soothing, comforting*)

I know they do, honey. I know they do. But listen, if this doesn't work out, it's no big deal. You'll get a show on the air. Eventually. Maybe not this one. Or the next. But the one after that. Probably.

ME   But the testing . . .

MY AGENT   Shut up about the goddamn testing! It's meaningless!

ME   But why would the studio spend money on something that was meaningless? Why would they waste their money?

MY AGENT   You're not seriously asking me that question, are you? It's a *studio*.

ME   Oh.

MY AGENT   (*suddenly upbeat*)

But listen, if I'm wrong and they do buy the show, I have one client who's just great! He's just great! I'll set up a meeting!

DISSOLVE TO:

INSERT SHOT:

A page from Variety *listing all of the produced pilots in contention for slots on the fall schedule. Each is grouped by network, with its producer/creators listed, and a short log-line.*

My finger runs down the list and stops at our show, and its description:

Five guys live together in NYC apartment.

PULL BACK:

INT. OUR OFFICE – CONTINUOUS

I smile, close Variety. *Look up, concerned. Something is troubling me. I open* Variety *once more.*

CUT TO:

INSERT SHOT:

Same Variety *page. I look over the list again.*

My finger runs down the list and stops at another listing under our network's heading. The description reads:

Young people hanging out together in NYC.

PULL BACK:

INT. OUR OFFICE – CONTINUOUS

My complexion turns sickly green. I realize that the network has two similar shows in competition. Ours, 'Five guys . . .'; and theirs, 'Young people . . .'

ME   (*muttering darkly*)

We're dead.

CUT TO:

INT. MY PLACE – DAY

9 a.m. I am sitting in my underwear, drinking a cup of coffee.

SFX: phone rings.

MY AGENT   (*offscreen*)

I just heard. It didn't happen.

ME   Oh.

MY AGENT   Sorry, kid.

ME   Yeah. They went with 'Young people . . .', didn't they?

MY AGENT   They may want it for mid-season. Or they may just let their option expire.

ME   When does it expire?

MY AGENT   1 January 1995.

ME   What?

MY AGENT   But maybe sooner. I'll call you right back.

102

DISSOLVE TO:

INT. MY PLACE — DAY

I stare out over the Pacific.

DISSOLVE TO:

INT. MY PLACE — DAY

Later. I'm still staring.

SFX: phone rings.

MY AGENT (*offscreen*) I've got good news and bad news and just news.

ME You have bad news? I thought I already got the bad news.

MY AGENT There's always worse news. Always.

ME What is it?

MY AGENT The network released the show. They've given up their option.

ME Actually, right now, that sounds like good news to me. At least it's over.

MY AGENT It's not over. That's the just news. Your studio is starting a network of its own in a few months. They may want to order the show for their own network.

ME So it's not over?

MY AGENT Nope.

ME It'll never be over, will it?

MY AGENT Nope. And that's the good news.

CUT TO:

Which brings us to today. Today we are waiting for the studio to tell us if they want our show. If they do, then I have narrowly escaped eating that karmic shit sandwich. They will order a bunch of shows for their fledgeling network and I will be in the chips again.

In the end, of course, what happened to turn our hot pilot into a non-event was an inchoate, invisible force that governs Hollywood. Call it the Fade. It didn't die – nothing dies here, nothing, in the words of my agent, is ever over. Things just fade. The obituary page in *Variety* is the perfect embodiment of the Fade. No one who reads it ever exclaims, Oh, what a shock! So-and-so died! What one says is, Oh, what a shock! So-and-so was still alive until last Tuesday. I thought he died *years* ago.

Meanwhile, I do what I do best: I wait by the phone.

FADE OUT.

WALL STREET

Fade in: June/July/August 1994

The fundamental difference between a Hollywood novice and a sad-eyed veteran is that a novice calls a script a 'script', a television show a 'television show' and a feature film assignment a 'feature film assignment'. A veteran calls all of these things, simply, 'a piece of business'.

I have never been able to pull off that kind of tough business-guy talk without sounding like a complete dork. That, along with my childish insistence on the literal meaning of words such as 'contractual obligation', 'creative approval', and 'prompt payment', has kept me feeling like an outsider.

CUT TO:

INT. OUR OFFICE – DAY

We are still brooding about our failed pilot. I have scavenged through my garage, rooting through old boxes, to find my film-school-era enemies list. I attach a list of the network's upper-level executives. I show the list to my partner, Dan.

DAN You forgot one name.

He takes the list from me and writes the name of the guy from the studio who told us, after the test results came in, that we were on the air and in a good time slot.

He taps the list with intensity, then circles the studio guy's name with his index finger.

(*with great feeling*) Him I want dead.

107

SFX: phone rings

EXT. ORSO'S RESTAURANT — DAY

My agent is on the curb, talking on a cell phone, waiting for the valet to bring the car. Orso's has a notorious valet-parking problem.

MY AGENT   How are we looking?

ME   Sorry?

MY AGENT   Are you excited?

ME   About what?

MY AGENT   About what. About what, he says. About your show.

ME   You mean the show that didn't sell?

MY AGENT   It did too sell.

ME   No, it didn't.

MY AGENT   Not to the originally intended buyer, no.

My agent waves a valet-parking stub at the attendant. He takes Robert Shapiro's ticket first.

ME   You know what? This conversation is giving me a cluster headache.

MY AGENT   Have you tried reverse-reflexology shiatsu energy-massage?

ME   No.

MY AGENT   I have a person. He'll come to your house. I'll set it up.

ME   What's all this about the show being sold?

MY AGENT   Your show was sold? Great! Congratulations!

ME   I'm asking *you*.

MY AGENT   Hey, I haven't heard a thing. It's a quiet time.

People are out of town or watching the O. J. Simpson trial.

My agent nods curtly to Shapiro.

ME But –

MY AGENT What I *do* know is that when I started in this business, I had a little office over a sewing store on Ventura Boulevard.

ME And?

MY AGENT Look at me now. Not bad, huh?

A long pause.

ME But –

MY AGENT You didn't let me finish. When I started out in this business there were only two big buyers in town, only two big networks. ABC was the third, and that was the new kid on the block. And now look at it. The number one network. I'm happy for them, I really am. I wonder if I should retire soon?

Another long pause.

ME Hello?

MY AGENT The point is, if you could stop interrupting me for five seconds please, the point is that by January 1995 there will be *six* buyers for television products. Six. That's almost three times as many. Six big networks. Now, if we can't get your show on at least one of them, then . . . well, maybe you should change careers.

My agent laughs. Smiles and waves at Shapiro as he drives away.

ME Or maybe you should.

MY AGENT What did I do to deserve that?

ME It was a joke.

MY AGENT You should seek therapy. For the darkness.

ME   It was a joke.

MY AGENT   Your industry is in turmoil and you're cracking jokes. You've got a failed pilot that your studio is desperately shilling around town and yet you see fit to crack wise. Interesting response.

ME   But –

MY AGENT   Stop interrupting me.

ME   But –

The valet roars up with my agent's car.

MY AGENT   Gotta go!

CUT TO:

It is rare that a conversation with my agent has a clarifying effect and yet, as we zigzag from scenario to scenario, the picture that emerges – distorted, jangling, fragmented, chaotic – is an accurate depiction of the television business in 1994. My agent is correct: there are now, or are soon to be, six broadcast television networks. As I write this, at least two of the older ones, CBS and ABC, are rumored to be takeover targets. The anti-trust regulations that have prevented the networks from owning the shows – sorry, the *pieces of business* – on their airwaves are almost fully repealed.

CUT TO:

EXT. STUDIO PARKING LOT – DAY

Blazing sunlight. 2 p.m. I've just pulled into the parking lot. I run into a studio executive walking back to his office from lunch at the commissary. I am trying, through my body language, to imply that I, too, am returning from lunch, albeit off the lot. The truth is that I am coming into the office for the first time today.

We exchange pleasantries. I wonder if the exec notices my wet hair.

STUDIO EXEC   Are you happy in your office?

ME Right now?

STUDIO EXEC No, I mean in general.

ME I suppose.

STUDIO EXEC But they're not large enough for production offices, are they?

ME We're not in production.

STUDIO EXEC You will be soon.

ME (*interested*) Yeah? What have you heard?

STUDIO EXEC I hear they're about to order your show.

ME For which network?

STUDIO EXEC I'd rather not say.

ME Meaning you don't know?

STUDIO EXEC (*testy*) Look, do you want to move into a bigger suite of offices or don't you?

ME Yeah, yeah, sure, sure.

STUDIO EXEC Okay then. We'll move you over the weekend. Jesus Christ, your agent is right. You *are* impossible to deal with.

CUT TO:

And so we move – me, Dan, our assistant and six bottles of gin – to larger, nicer, fully decorated offices. The carpet is soft and fluffy. Our conference room (a conference room!) is tastefully arranged. The lighting is understated. I am struck with the realization that we have moved into production offices for a show that doesn't have a production order from a network that doesn't yet exist.

CUT TO:

INT. MAPLE DRIVE RESTAURANT – DAY

Lunch with an agent from another agency. I am suddenly struck by how far we've come in the business: this kind of thing no longer makes

111

me nervous, furtively tearing my bread into tiny strips, eyes darting around the place, looking for spies.

In fact, we're having lunch with this agent as 'industry professionals', since we, at least in theory, are looking to hire writers for a show that, in theory, might get an order from a network that, in theory, might start up in a few months.

Cheers *seems a million years in the past.*

AGENT   Do you have any idea how hot you guys are right now?

ME   How hot?

AGENT   Hot hot, that's how.

ME   Hot hot?

AGENT   When I started in this business there were only four buyers – just four.

ME   You're twenty-eight.

AGENT   Believe me, I know. I feel it every day. The point is, pretty soon there'll be six buyers – and that's just broadcast networks. All the big cable stations will have original programming too. And they all want to be in business with you two. You're hot. Hot hot.

ME   Why?

AGENT   Because you have an unsold pilot. Not everybody can say that.

ME   Yeah. Some people can say that they have a *sold* pilot.

AGENT   You know what I think? I think success is overrated. It ties you down. Which would you rather have: a successful show on a big network, grinding you down every day, every day a new crisis, a star tantrum, an affiliates rebellion, a script rewrite; or, would you rather have a dozen unsold pilots, each for a different network, each a new, fresh adventure?

112

ME   Ummm . . .

AGENT   You make more money in failure.

ME   Really? I would?

AGENT   Not with your agent, no. But if you sign with me, absolutely. You guys are hot. Hot hot hot.

ME   Hot hot *hot?*

AGENT   Okay, so I exaggerate.

CUT TO:

And so, as we wait for our production order from a network that has yet to birth itself, and after a few desultory afternoons rattling around our new suite of offices, we begin writing a feature film. It's July, when a young man's fancy turns to pieces of business. And we have lunch with a bunch of other writers.

CUT TO:

INT. CITRUS RESTAURANT

About five writers are sitting around a table, each eating identical chicken salads and gossiping about people in the business, some of whom are in the restaurant at the time, a few of them within earshot.

ME   Have you heard this thing about the six networks?

WRITER #1   I heard seven.

WRITER #2   I heard six, but with a seventh cable thing.

WRITER #3   (*spotting someone across the dining room*)

See that asshole? That fucking no-talent moron wrote some stupid movie about some goddamn bomb or something.

He waves cheerily across the room at the no-talent moron.

(*smiling through clenched teeth, waving*)

Hi, asshole. Hi, no-talent fuck.

WRITER #4   What do you care?

WRITER #3   It opened last Friday. Made $23 million its first weekend.

WRITER #4   Yikes.

WRITER #2   What am I doing in this business?

WRITER #1   Interactive, my friends. Multimedia. The wave of the future.

ME   What's that?

WRITER #1   I'm into a deal now in the interactive action genre for home-based multimedia distribution. And I'm making a mint, let me tell you.

ME   You mean you're writing video games?

WRITER #1   Basically, yes.

ME   Wow.

WRITER #1   The future is now, buddy. Seven networks. One hundred channels of programming. Decentralized feature film production. Video games, CD-Roms, Nintendo, Sega . . . somebody has got to write that crap. They can get a computer to direct it. A cartoon to act in it. But you need a living, breathing, actual hack to write it.

CUT TO:

You're no longer a TV writer or a feature writer or a home shopping club writer; you're a 'content provider'. And everyone wants to be in business with you, even if you suck. Maybe especially if you suck. This glorious industry, the business, the town – whatever we call it this week – is a huge, colorful mosaic made up of glittering, golden pieces of business.

CUT TO:

INT. OUR NEW OFFICE – DAY

114

The O. J. Simpson preliminary hearings are on television. Work has stopped for the day.

SFX: phone rings.

INTERCUT WITH:

INT. MY AGENT'S OFFICE – DAY

The TV is on there, too, and tuned to the hearings. The sound echoes strangely through the telephone wire, creating a weird old-movie-Nazi-siren kind of Doppler effect.

MY AGENT   Are you excited?

ME   Yes, actually. Did you know that with six new networks and cable and decentralized feature film production the business is swimming with opportunities for writers?

MY AGENT   (*sarcastic*)

Did I know that? How should I know that? I only spend ten hours a day on the phone with everyone from Michael Eisner to Alan Suess's maid.

ME   Who?

MY AGENT   Exactly! (*then, muttering*) Did I know that? Did I know that? (*loudly*) I'm the one who told you that! I'm the one who told you that the future of this business is wide open. You can do anything.

ME   We're writing a feature.

MY AGENT   Except that. There's no real money in features.

ME   Fine. We'll move on to another piece of business.

MY AGENT   Another *what*?

ME   Another piece of business.

Long pause.

MY AGENT   You took my advice and got yourself some therapy, right?

115

ME   Nope.

MY AGENT   You saw my reverse-reflexology shiatsu energy-massage guy?

ME   Nope.

MY AGENT   Well, whatever you did, you've got a whole new attitude.

ME   Thanks.

MY AGENT   That wasn't really a compliment. By the way, the studio called this morning. They're anticipating an order for your series, for thirty episodes.

ME   Thirty?

MY AGENT   Yep.

ME   Isn't that a lot?

MY AGENT   Yep.

ME   Won't that cut into my other . . .

MY AGENT   Pieces of business? Yes, it will.

ME   But I thought –

MY AGENT   Hey, no offense, but you aren't really big enough yet for pieces of business. Wait a few years, and maybe after this show fails, and another show fails, and maybe you have a few more unsold pilots, *then* maybe it'll be pieces of business time.

   CUT TO:

A friend and I are on the way to the studio one morning when we stop off at a local restaurant for a cup of coffee and a blueberry muffin. The restaurant is called Campanile, and at night it's a pretty swank place. But in the morning, in an effort to develop what we in the entertainment industry call 'ancillary markets', the proprietors serve a light breakfast. By 'light' I mean the food, not the price; coffee and a muffin runs around $10. In the parking lot, my friend bumps into an old friend of his, someone he has not seen in many years.

CUT TO:

EXT. CAMPANILE RESTAURANT PARKING LOT – DAY

The two old friends shake hands and smile.

MY FRIEND   Hello there.

HIS FRIEND   Hi.

MY FRIEND   How are you?

HIS FRIEND   (*shrugging*)

Movie.

CUT TO:

Movie. He's movie. By which, I slowly understand, he means, 'I'm working on a movie, thanks for asking.' In a way, he has simplified a worn-out Hollywood conversation: Hi-how-are-you-what-are-you-working-on? Dogs sniff genitals; we say 'What-are-you-working-on?'

The other possibility, one slightly more embittering, is that the old friend knows that my friend is working in television and has been for years, and that *he* is working in film, or what we call *features*, and that he wants him to know it. Television people and feature people have an ancient cold war of status always raging beneath the surface of any encounter. Feature people have a kindly, aristocratic disdain for television people. When they compliment us, it is usually with a condescending admiration – i.e. 'I can't *believe* that you go into the studio every day and work work work. Really, you people are just a little *factory*. How marvelous! I could *never* do what you do. I need time to *think* about my work, to *noodle*, to *refine*. How lucky for you that you don't!'

Television people comfort themselves with their larger paychecks. The bitterness, though, grows. Feature people – who seem to be able to make only movies based on television shows – look down on television people for the same reason that old money and the upper class shrinks from the middle class: we're new, we're loud and there are more of us. The balance sheet of any major Hollywood studio embroiders the point: huge losses in the feature side are balanced by huge profits in the television side. *Full House* covers *Waterworld*. (Or, almost.) The only reason TV people don't make more trouble is that they all want to work in features.

CUT TO:

INT. MY PLACE – DAY

Dan and I are fed up with waiting around the office for a series order from the network that our studio is starting – or saying that it's starting. We elect to wait around at home instead.

Rather than relax, I am seized with the need to telephone my agent.

I grab the phone, dial, talk to my agent's assistant, wait a few moments. My agent comes on the line.

ME   I'm thinking about writing a feature film spec.

MY AGENT   Wonderful. That's a terrific idea. Do you know why?

ME   Why?

MY AGENT   You'll get it out of your system. You'll write one, it won't sell and it'll be out of your system. And that will be good. Because you'll *never never ever* get another chance to write one.

ME   What?

MY AGENT   Please. You'll be busy. You'll be producing your television show or pitching another show or working on someone else's television show.

ME   But –

MY AGENT   We are not having a conversation. I am talking.

ME   But –

MY AGENT   It's a bad career move. It's a waste of time.

ME   But –

MY AGENT   Plus I don't handle feature scripts. It would be handled by someone else at the agency and do you know what? There's nobody here as nice as me.

CUT TO:

Wall Street and my agent agree on one thing: television is where the action is. The finance pages of the newspapers brim each day with the latest takeover gossip: Disney is going to buy CBS, unless it buys NBC, unless Time Warner buys NBC, which they won't if they can buy ABC, which won't be sold unless the buyer can come up with $15 *billion*, which no one can unless the Viacom/Block-buster deal goes through, which it may, which means that NBC is on the block, unless the Japanese sell MCA or Columbia/Tri-Star, which they'll have to, because to own a network you have to be an American, which is why Rupert Murdoch turned in his green card for a passport, and to own a network you need $15 *billion*, which is, how you say, *real heavy coin.*

Young people are heading to Los Angeles in the kind of droves that, ten or fifteen years ago, choked and clogged Wall Street. Doltish kids with no imagination don't want to be just investment bankers anymore; they want to be *entertainment sector analysts* and *new media venture capitalists* and *film industry bankers.* It's as if everyone in the 212 area code woke up one day and said, 'Hey, look at all those people in Los Angeles making all that money. Me too! Gimme!' and so here they are.

Two big studios are starting new networks of their own. One of them has had the good sense to schedule our little series.

The order came in for thirteen episodes. The new media world order was so far turning out to be a disappointment. It was a lot like the *old* media world order: things happened slowly, the number

119

of episodes was never as high as you expected and, ultimately, more networks meant only more network executives.

Nevertheless, we excitedly set to work. We hire a staff of writers. We hire a production crew and a line producer. We get busy writing scripts. Things are humming in our little beehive and, in quiet, reflective, cigar-smoking moments, Dan and I allow ourselves to daydream a bit. *What if*, we think to ourselves, *what if this new media world order means that everything gets organized? What if the fact that our studio is a part owner of a new network means that everyone acts like he's on the same team? What if the network executives are nice and easy to deal with? What if they order plenty of episodes – not teeny numbers like nine and twelve, but big, BIG numbers like twenty-two – which would be a full-season order – and forty-four.* Cigar smoke clouds the office as we muse: *And since the studio wants nothing more than to make enough episodes to syndicate the series, and since they own the network, why stop at forty-four?* Getting excited: *Why not make fifty right off the bat? Why not sixty? Why not one hundred? Sure,* we think, *being an obscure show on a start-up network isn't a prestige gig, but it will be lucrative as in lucre, lots of filthy lucre.*

CUT TO:

INT. OUR NEW OFFICE – DAY

SFX: phone rings

INTERCUT WITH:

EXT. RITZ CARLTON LAGUNA NIGUEL – DAY

My agent is sitting by the pool.

MY AGENT   Hi! The weather is great!

ME   Where are you?

MY AGENT   On vacation. For the holidays.

ME   Which holidays?

MY AGENT   The *Jewish* holidays.

ME   Which holiday?

MY AGENT   You're an Episcopalian. A WASP. What do you know from Jewish holidays?

ME   I know some Jewish holidays.

MY AGENT   What is this, the Inquisition? Am I on trial? My God, I am on trial. This I cannot believe.

ME   I'm just asking you which Jewish holiday it is that you're celebrating.

MY AGENT   The festival of Schmutblech.

ME   What?

MY AGENT   Okay, so I made it up. I'm not allowed a day off apparently.

ME   I was just curious –

MY AGENT   I called you with good news and you instantly attack me.

ME   What's the good news?

MY AGENT   I forget. I'm all turned around now.

ME   Was it . . . something about my feature spec? Because I've been thinking and it occurred to me that if I take a year off from tele–

MY AGENT   Oh, yeah. I remember. They just hired a head of the network. And the good news is that the guy they hired has never heard of you or your show.

ME   Why is that good news?

MY AGENT   Because the other person they were considering hates you and your work.

ME   Hates?

MY AGENT   Don't obsess. That person is no longer in the

121

running. Your job now is to maintain as low a profile as possible and shoot as many shows as possible as quickly as you can.

ME But –

MY AGENT I've got to go. It's time for the service.

CUT TO:

The next day, the *Wall Street Journal* reports that my studio is actively bidding for a network. This is confusing, because up to that morning I thought my studio was starting one of its own. *What if,* we daydream darkly, *what if all this talk about the new media world order is a load of crap?*

CUT TO:

EXT. STUDIO PARKING LOT – DAY

We run into studio executives as we are walking to our office from the studio commissary. (Now that we're in pre-production, we get in early.)

STUDIO EXEC Hi.

ME Hi.

A long pause. We walk in silence for a bit.

STUDIO EXEC I want you to come to a party.

ME I'd like to come to your party.

STUDIO EXEC Not *my* party. *A* party.

ME Okay.

STUDIO EXEC The new head of the new network is giving a party for all of the new shows.

ME All? There are only three.

STUDIO EXEC Two. One was cancelled this morning, so they're not invited.

ME Cancelled? But we haven't even premièred yet.

122

STUDIO EXEC   I didn't say it was going to be a fun party.

CUT TO:

The next week the *Wall Street Journal* publishes a special section on the new television industry. It handicaps the various takeover battles. Our new network is mentioned, prefixed by the adjective fledgeling. Our new network chief is mentioned, prefixed by the adjective demanding. Our show is mentioned without a prefix. I am unaccountably – and foolishly – cheered. Publicity, in that weird logic that only Hollywood and Wall Street appreciate, somehow protects us. They can't cancel a show, we reason, that's been mentioned in the *Wall Street Journal*.

CUT TO:

EXT. OUR NEW OFFICE – DAY

I am heading out the door.

SFX: cell phone chirps.

I look around guiltily and take out my cell phone. A few years ago, I didn't even own one. Until a few months ago, I never would have taken it out of my car. And until very, very recently, I wouldn't have left it on. But I've come a long way since Cheers, *longer since film school, vast distances since being an English major at Yale. So now not only do I own a cell phone, but I leave it on, people call me on it, I have conversations on it . . .*

I answer the phone; Yale and my Yankee roots fade further into the foggy past.

ME   Did you see our mention in the *Wall Street Journal?*

MY AGENT   See it? Who do you think planted it?

ME   You planted it?

MY AGENT   No, I'm asking you: who do you think planted it? It's not good.

ME   Not good? It's great!

MY AGENT   No, it's not.

ME   But everybody reads the *Journal*.

MY AGENT   No. Everybody reads *Variety*. New York money
people read the *Journal*. So they read about your show and
then they hype it. You're the guys from *Cheers*. You're hit
machines. You're cutting edge, new, now. The word goes out
that your show is a surefire hit and everybody expects great
things. Snag: you're on a brand-new network, and the best
– the very best – you can hope for is a 3 or 4 ratings point.
But the New York money people don't know that because
they don't know from this business – people who read *Variety*
know from this business, people who read the *Wall Street
Journal do not know from this business*! So when your show gets
a 4 and you're popping champagne, the New York money
people are wringing their hands and spreading doom and
gloom and the studio stock goes down and they get nervous
and cancel your show.

ME   Why am I not in the feature film business?

MY AGENT   What? You're not having fun?

CUT TO:

I hustle to my car and race home. I am the recent owner of an
eleven-week-old puppy, who, when not chewing on an electric
cord with 110 volts crackling through it, expresses his contempt
for me by shitting in out-of-the-way places in my house. I catch
him squatting over the special television section of the *Wall Street
Journal* and staring at me in a casual way. My dog, I realize by the
way he treats anything to do with television, is a feature person.
Ours will be a turbulent relationship.

FADE OUT.

EXECUTIVE INACTION

Fade in: October/November 1994

We are in production, fulfilling a thirteen-episode order. One year
has passed since our initial pitch, and the months in between have
led a rocky trail to this month, to production, to what, in our inno-
cence, we thought would be fun. It *is* fun, of course, but it is also
hard work. My father has two sayings he likes to repeat:

1. *Every* job is a sales job.

2. *Everything* you really want to do turns out to be hard work.

CUT TO:

INT. OUR OFFICE – DAY

*Our offices have been transformed. Where once we romped in solitary
splendor (three people, six rooms), we now need to find space for our
assistant, two writing assistants, a production assistant ('PA' in
industry parlance), two staff writers, a few consultants and another
producer.*

It's not a packed house, but it's close.

SFX: phone rings.

*The PA answers it, then heads down the hall to the writers' room,
shouting.*

PA   Run-through!

TRACKING SHOT:

*The PA brushes by the staff writers, holding mugs of coffee and the
'trades' –* Variety, *the* Hollywood Reporter *– as he passes them.*

127

Run-through!

The writers sigh, toss the trades, grab script binders and pencils, and head for the door.

The PA turns a corner and enters:

INT. THE WRITERS' ROOM – CONTINUOUS

I am sitting with Dan and a consultant.

PA (*shouting*) Run-through!

ME Yes, thanks. We heard. Give us five minutes.

PA But they just called 'run-through'.

ME Yes, and in five minutes we'll walk over to the stage.

PA But the director called it for now.

ME (*slowly, staying calm*) Yeah, I know, but it's going to take us five minutes to wrap up what we're doing here and walk over to the stage.

PA Won't that upset the director?

ME Excuse me?

PA Won't that upset him? Won't that undermine his authority?

ME What? Where did you learn that kind of shit? Huh, kid?

The 'kid' is four years younger than me.

PA Well, isn't the director in charge of the production?

ME *This* production? The one *my partner and I* are in charge of?

PA Um . . .

ME *That* director? The one my partner and I *hired*?

It's been a long, long, long time since Cheers.

PA Um . . .

ME Where'd you learn that crap, kid?

'Kid' again. I'm becoming an Industry asshole.

128

PA   Um . . . UCLA Film School, I guess.

ME (*suddenly chastened*)   Oh, yeah. Right.

SFX: phone rings. The PA lunges for it, happy to be out of our conversation. He answers it, waits a beat, turns to me with a sly smile.

PA   Your agent on line two.

I grab the phone.

MY AGENT   Hi.

ME   Hi.

MY AGENT   You sound busy.

ME   I am busy. We're shooting a show tonight. And they just called 'run-through'.

MY AGENT   Well, you sound busy. My advice is, take some time for you. Pamper yourself.

ME   Is that why you called?

MY AGENT   To tell you to pamper yourself? Give me a break.

Long pause.

ME   Then why did you call?

MY AGENT   I'm coming to the show tonight!

ME   And?

MY AGENT   And I need you to make sure that the PA stocks lots and lots of those small Evian bottles backstage.

ME   Why?

MY AGENT   In case I'm thirsty, that's why.

ME   Yes, I guess I can see your point.

MY AGENT   Plus, I'd like to take some home they're so convenient. Anyway, you'd better get to the run-through. You don't want to piss off the director.

Let me tell you a true story about Hollywood.

Two men have been friends and writing partners for many, many years. They have endured more than their share of career tumult. For many years they were successful writers and producers, and had earned the lucrative status of show-runner twice over. 'Show-runner' is the delightful and colorful phrase used by executives and networks to denote those few writers who can, in their estimation, run shows – that is, hire and fire writing staff, supervise casting and production, and guide scripts from conception to rewriting to post-production.

What show-runners Don't have to do is write. Naturally, all television writers aspire to be show-runners.

Back to the story.

After a few more ups than downs, the partners find themselves on the short end of a bad deal at a notoriously nasty studio, running six episodes of an egregious sit-com starring a clinically insane harridan has-been. This kind of thing happens all the time.

So somewhere mid-sixth episode, after ten weeks of studio and network interference, and after a particularly stressful conference call between the network executive and the studio executive, both of whom agreed on only one thing – namely, that neither partner was, in their estimation, much of a show-runner – one partner locks the other partner in his office and proceeds to beat him senseless with a desk lamp. The victimized partner (but aren't they both, in a sense, victims?) lands up in hospital, the lamp-wielding partner is fired (there is, amazingly enough, a no-starting-of-fights clause in that particular studio's standard contract), production is shut down for a week or two and every other writer in town has something to talk about at lunch.

That story, like most of the stories I tell in these pages, is *mostly* true. Who knows, really, what happened in that locked office?

And who knows, really, what the dynamic relationship was between those two partners? Maybe the guy who got cranked with the lamp, *deserved* to be cranked with the lamp. I don't know. When hauled before a judge, as a defendant in two lawsuits (one from the studio, for something called 'infringement and/or arrestation of production schedule due to malice and/or negligence'; and one from his former partner), the desk-lamp warrior gave this as his reason for the attack, 'He didn't back me up in a meeting with the network.' At lunchtime gatherings of writers, two camps quickly form: those who say, 'Okay, he didn't back you up in a meeting, fine, that's not so good, but perhaps you could have stopped just short of embedding glass splinters in his eye', and those who say, 'Okay, he didn't back you up in a meeting. Why did you let him live?'

Dan and I are currently four episodes into a twelve-episode order. Were he to beat me knee-walking bloody with a table lamp, I assure you, I will have deserved it. Producing a television show plunges even the slickest show-runner into a personal *Apocalypse Now*, with everything from budget overruns to explosive dysentery.

Production does something else, too: it delineates the outside edge of acceptable social behavior. I have seen producers dribble sauce from a takeout lunch on their chins and clothes, and then bark rudely at the nearest PA to fetch some napkins; I have seen producers too lazy to mutter even the most cursory 'thank you', and I have seen producers literally *walk away* while someone of a lower caste on the production budget tries to make polite chit chat. Thus, when Dan and I remember merely to mumble our 'thank yous' and maintain our zombie smiles, we develop the reputation of being 'really nice guys'. We don't intend to be 'really nice guys', we'd rather be 'really fiercely intimidating guys'. In a business famous for its screamers and tantrum-tossers, we feel guilty when we snap irritably at a PA.

The true fault-line, however, is the one that runs between me and Dan. We've been friends since college – a full ten years – and we woke up one day to discover that we weren't really friends in the conventional sense. What we are is business partners who happen to be friends. Early in our career, we spent a great deal of time together after work and on weekends; later, as the work got harder and the headaches more frequent, I would see him occasionally, usually at the instigation of his wife, of whom I'm extremely fond; at a certain point during the final season of *Cheers*, we barely functioned as partners at all, sharing the producing duties with two other writers. Now, with a year of development under our belt and a large production order to fill, the scale has tipped a bit, and with only each other to rely upon, we've strengthened the weave of our partnership. No one really knows the intricate dynamics of a writing partnership, especially the partners. They muddle their way through, happy to split a paycheck for the privilege of being allowed to play 'good cop' ('Sure! Sounds great! Let me check it out with my partner, though') and 'bad cop' ('No *fucking* way!') on alternate days.

The complexities of this particular partnership elude me, as I'm sure they elude Dan. Simply put, we check and balance each other. We are the pin to the other's balloon. Our partnership works because we can trust ourselves to be wrong at least 50 per cent of the time and, when we're lucky, one guy's time to be wrong coincides with the other's time to be right. Usually, we're both wrong at the same time.

Laughter is a universal indicator: as long as I can still make Dan laugh, things are okay. So far, we're still laughing. The purely creative part of the job – the sitting-on-a-couch-making-jokes part – has always come easy to us. But there's another part to running a show, a larger part, in which I've often failed him. Making critical judgments, organizing a staff, being judicious and careful – these are all areas in which I fall short, occasionally to his irritation, but more often to his undying patience. That he can do all that and still be a dazzlingly talented and funny writer can only be chalked up to luck. Mine, not his.

Truthfully, for us, production is a tropical cruise compared to development. And along the way, against all expectations, our relationship with the cast has developed into an easy, casual, very pleasant system – and in a few instances, outright friendship.

How different from *Cheers*! We're working with actors who are, to a person, poorer than we are. (Crass, yes, but this is Hollywood – these things matter.) And when we walk on to the set, we're regarded with a full measure of either fear or respect – I've never been able to tell the difference, if there is a difference.

CUT TO:

INT. OUR OFFICE – DAY

We're watching the second cut of an episode. We need to lift two minutes to deliver the show at the proper length. The show usually films about five minutes long, which allows us to cut out jokes that don't work, pick up the pace and fix technical problems.

I see the red light on my phone flash. Then, as the PA answers it, it stays a solid red for a few moments, then flashes again: whoever called is now on 'hold'.

The PA enters.

PA Agent on line one.

I take a deep breath and answer it.

MY AGENT I just saw a rough cut of your first episode.

ME Really?

MY AGENT Do you have a pencil?

ME Why?

MY AGENT I have some notes.

ME What?

MY AGENT In Scene B, after the woman exits, double cut to a reaction three-shot –

ME I'm sorry. I'm not clear on this. YOU have notes?

133

MY AGENT Yes, I have notes. Now, in Scene B, after the
reaction, play the rest of the run in a flat two-shot, lifting all
the intercuts –

ME I guess I'm having a hard time processing this. Since when
do agents give notes on a rough cut?

MY AGENT They don't. It's not in their purview.

ME So . . . ?

MY AGENT So it's in *mine* and I *do*. Get a pencil.

CUT TO:

The entertainment industry is run on pretty much the same
lines as the rest of corporate America, except in the entertainment industry job performance counts for a good deal less. It's
crucial, early on, to sniff out the cobweb of relationships among
studio executives and between them and the network. Sometimes the top executive has a better relationship with someone
way, way down the ladder than he does with his second-in-
command. So when the guy at the bottom has a note, you have
to listen – or, at least, fake listening more energetically. And
when the second-in-command has a note, you fix him with a
steady gaze, let your mind wander, organize your day, whatever.
Because the network holds all the cards, you have to do more
than pretend to listen. You have to actually listen. Actually
listening to network notes leads, over time, to attacking your
partner with a desk lamp.

Now that I think about it, a movie studio doesn't really resem-
ble another corporation so much as it does a large bureaucracy:
everyone has a big-shot title; everyone has a big-shot salary; no
one does anything. The explosion of titles has become ludicrous
– especially after the rash of mergers and buy-outs. The closest
thing to a big studio in 1994 is a really nasty African military dicta-
torship: 9,000 generals leading six infantry in a pointless war
against twenty nomad tribesmen. Only in this case, the nomad

134

tribesmen are writers, and instead of shooting them or starving them or letting them die of infectious diseases, they pepper them with notes on the script and questions about the rough cut.

Everyone gets to be a president of something – a division ('President of the Network Television Division'); a group ('President of the Domestic Syndication Group of the Network Television Division'); a concept ('President of New Media Concepts for the Domestic Syndication Group of the Network Television Division'); or a vague goal ('President of Entertainment'). Presidents report directly to Chairmen, who themselves report to the CEO of the holding company, who report to the Chairmen of the holding company, who report to the *WALL STREET JOURNAL*. Everyone else is an executive vice-president, except for the kids who deliver the mail, who are just vice-presidents. It's grade inflation gone mad: everyone gets firsts in every subject, except those people who have Nobel Prizes.

Luckily for us, we're on a start-up network without a meddlesome layer of terrified note-givers in place. And our studio executive is a nice guy about our age who calls once in a while with a note or two, and signs off with a hearty 'Cool!' when he's through. The best executives are those who have just reached the buck-slip moment of their careers. A buck slip is a piece of heavy-stock stationery about two and a half inches across and six inches long, with the company logo on top and, best of all, your name printed on the bottom. It is literally true that anyone who's anyone in Hollywood has a stack of buck slips. It's the first sign of success. It's the bottom rung of the status-symbol ladder that ends with a shower in your office and a personal chef. Freshly minted executives send out loads and loads of gratuitous mail just to clip a buck slip to the stack, as if to shout to the world, 'Hey, world! Look at me! I'm no longer a personal assistant!' Young sharks, slaving away in agency mailrooms or as PAs have been known to have their own buck slips printed up. It's a lot cheaper than leasing a BMW.

CUT TO:

INT. SOUNDSTAGE – NIGHT

It is Tuesday night and we're shooting our show. The audience is in their seats in the grandstand, but the floor of the stage is crowded with cameras, producers, the director and about a dozen agents, only some of whom have even the slightest right to be there. Mine, of course, has commandeered the only chair, and is nursing a small bottle of Vittel water – not, as requested, Evian, which was my little way of saying, 'Hey, you can't push me around.'

The network president and the studio president (or, I should say, one of the *network presidents and* one of the *studio presidents) are in a corner, trying to watch the show on a small TV monitor. My agent is between them, chattering merrily, blocking the screen with hand gestures, tugging on their arms to make a point, flailing wildly with the Vittel bottle.*

The presidents are trying hard not to hear, straining to see the monitor, working very hard to collect their thoughts and maybe give a few notes for the second take of the scene. But my agent is like a jackhammer at five in the morning: incessant, jangling, nerve-shattering, concentration-busting. The Vittel bottle takes on a new significance: it wards off dry throat.

TRACKING SHOT:

I walk along the stage apron, passing the cluster of executives and my agent.

MY AGENT   So the Republicans control the House and the Senate now. Should be interesting, no?

STUDIO EXEC   (*to network exec*)

Maybe this scene would be better if –

MY AGENT   My kid did the funniest thing yesterday –

I walk to the edge of the soundstage. In the corner of my eye, I can

see my agent still yabbering away, fracturing every attempt the
execs make at coherent conversation.

I walk back. And hear:

Want to hear something crazy insane? I liked the Frankenstein
movie and hated the Vampire movie. Nuts, huh?

NETWORK EXEC   (*clutching head*)

Maybe this scene needs –

MY AGENT   You want to know my favorite flower? The *iris*.
That's it. That's my favorite flower.

NETWORK EXEC   Is there any aspirin?

CUT TO:

Things get clearer to me. My agent suddenly becomes very wise in
my eyes. The evening ends early, and with no notes. I instruct the
PA to order several cases of small bottles of Evian.

FADE OUT.

MEET THE PRESS

Fade in: January 1995

I heard the following story a few weeks ago.

A while back – let's say, for argument's sake, the mid–1970s – the most popular sit-com on broadcast television featured as its star a famous and versatile comedian who played a character not unlike himself. One particular episode centered around the character's identical twin brother – played by the comedian himself, utilizing really cheapo split-screen effects.

So the day of the shoot, a few minutes after a guest audience has thoroughly enjoyed the dress rehearsal, the comedian comes stomping into the writers' room, eyes blazing, hands shaking, boiling over with the two most prevalent emotions in Hollywood: incandescent rage and piss-yourself panic. 'We're shutting down!' he screams at the writers. 'We're going to eat this episode!'

'Why?' they ask.

'Because my brother is getting all the laughs.'

Which, when you really think about it, makes sense.

We are seven days away from the première of our new television comedy. The phone rings in what sounds like one continuous chirp from the moment we walk into the office until the second we race to our cars and, worse, the fax machine burps every few minutes with fresh reviews, some from out-of-the-way places like Milwaukee and Baton Rouge, and some from scary places like New York City and Chicago.

When we hear that National Public Radio has called our show a 'smart little sit-com' we are elated – too elated, it turns out, for moments later the fax machine spits out a 'sit-com without snap' from *People* magazine and a 'semi-funny' from the *Washington Post*. After lunch, we get an 'attractive cynicism' from the *Wall Street Journal* and a 'promising new sit-com' from *TV Guide*. Cocktail hour finds us reeling from a 'will end up on the manure pile' from the *Boston Globe* and a 'skip it' from the *San Diego Union*. The evening comes to a close with a 'snappy little sit-com' from the *Hollywood Reporter*, which I enlarge on the office Xerox machine and place next to our 'sit-com without snap' from *People*, forming a collage testament to my personal bitterness.

It's strange how much the bad reviews hurt. It's also strange how widely disparate the reviews are – our little show about five guys who share an apartment seems to rub people either the wrong way or the right way, but whatever it does, it rubs them hard. The *New York Daily News* gives us a rave, as does *New York Newsday* and the *New York Post*. *Entertainment Weekly* calls us 'uncommonly well written and acted'; *Variety* rips out our still-beating heart and eats it. The *New York Times* and the *Los Angeles Times* dismiss us so contemptuously that I expect to be arrested.

Our problem, we rationalize, is that our show *seems* tacky – the *Animal House*-like subject matter – and is on a tacky network, so most reviewers have an awfully hard time getting past the particulars to review the show itself. Also, what fun is it to write a good review, or even a balanced review? I've written reviews before. I know. It's much more fun to draw blood.

CUT TO:

INT. MY CAR – NIGHT

I am heading west on San Vicente Boulevard.

SFX: cell phone chirps.

I answer it.

INT. MY AGENT'S CAR – NIGHT

My agent is heading down Beverly Boulevard.

MY AGENT   Congratulations.

ME   On what?

MY AGENT   Just on being you. On having done it.

ME   Done what?

MY AGENT   The whole thing. It's marvelous.

ME   What are you talking about?

My agent searches the passenger-side seat for a slip of paper.

MY AGENT   Look, all it says here on my call sheet is Call R. – re. congratulations. So c'mon, meet me fucking halfway here.

ME   Look, all I've done today that merits congratulations is not put out a contract on the guy who writes television reviews for *People* magazine, okay?

MY AGENT   Well, see? That's something.

ME   Yeah, well, wait until we hear from the rest of the reviewers.

MY AGENT   Wait, wait, wait. What do you care what the reviewers say?

ME   What do I care? What do I care what the reviewers say?

MY AGENT   What is this? A David Mamet play? Yes! *What do you care what the reviewers say?*

ME   Well, I –

MY AGENT   Did you *really* think Dustin Hoffman was that great playing the retarded guy in *Rain Man*?

ME   Well . . .

MY AGENT   And wasn't *Schindler's List* kinda *boring*?

ME   Well . . .

MY AGENT   And let's face it, *Murphy Brown* is a bad show. She's got no range and all the other characters do is shout and mug.

ME   But –

MY AGENT   Two words: grow the fuck up.

ME   But I –

MY AGENT   I am not having this conversation. We are not having this conversation. This conversation is not being conversed.

ME   You know what? This day is hard enough without this phone call.

MY AGENT   Don't get huffy. I was calling to congratulate you and I'm attacked. Interesting.

ME   You called to congratulate me?

MY AGENT   I did.

ME   About what?

MY AGENT   Do you know who this is?

My agent mentions the name of a famous trio who have just started their own studio.

ME   Yeah, I've heard of them.

MY AGENT   It just so happens that they love you, love your partner, love your work and want to make a deal with you. I told them that you were busy, that it was out of the question, that you'd never leave the studio you're at for any amount of money. Congratulations!

DISSOLVE TO:

INT. MY CAR – NIGHT

Late at night, when I can't sleep, I drive from my house at the beach into Hollywood to browse through the only late-night bookstore in town, Book Soup.

144

DISSOLVE TO:

INT. BOOK SOUP – NIGHT

I feign interest in the New Fiction table, make a few desultory stabs at the New Non-Fiction shelf, but I'm drawn, like a porn freak, to the dark-curtained corner of the newsstand, to the section labeled Movies/Television/Industry *and to a book entitled* The Encyclopedia of Short-lived Television Series. *I always do the same thing: I check the index to make sure that my name still isn't there.*

CUT TO:

INT. MY BEDROOM – NIGHT

The room is dark.

SLOW-TRACKING SHOT:

Through the darkened room. We hear the sound of a pen scratching against paper.

THE BATHROOM DOOR, AJAR

A shaft of light blazes into the bedroom.

TRACKING SHOT INTO THE BATHROOM

The scratching noise gets louder and louder. Some splashing.

Pan up to reveal me, in the bathtub, sipping Bourbon from the bottle, a stack of newsclips forming a soggy pile on one side, a wrinkled old sheet of paper on the other.

INSERT SHOT:

The wrinkled sheet of paper – It is the old Enemies List, with the original names scratched out, and new names, assorted television critics' names, in splotchy columns. Some names are underlined several times.

CUT TO:

Most of the following day is spent furiously courting the press. We're in a tight spot: our show is premièring on a brand-new network. Scrutiny is close. The critics are expecting to see a parade of crap. It's hard to convince them otherwise. We spend the day at something called the Television Critics Association Day at a fancy Los Angeles hotel. The event is a high-grade junket: the China White of press tours. The critics get supped and schmoozed and stroked and gifted – a leather binder here, a bottle of wine there, a pen and pencil set, a useless baseball cap – and in return they write snide things about our show, tipsy, no doubt, from our wine, bloated from our deli spread. At a certain point in the day, the cast, Dan and I assemble as a ragtag panel on the dais and field questions from whichever critics aren't in the lobby trying on their new leather jackets – gifts from a large cable channel. The questions are mostly nice, mostly positive. I scan the nametags for a name that matches the New Updated Enemies List. I don't see one, so the afternoon passes without incident.

The next night, we shoot the third-to-last episode of our new series. We hope, of course, that it isn't really the third-to-last; it's the tenth episode of a thirteen episode preliminary order. We hope, maybe foolishly, that the American public is more in sync with National Public Radio than it is with *People* magazine. We hope that the reviewers from Milwaukee and Boston and San Diego are wrong, and that it is a case of what Dan calls the revenge of the people who want to write for television, but never had the courage. We know, of course, that sheer statistics will keep us unknown to most of America. The baby network on which we appear barely covers 75 per cent of the country, and our show will be run at odd times on odd channels ('Channel 67, the Voice of Chicklet Valley!'). So we start out with a sense of certain doom, dotted here and there by the faintest sparks of hope. We will certainly be at the bottom of the heap, but perhaps we won't be at the *very* bottom. What we hope for is an Industry litotes – that the media won't not like us, that the American people won't unnotice us and that, ultimately, the fledgeling network on which we appear won't not have nothing to replace us.

146

CUT TO:

INT. SOUNDSTAGE – NIGHT

We're shooting episode eleven of the thirteen-episode order.

This particular episode features roughly six dogs who must, on command, run, jump, sit and howl. We have been told throughout the week, as the dogs ran wildly through the soundstage licking and nipping and mounting every Teamster electrician on the premises, that they were just nervous, or disoriented, and that come shoot night all would go well. As the cameras roll and the dogs begin licking, nipping and mounting, I feel a tug at my sleeve.

MY AGENT   Hi hi.

ME   Hi.

MY AGENT   Aren't those dogs the cutest?

ME   They'd be cuter if they could hit their marks and do the scene.

MY AGENT   If they could hit their marks and do the scene they wouldn't be dogs. They'd be actors.

I laugh at this. My agent laughs too.

See? I can be funny.

More mayhem on stage. The dog wrangler has cornered most of the dogs in the prop shed. Our regular dog – that is, the lead dog – is sitting on the set quietly fuming. The guest dogs aren't behaving professionally.

Hear that?

ME   Hear what?

MY AGENT   Listen.

My agent's head cocks to one side, indicating the studio audience. I notice, for the first time, that they're all laughing uproariously at the skittering dogs. Big, rolling, chunky laughs – long, air-rich guffaws.

147

Do you hear? You're a hit!

ME   But they're not laughing at our show. They're laughing at some dogs that are screwing up our show.

MY AGENT   Same diff.

ME   What?

MY AGENT   Look, they're *laughing*, okay? When you get laughs you take them, no questions asked. I hope you're getting this on the track. You never know when you'll need to goose what you get during the real show.

ME   But they're not laughing at what we want them to laugh at.

MY AGENT   They never are.

> CUT TO:

A few nights later, we gather the cast and writing staff together for our première party. It is a low-key event; the cast brings their families and friends; we all sit around drinking and eating until it's time to watch our television show broadcast for the very first time.

> CUT TO:

INT. PREMIÈRE PARTY – NIGHT

People stand around in casual groups.

SFX: party noise – ice in glass, laughter, music.

Dan pulls me aside.

DAN   Take a look at this.

He hands me a small datebook, '1990' emblazoned on its cover.

I've kept this thing for five years. Look up what happened five years ago today.

I flip through the pages.

> CUT TO:

INSERT SHOT:

Pages flipping by.

My hand stops at 'January'.

Flips to '23 January 1990'.

    CUT BACK TO:

INT. PARTY – NIGHT

I look up at Dan.

ME   (*softly*)

Man . . .

    CUT BACK TO:

INSERT SHOT:

Datebook. Below the entry for '23 January 1990' is written:

    Pitch Meeting @ Cheers 2.00 p.m. Go in through Melrose Gate.

    CUT TO:

It was five years ago, to the day, that my partner and I had our first meeting at our first job in television, and took our first step on the long path to this night, to *our* night, to watching our show on broadcast television. I am struck, as I watch the end credits and listen to the toasts of the party-goers, that this is all really happening. That millions of people – not many millions, maybe three – are watching the end credits at the same time. Somehow, all those years on *Cheers* never seemed as real as tonight. Tonight, I can feel it in my bones – tonight I have a *career*. Of course, in retrospect, the past five years have been leading inexorably to this night; still, to me it comes as a surprise. Perhaps it's a symptom of being in one's late twenties: tonight I feel like I've turned a corner, but in fact, I turned that corner long ago – I just didn't notice it at the time. I turned it five years ago, when I tossed out my stack of law applications; I turned it again when I became a producer of *Cheers*. Lucky for me, I didn't notice. My WASP emotional repression has stood me in good stead – had I thought about it, really *thought* about it, I never would have allowed myself the failure, to risk playing in the big ring. And tonight I'm very glad that I did.

FADE OUT.

DISSOLVE TO

Fade in: May/June 1995

While it is a gross generalization to suggest that comedy writers are mathematically ignorant, it's a fairly safe bet that most of them aren't trained statisticians. Nevertheless, when the ratings come burping out of the office fax, a writer who cannot tell time and who routinely tips 100 per cent in restaurants ('Easier to figure out . . . just *double* it') instantly becomes a Compudyne 17MHz 586K Pentium Math Co-Processor Unit.

CUT TO:

INT. OUR OFFICE – DAY

Our second week's ratings come in. Early in the day, we get something called the 'Overnights' – a rating based on a dozen or so key major markets (i.e. cities), designed to give a quick snapshot. Later that afternoon, after it has tabulated its other information (from phone polling, diary sheets and set-top boxes), the Nielsen Company releases the 'Nationals' – which become the basis for the weekly rankings.

Each rating is divided into two numbers: the 'rating point' – the number of television sets tuned to that program; and the 'share point' – the percentage of televisions in use that were tuned to that program. Cheers *regularly garnered a '25' ratings point (each point representing, roughly, 900,000 viewers) and a '32' share.*

We are loafing around the writers' room.

The PA enters, holding a few sheets of fax paper.

153

PA Ratings are in.

I take the papers from him, glance at them, then look up.

ME Great numbers!

We have received a '3' rating and a '5' share.

PA What did we get?

ME *(insanely cheery)* A 3–5.

PA A 35? Great!

ME No. A 3 rating, 5 share.

PA Oh.

ME Hey, hey, hey. This is good news. We're on a start-up network that only reaches 80 per cent of the country. We're on at nine-thirty, we have a crappy lead-in – I mean, this is better than they *expected*. They promised the advertisers a 4 share, so we're all way, way ahead. Plus . . .

I begin shuffling through the pages in sweaty earnest.

. . . plus, look at our numbers in the key major markets – the urban markets, where our signal is strongest. We're getting a 6 or 7 in the Midwest, parts of the South give us a solid 4 rating, New York City loves us . . .

I reach for a calculator, begin pounding away.

(high-pitched, frantic) . . . and we're retaining, in most of the major markets anyway – but after all, that's what we're *talking about here* – we're retaining about 95 per cent of our lead-in, which is *pretty fucking good! I mean, we should be celebrating –*

Dan slowly removes the sheets from my hands.

DAN *(quietly)* The ratings suck, Rob.

ME *(shouting)*

I know! Don't you think I know that?!

CUT TO:

Our ratings hold in the 3–5 range for the duration of our run. We complete production on our initial order by the middle of February. What we do now is wait: wait for the network to make up its mind about ordering new episodes; wait for the studio to swing into action twisting the network's arm; wait, finally, for America to wake itself up and say, 'Hey! That's a damn funny show!'

The point of doing a show for a network that is co-owned by the studio is that business partners aren't supposed to screw each other. The point, all those months ago, was that maybe this kind of enterprise signaled a new way of doing business.

What happened was this: in an effort to reduce its near-term losses and reduce its debt after an expensive buy-out, our studio sold its interest in the network, essentially cutting us loose. So now we're getting jerked around like everyone else in the business, only in this case for a fledgeling network with just two nights of programming instead of one of the big boys. I don't mind getting screwed over – hell, I *expect* to get screwed over; but I'd like it to be done by a better class of network. Waiting around to hear yes or no from a disorganized mess of an enterprise run by an ir-rational lunatic for breadcrumb-sized stakes takes the joy out of this most joyful business.

We will be waiting for several months. It is axiomatic in Holly-wood that any decision that must be made can be made only at the last legal minute. We will hear from the network scant minutes from the moment of (5 p.m., 1 June) that our options on the actors' services expire. Unless, of course, America *does* come to its senses and watch our show in busloads, in which case the studio will drag *its* feet in an effort to extort more money from the network. Notice the absence of me in either scenario? It's because at this point, I don't count.

CUT TO:

INT. SANTA MONICA. STARBUCKS COFFEE SHOP – DAY

I enter, wearing a pullover emblazoned with the logo of our television show – a 'wrap-party'gift to the cast and crew.

The wrap-party gift is a crucial part of the business, and one fraught with class implications. Feature films always provide a jacket of some opulence, either leather or heavy cotton, always lined, always expensive. Television shows, depending on their relative success and longevity, satisfy the requirements with a baseball cap, a pullover or a cheap nylon attaché case. Certain shows (your Seinfelds, your Cheers) can't get away with cheaping out and then you see sprouting all over town Seinfeld car coats and Cheers jean jackets.

We're in the very early stages of success (so early, in fact, as to be unrecognizable from failure) and so we passed out pullovers.

I walk up to the counter and order.

ME   Tall latte, please.

GUY BEHIND COUNTER   Sure thing.

He sets about making my coffee, then spots the pullover.

Hey! You work on that show?

ME   Yes.

GUY   I love that show! What do you do?

ME   I'm a writer.

GUY   Wow! That's a funny show! That's the funniest show I've ever seen!

ME   Gosh, thanks.

GUY   No, no. Thank *you.*

He hands me my tall latte.

So, are you guys, like, looking for any new writers? Because, you know, I'm real good with dialogue and story is . . .

A writer friend of mine offers this moral puzzler. You are traveling in the Brazilian rainforest. You come across an aging, though still spry, Adolf Hitler. You tell him that he is the greatest villain of the twentieth century and that it will give you great pleasure to turn him in to the authorities. He tells you that he's seen your show and he thinks it is 'wunderbar'. Do you turn him in?

Faced with five months of unoccupied waiting time, I become horrendously ill. This takes all the fun out of staying home all day.

CUT TO:

INT. MY BEDROOM – DAY

I am watching the Charles Perez Show. *Charles has on 'Men Who Left Their Girlfriends for Their Girlfriends' Brothers'.*

SFX: phone rings.

I groggily answer it.

MY AGENT   (*offscreen*)

How are you feeling?

ME   Well, I'm running a fever and –

MY AGENT   That's terrible.

ME   And I'm dizzy and –

MY AGENT   But it sounds a lot better than what I had last week. I was dizzy. I ran a fever. Have you seen a doctor? You should get some Percocet.

ME   What is Percocet?

MY AGENT   It's a powerful painkiller. It freezes out the pain receptors in the central nervous system and floods the cerebral cortex with neurological impulses that create a completely restful, drowsy state.

ME   I don't think I need that.

MY AGENT   I wasn't saying get it for *you*.

ME   Why are you calling?

MY AGENT   Well, I know you probably didn't see this week's rankings. So let me be the first to say it: Congratulations! Your show is a hit.

ME   A hit? What were we? Ninety-second?

MY AGENT   Ninety-third, actually.

ME   And how is that a hit?

MY AGENT   Because who cares about what the ranking is? a), it's all about demographics; and c), the people who need to see the show have seen the show and they call me every five minutes because they love you and they want to be in business with you.

ME   Who are these people?

MY AGENT   Never you mind. You just concentrate on getting well. Get out of town, go on vacation. Because come 1 June, my friend, things'll start popping.

ME   You mean we'll be in production on our series?

MY AGENT   God, only as a last resort.

ME   What?

MY AGENT   It's not about *this* show. It's not about *this* move. It's all about the move *after* this move.

ME   What?

MY AGENT   Chill for the next few months. Then we decide if you stay at this studio or trade up.

ME   But I still want to do more episodes of our series.

MY AGENT   My advice: get to work on the Percocet. I'm running out of prescription pads.

CUT TO:

Our overall deal with the studio is up 1 June 1995. Which is, ironically, around the time that the network must either order our show or cancel it outright. We wrapped production on our show on 17 February 1995. What we have been doing since is what's known as letting our deal run out.

The theory is as follows. With a show on the air – anyone's air, even a new, unwatched network's air – you're sought after by all the studios, even some brand-new studios with hugely famous owners. So while you wait for the network to make up its mind, you take meetings, you have lunches, you hang around the house a lot with dirty hair and five o'clock shadow.

For years, I have wondered about the huge numbers of people that throng the city in the middle of the day – driving around, shopping, lingering over lunch, playing tennis, hanging out at the beach. This city is jammed in the middle of the day with all sorts of layabouts and lazybones. This is not Manhattan, whose down-town streets in the middle of the day are neutron-bomb quiet. LA is busy all day long, the golf courses and tennis courts and gyms and supermarkets and shops filled to capacity by mid-morning. Who are these people? I have wondered. I have finally figured it out. They are all television producers, waiting to hear from the network. They are all letting their deals run out.

CUT TO:

INT. MY PLACE – DAY

Morning. I have just returned from a three-week trip through Central America. I am drinking coffee in my underwear, staring at a pile of unpacked luggage.

I've lost track of time: it's May, network-scheduling season.

SFX: phone rings.

MY AGENT   Hi. Welcome back.

ME   Thanks.

MY AGENT   Did you have a good time?

ME   I had a great time, thanks.

MY AGENT   Great, great.
  Pause.

ME   Um . . . any reason why you called?

MY AGENT   Of course there's a reason I called. Your show was canceled this morning.

ME   You're kidding.

MY AGENT   I am? I don't think I am. I think I'm serious.

ME   Damn.

MY AGENT   May I be honest with you? Your show did not deserve to be canceled. Some shows deserve to be canceled. Your show did not deserve to be canceled. May I be honest with you? *I wish the network ill.* Seriously. I wish them *ill.* And I wish that on people very, very rarely, if ever.

ME   Damn.

MY AGENT   Stop saying damn. Say fuck. It'll feel better.

ME   Fuck.

MY AGENT   Feel better?

ME   No.

MY AGENT   I told you that you wouldn't. Look, don't wallow in this. I have a call I have to take. Stay by the phone.

CUT TO:

INT. OUR OFFICE – LATER

Dan and I are deep in thought. We have been mulling over a number of offers from competing studios. As we near the official end of our deal, and with this morning's news still rattling around our heads, we try to divine a next move.

160

SFX: phone rings.

The PA enters, nervously. He knows what's been going on, and he knows who would be the first to go in the event of a cancellation.

PA   (*nervous*)

Front office on line one, from New York.

It's an executive from our studio, calling from New York, where, for some reason still unclear to me after five years in the business, the various network heads travel every year from Los Angeles to announce their fall television show schedules, which means the various studio heads and various agents and various producers also travel from Los Angeles to lobby and cajole and make last-minute pleas. It could all be accomplished at half the cost if everyone decided, hey, we're all in Los Angeles, let's just stay in Los Angeles, which wouldn't make the owners of the St Regis, Regency, Carlyle and Four Seasons hotels very happy, but would make their employees very happy, since no one likes to have a bunch of nervous wrecks in fancy suits screaming, 'Where's the Ty Nant water?!' at them for two weeks straight.

Aren't you going to get it?

I nod and answer the phone.

ME   So we're canceled?

STUDIO EXEC   Who said that?

ME   The network did. At their press conference.

STUDIO EXEC   That's what they said then. What they say now is very different.

ME   What do they say now?

STUDIO EXEC   It's unclear.

ME   Look, are we canceled or not?

STUDIO EXEC   Absolutely not.

ME   Really?

STUDIO EXEC   Listen, who knows, really? Canceled? Not canceled? Maybe a mid-season back order for thirteen? I'm not in the predicting business. I *was* in the predicting business, but then, know what? *I got out of the predicting business.*

ME   I think there's something wrong with this phone. I couldn't quite understand a word you said.

STUDIO EXEC   Listen, I predict they order thirteen episodes as a back-up.

ME   When?

STUDIO EXEC   I predict in two weeks.

ME   Oh.

STUDIO EXEC   Got a sec? Think with me a minute. Hypothetical time. Say they don't order the show. Say your show's canceled. Now what?

ME   Now what, what?

STUDIO EXEC   Now what where do you guys go? Where's the fit? Do you know where the fit is? I'll be honest with you. I know you've been taking meetings around town. But where's the fit? Do you know where the fit is?

ME   It's here. I'm having it.

STUDIO EXEC   Let me call you back.

CUT TO:

We sit in our office for another hour or two. Our show, our little show, has been a difficult case from the start. We shot the pilot episode a year ago, for one network, they passed on it, a start-up network bought it and ordered twelve more episodes, which we shot in the autumn and early winter, it premièred in January, ran until a week ago, canceled this morning, maybe uncanceled this afternoon . . .

162

In my wallet, stapled to my driver's license, I have an organ donor's card, which means, in the clearest possible terms, that if I'm in a hideous car wreck (which in Los Angeles is a matter of living here long enough), the hospital personnel are empowered, upon my death, to scavenge my body for usable organs. There's also a box marked DO NOT RESUSCITATE, which instructs the hospital personnel on what to do if I'm brain dead but still clinging to life. I have checked the box. DO NOT RESUSCITATE is my motto – in life, love and business. It isn't much, but it's mine. If I knew Latin, I'd have a coat of arms made up.

CUT TO:

INT. OUR OFFICE – DAY

Thick clouds of cigar smoke.

SFX: phone rings.

I answer it myself for two reasons: a), because I'm closer to it; and b), because the PA and the other office employees are all off Xeroxing their résumés.

MY AGENT   I have great news.

ME   We got an order?

MY AGENT   No.

ME   We're canceled, and that's that, it's over, we can move on?

MY AGENT   No.

ME   What, then?

MY AGENT   Keep guessing. I like seeing how your mind works.

ME   What?

MY AGENT   The good news is that the studio called me and made me an offer to extend your deal two more years. At what I can only describe, after thirty years in this business, as a *serious escalation of monies.*

163

ME   How serious?

MY AGENT   First let me caution you against your tendency to equate money with happiness.

ME   How serious?

MY AGENT   Your life, your life*style*, is something that you and you alone can make into happiness. And no amount of money will alter that.

ME   How serious?

MY AGENT   Life is to be lived here, on earth. Not in some bloodless ledger book.

ME   How serious?

My agent then mentions a figure that is large and round and Rubenesque. My partner and I look at each other.

Why?

MY AGENT   Why what?

ME   Why did they call and offer to re-up us at such a premium? We just got canceled. We failed.

MY AGENT   In the first place, you did not get canceled. You *maybe* got canceled. In the second place, even if you *did* get canceled, by getting canceled you've proved that you're players in the big game, and c), don't ever say we've failed to me again. You did not fail. It was a good show that deserved better from its auspices. And fourth, the reason that they re-upped you at such a premium is because you have unquestionably the finest agent in this or any other universe, and rather than draw this out any longer, let me just say, you're welcome, it was my pleasure.

CUT TO:

The network calls later to say that while our show is not on the fall schedule, it is not canceled. They need two weeks to decide up or down, yes or no.

DO NOT RESUSCITATE, I think to myself. But it's no use. In Hollywood – in *my* Hollywood, anyway – that's a useless motto. This business is about lingering, about near-death, brain death and last-minute doses of adrenalin and shock pads. Projects go from here to there to life to dormancy because they linger, because they survive. And out here, just surviving gets you a *serious escalation of monies*.

CUT TO:

EXT. HARVARD BUSINESS SCHOOL – DAY

I am back in my home town, Boston, to watch an old friend graduate from Harvard Business School. We still have not heard from the network. At the many graduation parties I attend, no less than two dozen young newly minted MBAs saunter over to me and announce, with charming arrogance, that they are moving to Los Angeles to get involved in the entertainment industry. I smile and encourage each one with great intensity. 'Fuck 'em,' I think to myself, 'let 'em learn the hard way.'

As the students approach the dais, spread out on the splendid lawn in the middle of a beautiful New England spring morning, a noise snaps me back to present day.

SFX: cell phone chirps.

I answer it, unashamed. I am, after all, at Harvard Business School.

MY AGENT Sorry, kiddo. The show is officially canceled.

ME Oh.

MY AGENT What's that noise in the background?

ME I'm at Harvard Business School.

MY AGENT   Jeez. Isn't that a little drastic? I mean, you still have a very promising career, you know.

ME   No, not that. I'm here watching a friend graduate.

MY AGENT   You flew all the way back to Boston for that? Nice guy.

ME   That, and to celebrate my birthday with some friends.

MY AGENT   Oh! Great! When's your birthday?

ME   Today.

MY AGENT   How old are you?

ME   I just turned thirty.

MY AGENT   Happy birthday!

ME   Some birthday.

MY AGENT   Wait, wait, wait. You're *thirty*, not *fifty*. I know guys who are fifty, and have never had a show on the air, let alone a deal like you just signed. So just blow out the candles and shut your trap and get back here and get another show on the air. Happy birthday!

I hang up the phone.

SFX: cell phone chirps.

I answer it.

STUDIO EXEC   I assume you heard?

ME   Yeah.

STUDIO EXEC   Look, I'm sorry. We did what we could. They're idiots over there. Idiots.

ME   Thanks.

STUDIO EXEC   I'm out of town for the weekend. My daughter just graduated from Harvard Business School and so I'm in Boston –

ME   You're at the HBS graduation?

166

STUDIO EXEC   Yeah. Why?

ME   So am I.

STUDIO EXEC   What?

I stand up on my chair and scan the crowd. I spot the studio exec in the last row, leaning up against a tree, talking on his cell phone.

I wave.

ME   See me waving?

The studio exec looks up, sees me, waves weakly.

STUDIO EXEC   So this call is going to my office in LA, where my secretary transferred it to your phone in LA, which bounced it to you here?

ME   I guess so.

STUDIO EXEC   What a fucking world. By the way, what you doing here?

ME   I have a friend who graduates today.

STUDIO EXEC   You have a friend in my daughter's class? How old are you, anyway?

ME   I turned thirty today.

STUDIO EXEC   Fuck you.

ME   I'm serious.

STUDIO EXEC   Fuck you. I was feeling sorry for you, but fuck you.

CUT TO:

INT. AMERICAN AIRLINES FLIGHT 94 – DAY

I'm flying back to LA. I am locked into a conversation with an elderly woman in the next seat.

OLD LADY   What do you do?

167

ME   I'm a television writer.

OLD LADY   How interesting. Have you been doing it long?

ME   No, not really. About . . .

I start adding up the years in my head.

(*stunned*)   Jesus. I've been doing it for over five years.

OLD LADY   And is Los Angeles your home?

ME   No, not really. I've only lived there about . . .

I start adding up the years in my head.

(*stunned*)   Jesus. I've been living in LA for seven years.

My eyes glaze over. The old lady leaves me to my thoughts.

CUT TO:

Something occurred to me on that plane ride: I grew up in Los Angeles. I arrived as a very young twenty-three, and I arrive this day a still-young-but-wiser thirty.

It's all blurred: film school, getting an agent, *Cheers* . . . It's all blurred except for *our* show, which failed in only the narrowest sense, but succeeded in so many others: we learned a lot, we showed whomever we needed to show that we could do it, and I became whatever passes these days for an adult. And adulthood – or *my* adulthood, anyway – is characterized by a sense that life is an episodic comedy: funny little scenes connected by the thinnest tissue of meaning, characters you like and want to spend time with, and a big pay-off at the end.

Screenwriting format allows for two ways to end a scene: the 'fade' and the 'dissolve'. The 'fade' is final: fade to blackness, the picture slowly transforming to a solid black frame. The 'dissolve' is what we use in television. It's more forgiving. A 'dissolve' is a transition between one thing and the next – between scenes, say, or moments in a script. When you 'fade', you 'fade *out*'. When you 'dissolve' you 'dissolve *to*'.

CUT TO:

INT. MY PLACE – DAY

Late afternoon. I've just arrived from the airport. I set my bags down, greet my dog, flip through the mail, pour myself a beer and walk out on to my balcony.

SFX: phone rings.

I know who it is. I let the machine pick up.

DISSOLVE TO:

SET UP, JOKE,
SET UP, JOKE

The First Meeting, Monday Morning, 10:30 a.m.

'Hi.'

'Hi.'

'We'll be right with you. Did someone offer you coffee?'

'Yeah, I think it's coming.'

'Great, great. Well. Anyway. They'll be right with you. I'm sorry it's taken so long. But it's a conference call, so . . .'

'Right, right.'

'I'm Josh, by the way. I'm new in the comedy development department.'

'Oh, great. Nice to meet you, Josh. But, wait a minute . . . wasn't the guy before you . . .'

'Also named Josh? Yeah.'

'And where did he go?'

'Nowhere. He's my boss.'

'Oh.'

'That's Josh now. He's waving us in.'

'Okay, then.'

'Don't forget your coffee.'

'Hi!'

'Hi!'

'Hi!'

'Hi!'

'Hi!'

'Hi!'

'This is Josh, and you've met Josh, and this is Trish and Trish's assistant Tori, and Eli and Beth and Jamal.'

173

'Hi, Josh, and Trish, and Tori and Eli and Beth and . . . I'm sorry . . .'

'Jamal.'

'Jamal, right, right. Sorry.'

'Don't be sorry!'

'Josh still hasn't learned our names. And he's the boss!'

'So I heard. Congratulations, Josh.'

'I'm Eli.'

'Maybe it'd be easier for me if you all wore name tags.'

'Hahahahahahaha.'

'Hahahahahahaha.'

'Hahahahahahaha.'

'Funny! You're a funny guy. So why don't you tell us what you've got today?'

'Great. Great. See, I was thinking about something–'

'Can I interrupt you for a moment?'

'Of course, Josh.'

'I just want to say how much I've loved your work and how really grateful I am that you're here today.'

'Me too.'

'Me too.'

'Gosh, thanks, Josh and . . . Eli and . . . Trish and . . . all of you.'

'Big fan.'

'Thanks.'

'So, sorry, continue.'

'Well, what I was going to say was that one of the things that I've been thinking about is how, well, how mysterious all of this . . . business, this television producing business, is to most people, and I was thinking about some kind of . . . I don't know . . . kind of half-comic half-tragic look at this business through the eyes of a writer, maybe a guy like me.'

'Yeah.'

'Okay.'

'Let's think about this for a minute.'

'I agree with Josh.'

'Me too.'

'Well, okay, I was thinking it could be in, like, a pastiche of forms – maybe part of it will be in screenplay format, maybe part of it will be in the form of stories and anecdotes – I mean, you guys know how much people in this town like to sit around and gossip and tell war stories, right? – and that maybe it'll form some kind of accurate picture or snapshot – kind of an impressionistic thing, I guess – about the inner workings of and the state of our business. I mean, not this – I'm just throwing this out – but what if the spine of the story was, like, the life cycle of one television series?'

'Hmmmm.'

'Hmmmm.'

'Hmmmm.'

'Hmmmm.'

'I love it.'

'I agree with Josh.'

'I do too.'

'Me too.'

'The only thing I'm not crazy about is that it's about the television business and that it's about you.'

'But does it have to be about the television business?'

'I think Trish raises an interesting point. Does it?'

'And does it have to be about you?'

'Does it?'

'Does it?'

'I . . . well . . . I mean, it's . . .'

'Doesn't matter, really. Let's try it. Let's see how it goes. Let's play around with the area and see what happens. Is that okay?'

'Can we play around with the area?'

'I love the area.'

'It's a great area.'

'It's a really interesting area to play with.'

'So let's play with it.'

175

'Okay?'
'Okay?'
'Okay?'

SPRING: 'ON THE BUBBLE'

Fade in:

A famous actor once tried to describe the rigors of being in production. The hours are long, the food is mediocre, the living quarters are cramped. 'Basically,' he said, without a smidgen of irony, 'it's like Auschwitz.'

Of course, a holocaust is in the eyes of the beholder, and for him I guess hell was a double-wide trailer and three catered meals a day. For the rest of us, though, being in production is *not at all* like Auschwitz. It's not even like taking the *tour* of Auschwitz. It's not even, at its worst, like taking a trip to Poland. The only thing even remotely similar between those two things is that in each case, one's first impulse is to hide in the attic.

We have just finished producing twenty-two episodes of a half-hour television series. We are *on hiatus*, as the lingo goes. If your show is a hit – or even, in these days of diminished expectations, a moderate success – the concept of a *hiatus* is identical to the concept of a 'holiday.' Your show is definitely going to be on the network's fall schedule and you have about eight weeks to relax and go to Hawaii. If your show is not a hit – that is to say, if your show is written and produced by me – the concept of *hiatus* is closer to the concept of *frantic period of intense speculation and worry*. The production schedule of a normal twenty-two-episode season ends around the first week in March. The networks make their decisions about which shows to keep and which shows to drop in the middle of May. You see the problem here? Two-and-a-half months of speculation.

Our sitcom premièred to generally good reviews – some outright raves, from influential critics in the *Los Angeles Times*, *New York Newsday*, and *Media Week* – and low but not shabby ratings. Our situation, though, in the last four weeks before the networks announce their new schedules, is precarious. Because we cannot claim to be an outright ratings success, and because the network on which our show appears requires, above all, an outright ratings success, the word on our show is murky. *Variety*, the entertainment industry trade paper, has more or less written us off as a 'promising rookie' that has had trouble 'delivering'. I have been in the television business for six years and I am still waiting to attain the necessary diffidence to be able to read things about myself in *Variety* without lapsing into a kind of enraged hyperventilation.

CUT TO:

INT. MY OFFICE – DAY

I am at my desk smoking a cigar. That afternoon our office received a strongly-worded memo reminding us that California state law prohibits smoking in office buildings.

SFX: phone rings. It's my agent.

ME   What have you heard?

MY AGENT   Okay. No pleasantries, I guess. Hi. How are you? I'm fine, thanks. Me too. Not bad weather we're having. I agree, it's very pleasant. Especially in the evenings. Yes, they're very–

ME   I'm sorry. I guess I'm just a little tense. The waiting.

MY AGENT   I understand. It's a complicated time. Have you heard anything from the network?

ME   I haven't heard much. The numbers were pretty good – we're 'trended up', the studio says. We did better than the show that had our time slot before us. The reviews have been

180

gratifying. All in all, I'd say we're in good shape to get on the fall schedule.

MY AGENT   Oh. Gosh. I was hoping you were going to say that the ratings were sluggish and disappointing, that the network had higher expectations, and that you're a long shot for fall.

ME   Why were you hoping I'd say that?

MY AGENT   Because it's the truth. And I wasn't in the mood to deliver bad news.

ME   Um . . .

MY AGENT   It just brings the whole day down, you know?

ME   Yes, I suppose I can see how it would.

MY AGENT   Look, you're on the bubble, what can I say?

ME   Nothing, I guess.

CUT TO:

Our show is *on the bubble*, which is an industry term I've never really understood. *Bubbles* are fun, gassy things – they bring to mind balloons, champagne, celebrations. Yet to be *on the bubble* – which sounds like a Bertie Woosterism for *a little bit tipsy* – is to be neither officially cancelled nor officially picked up. It means they're still trying to decide about you. Still trying to figure out whether to order your show for one more year and give you a shot at the apartment in Paris, or dredge up a sad-sounding voice and get their assistant to track you down.

What you do know, though, is this: the official call, when it comes, will come at the last legal minute. You also know this: the official call, when it comes, will come about five or six days *after* you've already heard, from agents, studio executives, and, probably, the girl at Peet's Coffee. And you also know this: there really is no *on the bubble*; uncertainty is just bad news that's taking its time. If you're a hit – and to get a second season these days, you must be at least someone's definition of a hit – you know it. And if you don't know it, well, there's a reason for that.

If there is one rock-solid axiom in this business – maybe in every business, I don't know – it's that when you hear the rumor of bad news about your show, your money, your career, your livelihood, that rumor is always true. *Always.* At the risk of inciting legal action from certain major celebrities who have battled certain major rumors for years, let me stick my neck out further: those rumors are true, too. Or true enough. Essentially true.

This is, after all, the least imaginative place on earth. This is where people agree to spend hundreds of millions of dollars on movies because they remind them of other movies that have already been made. This is where old sitcoms are turned into either big budget feature films or low budget reality television shows. Do you really think people have the inclination or the imagination to *invent* rumors out of whole cloth? Of course not.

When you hear that your show is being cancelled and replaced with *Candid Camera Uncensored!* it may in fact turn out to be cancelled for *Family Candid Camera* or *Kids 'n' Candid Camera* or even something completely different. But it is going to be cancelled. The essence of the rumor is true. And the truth hurts. That's how you can tell it's the truth.

CUT TO:

EXT. SANTA MONICA STREET – DAY

I am wandering around in the middle of the day, walking the dog. I bump into a friend. She looks at me for a long time with a sad and confused expression.

FRIEND   Hi?

ME   Oh hi. How are you?

FRIEND (*disconcerted*)   Fine. And how about you? Are you okay? Is everything . . . okay?

182

ME Yeah.

FRIEND You look . . . different.

ME Oh, yeah, well I haven't shaved in a few days.

FRIEND And tired.

ME Yeah, well, we just finished twenty-two episodes, so I guess I am a little tired.

FRIEND And you've gained weight.

ME Well, see you around.

CUT TO:

Of course, she's right: I do look tired and I have gained weight. Unfortunately, the solutions to those two problems are mutually exclusive, so I have elected to remain tired for a few weeks while I try to work off the twenty-two episodes I have gained since the start of production. I have a writer friend who claims to own a pair of 'hiatus alarm trousers.' When he must lie down to button them, it's time to go on hiatus.

CUT TO:

EXT. SAN VICENTE BLVD – DAY

I'm driving to the gym. The phone rings.

MY AGENT I ran into the head of the network at lunch.

ME And?

MY AGENT You don't want to know where?

ME No.

MY AGENT The Grill. He was at The Grill.

ME And?

MY AGENT We had a conversation about the show.

And his tone was interesting.

ME What was his tone?

MY AGENT   In a word, *elegiac*. His tone was *elegiac*. Some, with a smaller vocabulary and a lack of appreciation for nuance, which is not something I do not have, might say *funereal*. But I think *elegiac* conveys the proper ambiguity.

ME   Actually, it doesn't sound all that ambiguous.

MY AGENT   Meaning?

ME   Meaning, it sounds like we're dead. I wish somebody would just call me up and tell me that, straight out. Just say, 'Sorry, didn't work, we're cancelling the show,' rather than all of this . . . this mystery.

MY AGENT   Not following you.

ME   Why can't they just say it now? Why do they have to wait until May?

MY AGENT   Because May is when they announce.

ME   Why can't they announce *now*?

MY AGENT   Because it's not May.

ME   Yeah, but–

MY AGENT   You're breaking up. Hello? I think I lost you? Hello? Can you hear me? Can you hear me now?

CUT TO:

Our show started strong. We premièred to good numbers, held a respectable slice of the previous show's audience, and in general behaved in a fashion that could best be called 'diligent.'

But these days, ratings described as 'diligent' and 'solid' are not enough to keep a show on the air. The stakes are simply too high. To stay on the air these days, a show must either show ratings growth, or be owned by the network on which it airs. Our show can boast neither. The weird thing is, these days a show garnering a 12 or 13 per cent ratings share can be considered a hit. Five years ago, it would have been yanked during the first commercial break. Our show delivered what will, in a few years, be considered stellar smash-hit numbers. The problem is, it's not a few years from now, it's now. We're ahead of the curve.

CUT TO:

INT. CITRUS RESTAURANT – DAY

I have cleaned myself up for a business lunch (dry salad, grilled fish, fizzy water) with a network executive. Although the network won't announce their fall schedule for four more weeks, I am consumed with curiosity about the fate of our program. The wisest thing would be to simply decline the invitation and pretend to be out of town – after all, the decision is out of my hands completely and I'll just drive myself crazy trying to work the various angles. But since I'm not out of town and I've shaved and taken off about seven episodes so far, I go – vowing to play it cool.

ME   So, are we cancelled or what? Just tell me.

NETWORK EXECUTIVE   Well, you're not cancelled.

ME   We're not?

NETWORK EXEC   Not so far. But it's early still. We haven't even screened some of the new pilots we're considering for next fall.

ME   What if those all turn out great?

NETWORK EXEC   C'mon! You know that never happens. We develop thirty scripts and shoot about ten pilots. We're lucky to get two or three that have potential.

ME   Oh.

NETWORK EXEC   It's a great show. You guys have done a terrific show. Everybody at the network loves it.

ME   But?

A long pause.

NETWORK EXEC   It's complicated.

185

ME Complicated how?

NETWORK EXEC Let's just leave it at 'it's complicated.' (*then, brightly*) So, any big hiatus plans? You look great, by the way. Have you lost weight?

CUT TO:

In Hollywood, when things are described as 'complicated', the news is rarely good. Tumors and cancerous lesions are 'complicated'. Mega-hits and sure things are simple. Big fat checks are simpler still.

What's complicated, in a town like this one, is that information is rarely informative. In the weeks between March and May, so much gossip is tossed back and forth, so many projects are *sure things* on Monday that become *dead on arrival* by Thursday, that the best, sanest, course of action is to muffle out all the noise altogether.

Still, the great thing about rumors is that there's always one to hang on to. For the ninety-nine pieces of negative information you hear about your project, there's always at least one more that you can embroider and inflate in your mind that means, *We're a sure thing for the fall schedule. I heard it from a guy who was in the meeting.*

Also: gossip, when it's about other people and their troubles, is fun.

For instance, here is the latest, hottest, most impossible-to-substantiate rumor racing through town:

A hugely rich media mogul and his wife engage in a kinky three-way involving bondage, light sadism, and a young lady from Thailand. In an act of monumental foolishness – almost biblical in its irony – the mogul videotapes the entire session (dirty talk, leather masks, *everything*) forgetting that these days everything that's recorded eventually finds its way into the hands of the press.

Call it 'Flynt's Law,' named for Larry Flynt, publisher of every fifteen-year-old boy's favorite read, *Hustler*. Any humiliating act, caught on film, audio- or videotape will be revealed, like water seeking its level, in the most excruciatingly painful way. If you cheat on your wife, she will not receive the incriminating photographs in a scruffy envelope in private. She will see them in a newspaper brought to her attention by your children. If you confess strange passions to a good friend in a neighborhood bar, the audiotape will be played coast-to-coast and your mother will hear it first.

The rumor continues: somehow, the video cassette slips out of the mogul's house (they have a way of doing this) and into the hands of one of America's most notorious pornographers. This is hot stuff, he thinks to himself, and prepares to publish stills from the videotape in a multi-part, multi-issue format entitled, no doubt, *A Hollywood Sextravaganza!*

Faced with the kind of embarrassment that would make anyone – even a billionaire media mogul – want to crawl up his own ass, the mogul makes a final, desperate plea. He calls the pornographer up and begs – *begs* – him not to publish the photographs. The two men are, he says, in essentially the same business. They have, he says, many things in common. There is, he declares, no end to the respect and esteem which he, billionaire media mogul, has for the man who made a hundred million dollars selling what are essentially gynecological illustrations.

The pornographer relents. He promises not to print the photographs and has the original video cassette messengered back to the mogul's office. He makes a few copies for private viewing, of course. Or so goes the rumor.

CUT TO:

INT. AOC RESTAURANT – NIGHT
I am out to dinner with an old friend. She is a reporter for a couple of national publications, and has developed what the colorful phrase-makers out here call 'a brand identity'. She is known as an excellent journalist, a witty writer, and, best of all, someone with the ability to

explain this confusing city to the rest of the country, or, at least, to New York. In her latest column, she refers knowingly to the rumor about the media mogul and the pornographer, claiming to have seen the tape herself and recognized the mogul's 'distinctive voice'. But she doesn't name names. So I have invited her out to a swish dinner for the sole purpose of finding out who it is. From the first drink to the salad course, I feign interest in her career. Over the fish, I ask thoughtful questions about her child. Then, finally, over dessert, I pounce.

ME   Tell me who it is.

MY FRIEND   I can't. I'm sworn to secrecy.

For some reason, I'm unable to accept this. It's as if, faced with a career in an industry that renders me powerless – tossed around by the whims of actors, executives, marketing guys, and, ultimately, one hundred million distracted television viewers – I need to know which mogul did what to whom and with what in his mouth when he did it. I've been at the mercy of rumor-mongers and gossips for months – 'Your show is looking great!' 'Your show is history!' – so I need something to chew on that involves somebody else's ass. Literally, in this case.

ME   Tell me! Tell me tell me tell me tell me!

She looks at me brimming with pity. She closes her eyes and sighs.

MY FRIEND   You're pathetic.

ME   I'm a writer in Hollywood. How is this news?

She takes a sip of her wine, looks around the restaurant furtively, and then:

MY FRIEND   Okay. Okay. I'll tell you. But you have to promise me that you won't tell anyone who it is.

ME   I won't. Tellmetellmetellme.

MY FRIEND   Because this guy is *very* powerful. This isn't just some Hollywood rumor, okay? This is BIG stuff. I could lose my job over this.

188

ME   I understand.

I try hard to shrug nonchalantly.

ME (CONT'D)   Tellmetellmetellme.

She leans forward, and then in a voice barely audible, low and sad, she tells me the name of the mogul who taped his three-way and begged the pornographer and barely missed being flattened by the giant anvil of shame, humiliation and embarrassment that hovers above us all, suspended by the slenderest thread imaginable, ready for Flynt's Law to bring it crashing down.

And let me tell you, it's one big fat juicy name. I mean, wow! I only wish I could tell you who it is. Can't though. You'll just have to guess.

Let me tell you another story that's making the rounds in Hollywood. It's a 'salad course' story – it lasts just long enough to finish a salad at lunch, and is flexible enough to segue easily to the 'main course' story, which lasts a little longer, until the 'decaf cappuccino' portion of the lunch, which is when we get down to business.

A young actor discovers that his girlfriend – with whom he thought he had an exclusive arrangement – is seeing another guy on the side. He learns the identity of this 'sloppy seconds' character – an agent's assistant at a powerful agency – and heads over to his place of work for a man-to-man chat. Once in the agency lobby, he belligerently demands that the assistant come down and face him. Finally, the assistant appears, all six feet, 190 muscled pounds of him. The actor gets his ass kicked all over the lobby. The assistant gets promoted, because his bosses are agents, and all agents secretly hate all actors.

CUT TO:

INT. MY OFFICE – DAY

I am on the phone with an acquaintance, a notorious gossip who prides himself on knowing everything first. He has just told me that the president of one of the large television networks is about to be fired.

MY FRIEND   Got anything for me?

ME   Nope, sorry. We've been in production on our series for the past year, so I'm sort of out of the loop.

MY FRIEND   (*disappointed*)
Oh. But I just gave you a really juicy titbit.

ME   Sorry.

I feel terrible. I've received but not given. So I decide to make something up, something unverifiable. I mention a powerful media banker in New York.

ME (*cont'd*)   Know him?

MY FRIEND   Know him? Sure!

ME   I heard that he has cancer.

MY FRIEND   Oh, is that out?

CUT TO:

My friend will never be caught unknowing. He's heard everything first, even if it's a lie that I just made up.

CUT TO:

INT. CITRUS RESTAURANT – DAY

I'm having lunch with my agent. I mention the gossip about the network president.

ME   Did you hear about it?

MY AGENT   Hear about it? It was in the paper for Godsakes.

ME   It was? Where? In the business section?

MY AGENT   No! In the real estate section. There was an item in it about [*my agent mentions the name of a major player in the television business who has, up until now, lived in New York*] and how he and his family are moving back to LA. They bought a

190

huge house in the Palisades which means he got a big signing bonus. That can only mean one thing. C'mon! Don't you read the paper?

The main course arrives.

MY AGENT (*cont'd*)   Did you hear about [*my agent mentions the name of a New York media banker*]? He's dying. Of leukemia. They're giving him three months.

CUT TO:

Gossip is only truly interesting if it's about people and situations that have no direct impact on the listener. If it was our network president being replaced, it wouldn't be gossip. It would be bad news.

CUT TO:

INT. MY OFFICE – DAY

Later that week, we discover that the network president may quit, be fired, or stay, but in any case, someone is being brought in at a higher level. It is an indication of the current Hollywood mania for fancy titles that there is a position above 'Network President'.

My agent calls. I ask about the situation.

MY AGENT   How the hell should I know? I was just over there with another client, pitching a new series.

ME   Really? But aren't things up in the air over there? Aren't they in disarray?

MY AGENT   Yeah. But how is that different from every other place?

ME   Well . . .

MY AGENT   Look, I salute the uniform. No matter who's wearing it this week. They want to make a donkey a network president, you know what? I'll tell my clients to pitch to the donkey.

ME   I guess that makes sense.

MY AGENT   Now, on to other matters. Let's talk about your show. The rumor is that . . . which . . . –st . . . and they think . . . tried to tell them . . . you should . . . to stop . . . wh . . .

ME   I can't understand you.

MY AGENT   What . . . can . . . into canyon . . .

CUT TO:

I hear later that the actor who got cranked in the agency lobby was not, in fact, cranked in the agency lobby. His two-timing girlfriend, I hear later, was not, in fact two-timing him, but was a committed serial monogamist. The agent's assistant, I learn later, wasn't six feet tall, wasn't buffed and cut, wasn't involved with the girl at all, except for a desultory dinner date months ago, after which the girl declared her non-interest and the agent's assistant began stalking her and sending nasty letters to her boyfriend, the actor.

The actor shows up at the agency lobby with one of the letters and a polite request to the agent's assistant to stop sending them. No one is beaten up. No one is promoted. The agent's assistant, though, is fired weeks later for being 'creepy'.

I'm pretty sure this is an accurate account, but I'll keep reading the real estate section to be sure.

CUT TO:

INT. FOUR SEASONS HOTEL ROOM, NEW YORK CITY – MORNING

SFX: *Phone rings.*

ME (*groggy, waking up*)   Hello?

MY AGENT   I'm going to a Hillary Clinton fundraiser tonight!

ME   Oh, gosh. Well. That's very nice but I'm meeting an old friend from college for dinner and–

MY AGENT   I wasn't inviting you. Do you know who gave me these tickets? *Tom Hanks*. He *gave* me these tickets.

ME   Then why are you telling me this?

MY AGENT   Are you kidding? I'm telling everybody this.

ME   But–

MY AGENT   Look, the reason I called is to tell you that I haven't heard anything official yet.

ME   What have you heard?

MY AGENT   Nothing official.

ME   What have you heard that's unofficial?

MY AGENT   Unofficial?

ME   Unofficial.

MY AGENT   Nothing unofficial.

ME   What's the rumor?

MY AGENT   Don't talk to me about rumors. Rumors are rumors. They *swirl*. That's what they do. They *swirl* and they *fly*.

ME   But isn't the rumor always true?

MY AGENT   Where did you hear that? Where do you pick up this *bullshit*?

ME   Name me one time when the rumor turned out not to be true. One time.

MY AGENT   Okay. That's easy.

A long silence.

MY AGENT (*cont'd*)

What, you mean now?

ME   Yeah.

MY AGENT   Can it wait until I'm back in my office? I need to refer to my notes.

ME   See?

MY AGENT   Okay! Okay! The rumor is your show is dead, okay? Are you happy? And yes, yes, it usually – okay, mostly – okay, *always* – turns out that the rumor is true. There. You made me say it. Satisfied?

ME (*after a pause*)   But there's still a chance, right?

MY AGENT   Of course! Of *course*! Yes. Yes, there is still a chance.

ME   Really?

MY AGENT   Yes!

ME   *Really?*

MY AGENT   Why are you doing this to me?

CUT TO:

The format of the American sitcom is so indelibly etched into the consciousness of its audience that it's easy to forget that the whole thing was invented in the 1950s by Desi Arnaz.

Desi – now and forever known best as 'Lucy's husband' in the long-running Ur-sitcom of the 1950s, *I Love Lucy* – came up with the money-saving system of shooting a sitcom all at once, like a stage play, while three cameras zoomed back and forth filming the action from three angles.

Desi wasn't much of an actor. *I Love Lucy* has been in continuous reruns since the 1960s, and his over-the-top reactions and finger-in-a-light-socket doubletakes don't get better with age. And when one considers that Desi Arnaz, a Cuban-American band leader married to a redhead named Lucy, was unconvincing in his portrayal of 'Ricky Ricardo', a Cuban-American band leader married to a redhead named Lucy, well, in the words of a studio executive acquaintance describing a young male star, 'It's hard to know what he brought to the party, talent-wise.'

What Desi brought to the party, talent-wise, was something unheard of since in on-screen talent: he brought financial sophistication. He knew what a half-hour television show should cost, and he knew how to make it cost just a few dollars less. He put the cameras on wheels because it was a cheap solution to cost-prohibitive multiple takes of a scene, and because it guaranteed that a sitcom could be shot in one evening with one audience.

St Desi, the patron saint of sitcom producers, is the stuff of legend. In the old Nicodell restaurant on Melrose Avenue – now, fittingly, flattened into a parking lot – people in the business would point to a certain booth (never the same one, but that's not important) and say, 'That's where Desi told William Frawley that if he ever showed up drunk to an *I Love Lucy* rehearsal, he wouldn't get paid for the day.' And the most famous Desi tale: when he and Lucy wanted to leave Manhattan – which was, at the time, the center of television production – for Los Angeles – which was, at the time, too far away from network headquarters for adequate supervision, the network demanded that he and Lucy agree to a pay cut, which they did, but in return, Desi asked for 100 per cent ownership of all episodes of *I Love Lucy*. The network readily agreed. After all, it reasoned, what possible value could there be in an already-broadcast episode of a sitcom?

Desi was no fool. He knew he wasn't an actor. Or a band leader. He was a businessman, or as my friend the studio executive puts it, 'a businessman in The Business.'

I am in The Business, but I'm not a businessman, and this perhaps is why I'm in New York, at the Four Seasons Hotel, waiting to hear officially that the show I have been working on for the past year is cancelled.

For some reason, the major networks announce their new schedules in New York, though they have all long-since followed Desi and Lucy to Los Angeles. Traditionally, these decisions are made in New York by Los Angeles-based executives for two reasons: one, the various media buyers and advertising executives are planted in Manhattan; and two, executives of all stripes in all industries get an erotic charge from eating a $35 room-service breakfast.

But because they've flown out here, we've flown out here. And so did all of the big agents. And the studios. And the other producers and writers who are vying for spots on the fall schedules. We're all here because . . . well, we're here ostensibly because if the network wants a last-minute creative meeting, or an adjustment or two to an existing series, we'll be available. But as far as I can fathom, we're really all here for two reasons: to get wildly, lower-lip sagging drunk, and to give money to Hillary Clinton.

The following happened a year or two ago:

A television network was thrashing out its schedule but the executives hit a snag. With only one slot to fill, and three possible choices, they simply couldn't identify the most promising candidate. The execs dithered for a day or two in their New York hotel rooms, screening and re-screening each pilot, trying to develop some kind of intuitive, gut-based sense of each show, and trying, if you'll permit the phrase, to rely on their own taste when they gave up and made a courageous decision: they ordered up another focus group. But it would have to be a fast one.

Each network unveils its fall schedule to great fanfare and huge expense, jetting in the stars of the show, laying on a buffet spread heavy on pricey shellfish, all to convince the advertising community that an upcoming show about, say, four young people interacting in a sexy fashion will be different, better, funnier, and longer-lasting than the dozens of other shows that the other networks are offering about, say, four young people interacting in a sexually-charged but basically chaste arena.

196

But to do that you need to decide *which* show you're going to schedule so you can know *which* actors and actresses to jet into Manhattan for glad-handing and ass-kissing the advertisers.

You see the dilemma: the network under discussion hadn't made its final decision with the press conference only twelve hours away. The solution? Fly the casts of ALL *three* programs to New York on the *same* plane. In the intervening six hours, collect the results of the last-minute focus group and make the decision. When the plane lands, gather the casts in the airport lounge, whisk some of them into Manhattan and into stardom; tell the others to slink home.

This solution contains all you need to know about Hollywood. It has it all: extravagance, procrastination, cruelty masquerading as efficiency, and focus groups.

CUT TO:

INT. REGENCY HOTEL BAR – MANHATTAN – NIGHT
I am sitting at the bar waiting to meet a friend. I know personally, or have worked with, or know people who have worked with, every single person in the bar. An agent slaps me on the back. His eyes are red and his tie is askew.

AGENT   Hey man.

ME   Hi.

AGENT   Let me buy you a drink.

ME   Thanks, but I'm on my way out.

AGENT   Then let me give you two tickets to the Hillary Clinton thing.

ME   Gee, that's very generous of you.

AGENT   Look, from me to you, let me just say, I'm sorry about your show, man.

ME   Why do you say that? What have you heard?

AGENT   Ooops. Hey man, if you don't know then I don't know, okay?

I look down at my drink. The agent looks around, guiltily.

AGENT (*cont'd*) I feel terrible that you heard it from me, man. I mean, not that you heard it from me, but that you heard it from me when I'm so . . .

The agent begins staring at an attractive young woman who has just entered the bar.

ME So . . . wasted?

The agent moves off.

AGENT (*to attractive woman*) Would you like to meet Hillary Clinton?

CUT TO:

A few years back, a well-known comic actor hosted his own late-night talk show. The show received dismal ratings, terrible reviews, and midway through its thirteen-week run, it was cancelled.

So it was odd, only a few days after such a spectacular and public failure, to see the actor sitting at an outside table at the old Columbia Bar & Grill – now something called *Pinot Hollywood & Martini Bar* – having lunch with a couple of friends. Odd because in his shoes I'd be thousands of miles away for months; and odd because he didn't look that great. He didn't look tanned or rested; hadn't had a quick eye tuck or chin implant; didn't laugh loudly or smile nonchalantly. He looked, instead, like a guy who just got his ass handed to him on national television.

It was a heroic performance – the bravest lunch I've yet seen eaten. And as he ate and chatted with his party, Industry types would pat him on the back or give him a 'thumbs-up' gesture as they passed. A few would murmur 'Good for you'; some would claim, loudly, 'I loved the show'; and some really smart ones would opt for the sophisticated surgical strike compliment: 'My *kids* really *were wild* about that show.'

In much the same way that the audience at an Oscar ceremony a few years ago gave Christopher Reeve a tearful, hand-reddening ovation – not for *Superman III* or *The Bostonians* but for, let's face it, falling off a horse – the lunchtime crowd at the old Columbia Bar & Grill wanted this actor to know that *they* knew how tough it was for him to eat lunch out on the sunny patio, and that they applauded his bravery and wished him the best. It's often said about people in this business, mostly by people *not* in this business, that we're heartless and unforgiving. Not true. We relish failure. We wallow in misfortune. We live to applaud the down-and-out.

So it was not surprising to see the parade of well-wishers file by that afternoon. One of them, a guy in the international television distribution arm of a large studio – a guy I *knew* didn't know the actor from a hole in the ground – walked by him, stopped, put his hands on the guy's shoulders, leaned down, and *kissed the failed talk-show host on the top of the head.* And while I could not bring myself to go that far, the spirit of full disclosure requires me to admit that, when our eyes briefly met across the restaurant patio as happens occasionally in public places (I wasn't staring at the man, honest) I caught myself giving him, a man I haven't met either, a raised-eyebrow-rueful-smile greeting.

CUT TO:

INT. HOTEL ELEVATOR – NIGHT

An executive from another network steps into the elevator after me.

EXECUTIVE Hi!

ME Hi.

EXECUTIVE I'm off to see Hillary.

ME Great.

EXECUTIVE What are you in town for?

ME Well . . . you see . . . our show is . . . we thought there might be a chance . . .

I trail off.

ME (*cont'd*)   To visit a sick relative.

CUT TO:

Because the thrill of raiding the minibar and ordering room service and gratuitously dry-cleaning my clothes at the studio's expense has worn off, I bite the bullet and actually go to the Hillary Clinton fundraiser. My enjoyment of the event is marred somewhat by two things: one, I'm not a Hillary Clinton supporter; and two, right before she starts to speak, an executive from our network approaches me with a sad, wan smile on her face, and whispers, 'You're not on the fall schedule' in my ear, and then, as the senator begins her speech, the executive adds, 'probably', and moves off.

I do not do the Desi-thing. The Desi-thing to do would be to head back to the hotel, catch the next plane home to Los Angeles, and start planning the next show. Instead, I head back to the hotel, get drunk, and send my pyjamas out to be dry-cleaned and pressed.

I don't have the Desi in me. I'll never be a businessman in The Business.

CUT TO:

INT. FOUR SEASONS HOTEL NEW YORK – DAY

I'm in my room. It's four in the afternoon. I stare at the phone. It rings.

ME   Hello?

MY AGENT   Still moping? Go out! Carouse!

ME   What do you want?

MY AGENT   I want to tell you that your show was officially cancelled fifteen minutes ago. I'm trying to use my sad voice, but it's hard, because I've got two other clients who got their shows ordered, and I've been using my happy voice most of the day, so forgive me.

ME   Thanks.

MY AGENT   Remember that you did a bunch of hilarious and excellent episodes of television, and for what it's worth, the conversations I've had with everyone are all about you and your partner and how great you are. In fact, the president of another network stopped me in the Bergdorf Goodman elevator to tell me that he would, in his words, 'pay anything' to get your next show for his network.

ME   He said that? Really?

MY AGENT   Really.

ME   Wow.

MY AGENT   As long as it's a male-driven comedy, because those are the only ones that make any money in reruns.

ME   I see.

MY AGENT   So get going! Start writing!

ME   I don't know. I don't know if I have another one in me.

MY AGENT   What? What are you talking about?

ME   I'm just saying I feel like I'm stuck in a bad pattern – we do a show, they put it on, they take it off, we do a show, they put it on, they take it off. It's like we're in this awful rhythm – do a show, get cancelled, do a show, get cancelled, like, like . . .

MY AGENT   Some kind of sitcom script?

ME   Yeah.

MY AGENT   What's wrong with that?

A long pause.

ME   I don't know what's wrong with that, actually.

MY AGENT   I mean, it works for half-hour comedy.

ME   Yeah, but I'm not sure life really follows the patterns of situation comedy structure.

MY AGENT   You aren't?

ME   You *are?*

MY AGENT   I have a teenager at home and an elderly parent in the early stages of Alzheimer's. Trust me. It does. It really really *really* does.

CUT TO:

Charlie Chaplin once explained that there are two ways to film the old guy-slips-on-a-banana-peel joke. The first, unfunny, way goes like this: cut to the guy walking, oblivious. Cut to the banana peel, lying in wait. Cut to a wide shot of the guy approaching the banana peel. Cut to a close-up of the banana peel, just as the guy's foot hits it. Cut back to the wide shot, as the guy slips on the peel and lands on his rear end, which as everyone knows from cartoons, is the funniest part of the human body and one which registers no real pain.

The second, funny, way to film that same sequence is as follows: cut to the guy, walking. Cut to the banana peel, lying in wait. Cut to a wide shot of the guy approaching the banana peel. Cut to a close-up of the banana peel, just as the guy's foot *almost* hits it. Cut back to the wide shot, as the guy deftly steps over the banana peel, smiling smugly . . . and falls into an open manhole.

Get the difference? The trick is to make sure the audience never knows which part is the set up and which part is the joke. Until they start laughing.

When I got back home, a friend of mine told me the story about the network and the three casts. After I finished commiserating bitterly, which in Hollywood means explaining how the situation is much *much* worse in my case, she told me the quaint finish.

Apparently, in the confusion, one of the actors from one of the castoff programs got mixed in with the chosen ones, and was whisked into Manhattan, where he dutifully attended the press conference, charmed the advertisers, gorged himself on grilled lobster, and ran up $13,000 worth of hotel charges, most of which, it was hinted at darkly, were for hotel-supplied hookers.

That's a guy who takes bad news gracefully.

FADE OUT.

A phone call, Friday, 4:30 p.m.

'Hi!'

'Hi.'

'I just wanted to say how much fun it was working with you.'

'Um . . . thanks.'

'I just . . . it's just such a pleasure to work with a writer who really feels passionate about his project.'

'Well, thanks, Trish.'

'Tori.'

'Tori.'

'And I wanted to say that I'll miss you.'

'Oh. Well, I'm sorry to hear that. I guess my next question is, which one of us is leaving?'

'Hahahahahaha.'

'No, seriously. Which one of us?'

'Me! Didn't you see it in the trades? I'm going to another opportunity.'

'Oh. Well congratulations.'

'Thanks. Please hold for Josh.'

'Hi!'

'Hi, Josh.'

'Hey there!'

'Hi, it's Josh, too.'

'Hi.'

'I'm in the car with Josh and you're on speaker.'

'And we're here in the office, me and Tori and Jamal and Eli, on conference.'

'Okay.'

'We read the pages.'

'Oh, okay. I just sent them along so you could get a flavor of . . .'

203

'You know, I always want to start out positive and keep things real collegial, okay?'

'Okay.'

'So on the positive side, we're no longer concerned that this thing may not be long enough.'

'Oh.'

'But we're a little concerned that it's just all about failure.'

'So far.'

'Right. Thanks, Eli. So far in the pages that you've given us.'

'And about how bad you feel getting another show cancelled and how many failures and setbacks you've experienced.'

'I don't think it's "many" failures, really. I've been pretty successful, I think.'

'The first thirty pages aren't very up, is what we're saying.'

'Oh. Right. See, what I was going for was . . .'

'It's just that we don't have a lot of success with projects about aging failures scrambling for money.'

'Aging failures?'

'I'm just responding to the pages.'

'We really want everyone who comes into contact with the project to like you.'

'I do, too.'

'Great!'

'Great!'

'Great!'

'So maybe I should make some adjustments in those pages and sort of lighten the tone, make me – I mean, the narrator guy – more likable.'

'I think it would really help it out a lot.'

'Let me work on that.'

'Great!'

'Great!'

'Great meeting!'

'Great meeting!'

204

SUMMER: 'IS THERE A SHOW IN THAT?'

Fade in:

Hollywood has two pompous nicknames for itself: 'The Business' and 'The Industry'. Both names pack an ironic punch: calling it 'The Business' must surely elicit a sickly smile from shareholders of the Sony, Vivendi, and AOL/Time Warner Corporations, who are probably still waiting for the spending to stop and the business to begin; while the nickname 'The Industry' – with its connotation of industriousness – is equally silly when one considers that the most prevalent activity on any soundstage or location shoot is the reading of magazines and the eating of pastries.

Still, the beehive that is Hollywood manages to churn out enough news, gossip and press releases to fill two daily newspapers, *Variety* and its scrappier cousin, the *Hollywood Reporter*. Around here, we call them the 'trades' – short for 'trade papers' – and they are read with bitter intensity every morning by anyone who's anyone, and anyone who's *trying* to be anyone, in The Business.

Walk through the various breakfast spots in Los Angeles, and it's easy to spot the out-of-towners. They're the ones reading the trades in public. Out-of-towners think that *Variety* and the *Reporter* are filled with interesting Industry news – stock quotes, reviews, box-office figures, that kind of thing – and, of course, they are. But the more practiced reader, the Industry denizen, reads the trades for one reason and one reason only: to find out how much other people are being paid. And as this leads almost inevitably to violently obscene language, reading the trades is something to be done in private.

CUT TO:

EXT. STUDIO PARKING LOT – DAY

I walk to my office.

My writing partner and I have recovered, slightly, from our recent cancellation and we are now back at work, trying to come up with another series. In Hollywood, failure is like childbirth – it's messy and painful and often requires hospitalization, but when it's all over, some magic amnesia takes place and you can't wait to do it again.

This isn't really an act of heroic non-sulking. It's our job, actually. We have what is called an 'Overall Deal' at a large studio. Which means, essentially, that they pay us a tidy sum to come up with, write, produce, cast, and generally generate television shows, which we then try to sell to the various television networks.

It's a great system, but it doesn't make much economic sense. In baseball parlance, we're being paid to 'swing for the fence,' to aim for a monster hit. Because one monster hit generates enough profit for the studio to pay for everyone else's failures. At least, that's how the system is supposed to work.

CUT TO:

INT. MY OFFICE – CONTINUOUS

My assistant tosses Variety *at me with sadistic glee.*

MY ASSISTANT   Page three.

ME   Good morning.

MY ASSISTANT   It won't be when you read page three.

CUT TO:

INSERT SHOT: PAGE THREE OF *VARIETY*

An article reports that a television writer – a friend of mine – has recently signed a deal with a studio for a whopping huge sum.

CUT TO:

CLOSE-UP: ME, READING

I am aware that my eyes are bulging out of their sockets. I am aware that my face is getting red. I am aware that the entire office staff – a staff, I'm sure, convinced that I'm an overpaid, under-worked complainer (a characterization that I do not dispute) – is watching me intensely.

I muster a smile.

ME (*croaky voice*)   Good for him! I'm happy for him. Really.

CUT TO:

Later, alone, in my office, I attack a pocket calculator with violent stabs of my finger. I am making a desperate and pathetic attempt to crunch the numbers in his deal and crunch the numbers in my deal and still come out ahead. I do this for several minutes. Huge rolls of calculator tape spill out over my desk.

It is only when I've run the calculator's batteries down that I stop this childish and deeply unattractive behavior. I should know better. I've been in this business long enough to have learned this immutable law: no matter how much money you make, someone is always making slightly more. It is hardwired into the circuitry of The Industry, and it is what makes things here hum with the ruthless efficiency that pure uncut greed produces.

The office upstairs is occupied by a television writer who also has a big contract at the studio. As I sit in my chair, heart rate returning to normal, angry facial rictus relaxing, eyes slowly changing from envy-green to normal-blue, I can hear the guy upstairs come into his office. I can hear him greet his assistant. I can hear him take a seat behind his desk. I can hear the rustle of *Variety*. And I'm pretty sure, if I tilt my head just right, I can make out the clickety-clack of his calculator as it works and worries the numbers.

209

CUT TO:

INT. MY OFFICE – DAY

The phone rings.

MY AGENT   How's the development coming? Any hot ideas?

ME   Hard to say.

MY AGENT   Hard to say? C'mon. Perk up here. This is show business. I want you to have fun.

ME   What?

MY AGENT   And you should want you to have fun.

ME   Well, to tell you the truth–

MY AGENT   I don't want to hear this. This is about the deal in the trades, right?

ME   Well, as a matter of fact–

MY AGENT   I don't want to hear this. But I'm right, right? Tell me I'm right.

ME   You're right. It seems that every day I read in the trades about someone else's big money deal at some other studio to do exactly the same job as I'm doing – no, a worse job, actually, because we get shows on the air, and these guys haven't done that – and I can't help but think that I'm a chump and you're too complacent.

MY AGENT   So when I say 'I don't want to hear this,' you hear what, exactly? 'Please tell me all about it?' I'm interested in the way your mind works.

ME   You know what? This isn't a fruitful conversation.

MY AGENT   Can I tell you something that I hope makes you feel better? The trades only report a fraction of the deals around town that are better than yours. There are more deals better than yours in town than there are stars in the heavens.

ME   Umm . . .

MY AGENT   Don't interrupt. This wind-up has a big finish, I
promise you. But those deals are just *temporary*, you see. They
won't last. Those guys will make a nice pot of change for a
year or two–

ME   Or three. Or five.

MY AGENT   Let me *finish*. I'm telling you, it's worth it. Anyway,
you guys have a great track record. You get shows on the air.
And you'll get another one on the air very *very* soon.

A pause.

MY AGENT   *Right?*

ME   Right.

MY AGENT   Let me *finish*. Anyway, the point is, you're building
equity in a big, big payoff – that *I* negotiated, *okay?* – after
only three or four years of your series, a payoff, may I just add,
that will make all of those development deals seem pathetic
and hopelessly threadbare. You can thank me now if you're
feeling gracious.

ME   Really?

MY AGENT   *Really.* Keep your eye on the brass ring, kid. Don't
get distracted by gold fever.

ME   But what if our show gets cancelled again? What if we never
make it to year three or four?

MY AGENT   Well, then you were right the first time.

ME   Excuse me?

MY AGENT   Then you *are* a chump.

ME   Interesting point. But what about a new studio deal?

MY AGENT   What about it?

ME   Well, we've got a year left on the current one. What I'm
asking is, if we don't get another show on the air this year, do
you think the studio will offer us another contract?

MY AGENT   What do you want me to say? That somehow the huge, industry-wide cost-cutting purge is going to sort of swerve around you? Make a you-specific exception?

ME   I'd like that.

MY AGENT   Did you spend all the money?

ME   No.

MY AGENT   Really?

ME   Really.

MY AGENT   *Really?*

ME   Really.

MY AGENT   Look, do you want me to be honest? Really honest?

ME   I don't know. Do I?

MY AGENT   Probably not. But I'm going to be anyway. The business has changed, okay? Radically, radically changed. There are no big studio deals out there anymore. The era of big deals is over.

ME   Then what about that deal in the trades? That guy's agent got him a lot of money.

MY AGENT   What is this? Dump on me day? Look, that deal in the trades? The one you've got such *tsuris* about? That's pretty much the last deal you'll be reading about for a while. The town is broke, okay? It's not a deal. It's a *death rattle.*

ME   So you're saying that when our deal is up the studio won't want to re-up us?

MY AGENT   I'm saying deals are over. And you've got exactly one year left on yours. So do you want to spend what could easily be your last year making guaranteed serious money moping and whining and making vicious personal attacks on me, or getting another show on the air?

ME So you're saying that it's unlikely that there's a deal after this deal?

MY AGENT I quibble with the term 'unlikely'.

ME So you're saying–

MY AGENT You keep saying 'So you're saying' like you're listening to what I'm saying, but you're obviously having a hard time with this. This is some kind of personality disorder thing. I'm telling you, okay, I'm telling you that you have one year left, okay, on a deal that no one is ever going to get again, okay? That's what I'm saying. I'm saying it, I said it, I'm done.

ME You're telling me this *now*?

MY AGENT Oh come on. What did you want me to do? Call you up a few months ago and say, 'Let me tell you what I'm hearing out in the marketplace. I'm hearing money is tight. I'm hearing that somewhere between TiVo and Osama bin Laden and fifty bazillion cable channels, things got squeezed pretty thin? That there's no more big money in television? That there are no more big-money studio deals? Make sure you save your money because in the not-too-distant future we're all going to be looking back on these days and thinking to ourselves, *Wow! We all lived through a truly historic era when writers were paid huge sums of money and now that era's over and it will never ever ever ever repeat itself.*' Is that what you have in mind?

ME Would have been nice.

MY AGENT I agree. But I hadn't put it all together until just now.

SFX: Click. Dial tone.

CUT TO:

In this business, timing is your most important friend. And in the television business, in which each issue of the *Wall Street Journal* seems to signal a new direction, the perfect time to sign a deal was anytime directly before, or directly after, we signed ours. And the *Journal* agrees with my agent on another important detail: the money wheel has stopped spinning. No more fat writers' contracts.

But I'm grateful to be working. A year left to go on a studio contract is a lot better than no contract at all.

I had lunch with an old friend of mine, a guy who has spent a Hollywood lifetime (that's roughly fifteen years) working in the television business. He hasn't had an easy time of it recently. He hasn't worked in two years.

I do know a lot of writers who are currently either not working, or working for a lot less than they used to. I'm sure some blame it on the recent popularity of reality shows, but I tend to blame it on the huge glut of sitcoms that were on in the late 1990s, leading to huge development deals and inflated salaries, leading to, inevitably, a market correction. Leading to no more development deals.

The people in trouble are the ones who made the same mistake overpaid people have always made, in all businesses: they spent the money. Or, worse, they *got used* to the money.

So last week, when my friend called me for lunch, I knew who was buying.

We pulled up in our respective cars at the same time, and as he was getting out of his, he smiled weakly.

'What do you think?' he asked, jerking his thumb at the car.

'Nice,' I said. It was a Chevrolet station wagon. The guy has kids. What was I supposed to say?

'Yeah, well,' he mumbles, 'I had to cut back. Dump the Lexus.'

'Still, that's a nice car,' I said.

'It's a *shitty* car,' he said bitterly. 'I have to tell everyone that it's my *wife's* car. And still they treat me like dirt.'

He turns to the valet parking attendant. 'Be careful with my wife's car, okay, *amigo*?' Then he turned and peered into the restaurant. 'Do you think they saw me drive up? If they did, sorry, man. We'll get a rotten table.'

'C'mon,' I said. 'People don't care about stuff like that. That's just an LA myth.'

He looked at me and shook his head sourly. Then he brightened. 'But they saw *you* drive up too. And your car is *nice*.'

The truth is, I have two cars – a silly Los Angeles extravagance, I know, but in my defense, one of them is a real shit pile. It runs intermittently, makes peculiar noises, and at speeds under 50 miles-per-hour emits an odor that smells like neither gasoline nor oil, but, instead, like burning human flesh. But I love that car, and can't get rid of it for some strange sentimental reason, so when I bought my German sleek-mobile, I kept the shit pile in the garage alongside it. I like to think that the two cars, after some initial sniping, have reached an understanding, sitting there quietly, side-by-side in the dark. Perhaps the shit pile keeps the German sleek-mobile honest and humble, in an all-flesh-is-grass sort of way. And the German car, in return, reminds the shit pile that he is, in fact, a shit pile, and too many won't-starts and sickly-smells and it's out the door.

A few days after that, I had lunch at a place that my writing partner and I go to at least once a week. It's a standard Italian restaurant (bad bread, illegible menu, obscure Italian fizzy water) but it's been a serviceable feeding place for years.

The valet guy looked at my car.

'Everything okay, chief?' he asked, in a tone of voice that, even through his thick Chiapas accent was clearly pitying.

'Yeah, fine,' I said, not quite getting it.

'Where's the other car?' he asked. 'The nice one?'

'Home,' I said, my voice strangely high-pitched. I mean, it *was* home. In the garage. But for some reason I decided to drive the other one to work, something I'd never done. I think of it as a weekend car, a drive-the-dog-to-the-beach car.

'So everything's goin' okay then, chief?' he asked again, with a face out of a Latin romantic tragedy.

'Yes,' I said, too indignant to be convincing. I pulled out of the restaurant. In the rearview mirror, I could see his face, his pitying, sad-eyed, poor-*gringo* face, peering at me.

And driving back to the studio, I realize that I'd been experiencing that scene, in varying tempos, all day. The pretty girl at Peet's Coffee that morning saw me drive up for the first time, and for the first time she was, like, diffident. People on the freeway wouldn't let me pass. At the time, I attributed it to heavy traffic, or a lurking highway cop, but the truth, as I now realize, is that people in Los Angeles *do not get out of the way for crappy cars.* It's Lexus or better around here.

And the guard at the studio gate – a gate I've been driving through with a cheery wave for *twelve* years – that day he gave me the fish-eye, the not-so-fast-fella, the you're-bringing-that-bag-of-bones-in-*here*? look.

The next morning, dashing off to work, I reached for my car keys. My hand stopped, suspended over the two different sets. I thought to myself: Am I going to play the silly money-obsessed game? Or am I going to thumb my nose at the foolishness of the Hollywood machine? Am I going to surrender to a tawdry set of values, to a sick craving for status and misbegotten respect? Or am I going to forge my own set of standards? Am I, finally, a man or a mouse? Who am I? (Or, at least, who am I *today*?) I'm not going to tell you which set of keys I took. I don't want you to think less of me. Or more of me. Depending, I guess, on you.

CUT TO:

INT. 'THE RODEO ROOM' BEVERLY REGENT HOTEL – DAY

I am at a large lunch for a United States senator. He is speaking about the 'sacred trust' that Americans place in what he calls 'the media professionals.' I am staring down at my sorrel soup, trying to avoid the gaze of his chief fundraiser, who is sitting opposite.

An agent I know is sitting next to me. He puts his hand on my shoulder and gives it a squeeze. I have been in Hollywood long enough to know that he will next slip his hand up to my neck and lean in to whisper into my ear. This is weird the first couple of times, and then, suddenly, it isn't weird anymore.

AGENT   (*whispering*)
So, what, you've got an overall deal somewhere?
I nod.

AGENT (*cont'd*)   When did you sign?

ME   Two years ago.
His face squinches up in agony.

AGENT   Oooo.

ME   Yeah, well.

AGENT   So you got the up tick but not the bonanza and it's killing you.

ME   Well, it's not *killing* me.

AGENT   I tell all my clients, 'Bank the dough because this will *never happen again.*'

ME (*mumbling*)   It's not *killing* me.
He squeezes my neck.

ME (*mumbling*)   I've got my health. I'm young.
The agent puts his finger to his lips.

AGENT   Shhh. I'm trying to hear the senator.

CUT TO:

I got the up tick but not the bonanza, which I hope will never be a suitable title for my autobiography.

The only sure way to reap the bonanza, unfortunately, is to come up with a great idea. Which is hard work. Who knows where ideas come from?

A screenwriter I know once wrote a script about a screenwriter who cheats on his wife. In the script, the screenwriter's wife is fat, shrewish, and is hit by a bus on page 97.

In real life, the screenwriter's wife is nice-looking, pleasant, and because she lives in Los Angeles, hasn't been *near* a bus in fifteen years. Still, she was deeply upset by her husband's script.

'Is that supposed to be me?' she wanted to know.

'No, no,' he assured her.

'Then who is it?' she demanded tearfully.

'It's my first wife,' he said.

'And who's this slut bitch your character meets at a Starbucks and fucks in the backseat of the Lexus?' she wailed.

'That's you,' he answered. Then added, helpfully, 'Don't you remember how we got together?'

She still wanted to know about the bus accident. In real life, his first wife was alive and well and collecting eleven thousand court-ordered dollars every month from him. So what's the deal, she wanted to know, with the bus thing?

'That, darling,' he said, 'is where I did some writing.'

A friend of mine told me the following story, which I assume is true because it doesn't involve money:

He and his partner had just worked out a treatment for a new animated series. Armed with drawings and sample dialogue, full-color renditions of all of the characters, and even some sample voices, they march to the office of the studio president to present their show.

The new series follows the life of a perpetual loser – a panicky guy who's a cog-in-the-wheel, lives with his parents, brims with unrequited lust, surfs the internet for free pornography, you know the type – and chronicles his triumphs (few) and his humiliations (many). Think Charlie Brown all grown up and you'll have the idea.

In an act of inadvertent cruelty, though, they based many attributes of their lead character – including, unbelievably, his appearance – on one of the presidents of the studio. Sometimes the creative process is like that: you can spend months and months

218

recreating what you already know, and bits of your familiar life appear, even in something as trivial as a treatment, as out-of-the-blue-sky wholesale fantasy. It never occurred to them that they had modeled a character after this guy until they were in his office with a few other executives getting 'notes' on the treatment.

'Getting notes' is a little like 'writing a treatment', only in reverse. It's the lazy executive's tool: it allows him to do what he does best and likes to do (talk), while freeing him from doing what he does poorly and doesn't enjoy (make sense). The writer's responsibility is to nod, jot down a few illegible notes, and pipe up, every now and then, with a cheerful 'you may be right' and a thoughtful 'we'll take a look at that.'

Halfway through the notes, the executive picks up the sketch of the main character – a sketch, essentially, of a younger him – and taps it thoughtfully. As he looks at the sketch and chews his lower lip, my friend's eyes dart back and forth between the two of them, and suddenly, like an ice cube down his back, he sees what he has done. His partner makes a similar realization and freezes, pen poised over pad.

'It seems a little familiar,' the executive says, slowly, and they know that they're sunk. He's insulted, hurt, furious – he'll take this whole episode as an elaborate insult delivered in his office and with his money. They'll have poisoned the friendly relationship they have with him and the studio – a relationship that allowed them a huge amount of autonomy – and nine months from now they'll be assigned to a crappy show they broadcast in the afternoons, aimed at kids with no friends.

'Familiar?' my friend asks. If it's possible for a voice to sweat, his was sweating. 'How so?' he continued. 'Do you mean "familiar" like as in "family?" As in "this guy looks like a part of our television *family*?" Or do you mean it like "I've seen this guy somewhere before?" Because, I mean, how could you? *How could you?* It's totally made up. Like from . . .' He snaps his fingers. 'Like from thin air,' he says.

The studio chief looked at him strangely. 'No,' he says, 'I mean that the colors that the artist used look a little *Simpsons*-y. Maybe we should go more neutral.'

'We'll take a look at that,' my friend says thoughtfully.

The meeting breaks up. The junior executives file out of the office and they pack up their notes. As they leave, the executive calls them back.

'I know what you're doing,' he says, breaking into a wide grin. 'And it's hilarious.'

The sweaty voice again.

'What?' my friend asks. 'What are we doing?'

The studio chief mentions one of the junior executives who was in the meeting. 'You're basing your character on him, right?'

My friend reiterates that it's all make-believe pretend.

'You writers!' the studio president says. 'You're so mean. Funny but mean.'

And they slip out of the office.

People rarely recognize themselves. I suppose this is why so many parents of writers are still on speaking terms with their children.

CUT TO:

INT. OFFICE – DAY

We are sitting around trying to come up with a new show. Our task, for the next ten months, is to get a big idea for a series, flesh it out, write a first, or 'pilot' episode, get a network to agree to film the pilot, then get the same network to agree to make twenty-two more just like it. Simple, really.

But for now, what we really need is an idea.

What we do, essentially, is sit in our office and stare out the window in silence. Each one of us silently hopes that the other will either throw out a brilliant idea for a show, or better still, begin an off-topic conversation. Then, we can chat aimlessly for a little bit, until the one who started the off-topic conversation says something like, 'I bought a new

220

shirt this weekend,' or 'There's a new Italian restaurant in Santa Monica,' or 'I'm getting another cup of coffee,' at which point the one who didn't start the off-topic conversation can say, bitterly, 'Is there a show in that?'

SFX: Phone rings.

MY AGENT   Hi hi.

ME   Hi.

MY AGENT   So? Anything?

ME   What do you mean?

MY AGENT   It's been two months! What's next?

ME   We're thinking. We're noodling.

MY AGENT   Bullshit. You're staring out the window brooding silently and wondering why everyone else has a show on the air and you don't.

ME   What makes you think that?

MY AGENT   Number A, because all writers are alike, and two, because I'm standing outside your office looking in the window.

ME   What are you doing on the lot? Did you come to take us to lunch?

MY AGENT   No, I'm taking another client to lunch. I'd stop in and say 'hi' but I'm in a hurry. My other client has a show on the air so he's really busy.

ME   Just so you know, we're not brooding anymore.

MY AGENT   Good.

ME   We're just trying to come up with something that people will respond to. It's not easy.

MY AGENT *(soothing voice)*   I know, honey. I know.

ME   So we're just taking it slow.

MY AGENT   Not too slow! You've only got a year.

ME   We're trying to figure out what people want.

MY AGENT   Oh God. Whatever you do, *don't do that*.

ME   Why?

MY AGENT   Just do a show that *you* want to watch. Just do a show that *you* think is interesting. That's hard enough.

ME   I'm not sure my tastes match most of America's.

MY AGENT   Want to hear something sad? I'm sure that they do.

ME   Really?

MY AGENT   Oh *please*. I'm so sick of people out here thinking they're so different.

ME   What?

MY AGENT   People are the same all over. You think you're the only one in America staring out the window thinking to himself, 'I hate my job?'

ME   Oh.

MY AGENT   Is there a show in *that*?

CUT TO:

An actor friend of mine tells the following story: he was working as a lunch-shift bartender at a swank Beverly Hills restaurant. The customers were all talking about a terrible plane crash that had occurred earlier that morning. A well-known agent stopped by the bar while waiting for his lunch guest to arrive. He overheard two customers talking about the crash. It was the first he had heard of it. 'How many people died?' he asked. They told him that the death count was somewhere between three and four hundred. He winced.

'Oh, man, how awful,' he said. 'So was there anybody on the plane?'

He didn't mean *anyone* anyone. He meant *anyone show business* anyone. He meant *anyone I have pretended to be best friends with in the past* anyone.

People who are not in show business – or, to be more specific, people who do not live in the 310 or 212 telephone area codes – are an impenetrable mystery to those of us who do. What movies they watch and why, what television shows they choose and why, what they eat, why they eat it, when they work, what they drive, and especially how on earth they seem to make do on such skimpy salaries – these thoughts obsess our waking hours. Figure them out and the world is yours. That's the chief irony of this most ironic business: only those with the common touch can afford to live like kings. Steven Spielberg is so tuned in to the sensibilities of ordinary Americans that he no longer needs to be around them. Ever.

But the truth is, America isn't all that remote from, say, Brentwood, as much as it pains Brentwood to admit it.

Once, years ago, a successful and well-respected television writer was asked by the *Los Angeles Times* to list her favorite television programs. They wanted to know, for some unfathomable reason, what someone who creates television likes to watch. She professed, like so many university professors, not to watch anything. 'You see,' she said, 'I *hate* television. Really. My husband and I *never* watch the damn thing. We don't even have cable.'

The interviewer pressed on. Surely she must watch something – the news, maybe, or the financial channel? Finally, she admitted to watching only two channels, CNN and the Discovery Channel, both of which are available exclusively on cable, which she professed not to have. Ultimately, she admitted to having cable in 'the upstairs television', but not the 'downstairs television', or the 'kitchen television'. By my count, that made three televisions in her house, all presumably hated and unwatched. Television has this effect on people. There it is against the wall, as big as your head, and yet no smart person ever seems to watch it. Perhaps because it conjures up a life of lonely idleness, secret snacking, and social isolation, people just don't want to admit to their TV habit. It's like masturbation for the eyes. It's not a pastime you want to advertise.

Rotten television is another matter. The same dinner companion who denies watching anything on the box will, without taking a breath, gleefully recount the latest episode of *The Littlest Groom* or *Temptation Island* or one of those talk shows where loathsome guests spew vile anger, and occasional blows, at each other. Ironic distance, I guess, makes the heart grow fonder.

Of course, I never watch the damn thing either, and certainly never waste my time with anything as awful as *Temptation Island*. This has less to do with my elevated sensibilities than my all-consuming jealousy. Why turn on the tube – even just to flip around the dial – and run the risk of seeing a show more successful and popular than any show my partner and I have ever written? Or, worse, *better* than any show my partner and I have ever written?

CUT TO:

INT. WASHINGTON, DC HOTEL BALLROOM – NIGHT

I am at a big Washington journalists dinner. I'm the guest of an actual White House correspondent, and until I walked into the dinner and saw 2,500 people milling around, I was thrilled and honored to get the invitation. Now, as I make my way to my table (off to the side, behind a pillar), I wonder who must have cancelled at the last minute and bequeathed my invitation.

My table is almost filled, and for a moment I'm cheered by the presence of an actual cabinet secretary two seats to my left, and not just any old cabinet secretary, but one who is currently under investigation for influence peddling. I am clearly at an important table. But my spirit quickly falls when I realize that I'm the only non-journalist at the table (I figure this out by noticing that I'm the only one – besides the cabinet

224

secretary – who is not wearing a pre-tied bow tie) and in a few moments I'm going to be asked what I do for a living (a standard and blunt question in this bluntest of towns) and I'm going to say, 'I'm a television writer,' and everyone at the table is going to shrug and say, in staggered turns, 'Oh, I never watch television,' and 'I just can't bring myself to watch it.'

CABINET SECRETARY   What do you do?

ME   I'm a television writer.
  Nods. Shrugs.

CABINET SECRETARY   Any show in particular?
  I mention a few I've worked on.

WOMAN TO MY RIGHT   Oh, I *never* watch television.

MAN TO MY LEFT   I just *can't bring myself* to watch it.

MAN TO MY SECOND RIGHT   Who has the time to watch the damn thing?

CABINET SECRETARY (*pointing to me*)   Hey, I liked that show.

  I decide to give generously to the cabinet secretary's defense fund.

WOMAN TO MY RIGHT   I saw a cute *Raymond* last night.

MAN TO MY LEFT   Anyone know who was voted off *Survivor*?

  DISSOLVE TO:

INT. WASHINGTON, DC HOTEL BALLROOM – LATER THAT NIGHT

I'm chatting with the cabinet secretary, telling him about the various Screen Actors Guild minimums, explaining the concept of residuals, and the stylistic differences between film and videotape – he asked, by the way.

CABINET SECRETARY   So, what's the deal with syndication profit sharing? Explain that to me.

ME   Well, that's where all the real money is, actually. The studio basically pays for a show and rents it to a network. The fee the

225

network pays, called a 'license fee', isn't really enough to cover the cost of the show.

CABINET SECRETARY   Wait, so the studio loses money?

ME   Yeah. Until the show has enough episodes produced to syndicate–

CABINET SECRETARY   Sell into reruns?

ME   Right.

CABINET SECRETARY   Interesting. So why don't the networks just make their own shows and keep them on and keep the profits?

ME   Well, they do. Now, anyway. There's been a lot of deregulation of that business, so . . .

CABINET SECRETARY   You know what would be a great show?

ME   What?

CABINET SECRETARY   The office of a cabinet secretary. Be hilarious. The things that go on. People would love it. What do you think? Is there a show in that?

CUT TO:

INT. THE GRILL – DAY

A busy Los Angeles lunch spot.

SFX: Cell phone chirps.

Everyone in the restaurant instinctively checks his own phone. So do I, which is a good idea, since it is my phone that's beeping. That's the strange thing about cell phones: the ring seems to come from everywhere at once.

I answer.

MY AGENT   Hi!

ME   Hi!

MY AGENT   So. Anything?

ME Not yet.

MY AGENT Well, don't panic. Just have a nice lunch and keep loose.

ME Okay.

MY AGENT Have a salad. You need the roughage.

ME Excuse me?

MY AGENT Physicalize the process. Pretend you're constipated. Relax. Eat some fiber. Don't panic. Then, gradually . . .

ME I'm eating, here.

MY AGENT I'm just saying don't push. I'm just saying let it come naturally.

ME And then when it does, we'll point to it and say, 'Is there a show in that?'

FADE OUT.

AUTUMN: 'I APPLAUD YOU'

Fade in:

FLASHBACK SEQUENCE

Years ago, we wrote a treatment for a television series. This was an unusual thing to do. For some reason, it's considered eccentric for writers to *actually* write. We're supposed to pitch ideas verbally – go into the network president's office and *act passionate about the project*. But that has always seemed vaguely humiliating to us.

So our agent sent the treatment to a network, and before we knew it we were sitting in the office of some kind of network vice president.

OPTICAL EFFECT DISSOLVE TO:

INT. NETWORK VICE PRESIDENT'S OFFICE – DAY

We are holding tiny bottles of expensive water and sitting on a soft leather sofa that is both oversized and slippery, so that it's impossible to sit without sliding slowly off the cushions. It's an infantilizing piece of office furniture. My bottle of water sweats tiny droplets on to the arm, which pleases me in a petty way.

The vice president sits facing us. She smiles mirthlessly. She taps the treatment.

NETWORK VICE PRESIDENT   This is hilarious. *Hilarious*. We loved it here. Didn't we?

She turns to her staff. They nod and smile robotically.

NETWORK VICE PRESIDENT (*cont'd*)   So . . .

ME   So . . .

NETWORK VICE PRESIDENT   Tell me about the show.

ME   Well, it's all right there in the treatment.

NETWORK VICE PRESIDENT   Yeah, but I thought the reason you wanted to come in was to *describe* the show. Isn't that why you came?

ME   Not really. We thought *you* wanted to see us, because you liked the treatment.

NETWORK VICE PRESIDENT   I didn't *like* the treatment. I *loved* the treatment.

ME   Great.

NETWORK VICE PRESIDENT   Great. But pretend you *didn't* write the treatment.

ME   Why would we do that?

NETWORK VICE PRESIDENT   I just want to get a sense that you're *passionate about the project.*

ME   But . . . I mean . . . we *wrote* a treatment. Isn't that passionate enough?

NETWORK VICE PRESIDENT   But that's just writing. I like talking.

OPTICAL DISSOLVE TO:

END FLASHBACK SEQUENCE

What she wanted, of course, was a pitch. Which we don't do.

We're fairly unique that way, actually. Most writers prefer to pitch an idea before they write it, but in our experience, this leads to difficulty.

The whole point of writing a treatment – or, better yet, writing an entire script – is that there's very little confusion left about what, exactly, the show will be about and who, exactly, the star or stars of the show will be, and what, precisely, is or is not funny about it.

But when you pitch a show, you pitch into the wide blue sky. You pitch the general idea, the concept – whatever that means

232

– and you naturally smooth the sharp edges and tailor the pitch to the involuntary reactive facial muscles on the face of the highest ranking decision-maker in the room. It's almost impossible not to. A pitch is like a performance by a raggedy subway clown. He just wants you to love him and toss him some change.

So the network hears what it wants to hear: that your show will be perfect for an actor they have a deal with; that it will concentrate on family life, snugly fitting into an open 8:30 p.m. slot; that its point of view will be single people, or urban dwellers, or blue collar, or married with children, or whomever the target audience is for that network, on that night, that week.

But you go back to your office, mysteriously forgetting the shabby desperation of your pitch. You start writing the idea that was in your head before you started talking to the impassive face of the network executive, before he or she started grinning slightly, before the first laugh, before you made the sale.

And in the ensuing weeks – and sometimes months – between the sale of the script based on the pitch (which usually takes place in October or November) and the actual writing and delivery of the finished draft (sometime in January or even early February), the difference between what they bought and what you sold becomes enormous.

The easiest way to explain the system is by describing when, exactly, a writer gets paid and for what.

If you pitch an idea to a network and they like it, they'll order up a script and pay you for that.

Once you turn in the script, they'll ask you to address a set of concerns – they call these 'notes' – and you'll get another small check when you deliver a second draft.

The network usually orders more scripts than they need to produce, so after you've turned in your script, you have to wait a few weeks, or months, to see if they want to produce your script. This is called a 'pilot order', and it comes with another juicy check.

You now have to hire a director, assemble a cast, and produce the pilot, all under the helpful supervision of the network and the studio. When this is done and delivered, usually sometime in April, you get another small check. And you wait until May, at which point the networks decide which old shows they still want, which shows they don't (see above), and which pilots they're going to order to series.

It's quite simple, actually, but we make it simpler. We write a script, usually over the summer, finish it in early autumn, send it out to the various networks, and hope that they want to buy it. No pitching, no back-and-forth notes, just writing and reading. To us, this has always seemed like a more sensible approach for all involved. If they like the script, they simply make it, without all the uncertainty and the waiting, and without the irritating flurry of small checks to cut. But to some in the business – certain *network executive* types – our system has a whiff of arrogance to it. *Take it or leave it*, we seem to be saying. (Well, not *seem*, really: that's exactly what we *are* saying.)

That's the way a couple of writers with big studio deals have always done it, anyway. But times change.

CUT TO:

INT. MY OFFICE – DAY

The phone rings. It is . . . well, you know.

MY AGENT   Hi.

ME   Hi.

MY AGENT   So.

ME   So.

MY AGENT   I'm trying to tell from your tone of voice whether or not you're wallowing in self-pity about how hard development is, but you haven't said enough yet for me or my assistant to tell.

ME Your assistant?

MY AGENT He listens in on every call I make. That's the only way he'll learn the business.

ME Hi.

MY AGENT But he's not allowed to talk.

ME Oh. I thought young agents got their start in the mailroom.

MY AGENT The *mailroom?* Why the mailroom? Who gets mail?

ME I just thought–

MY AGENT This is a *telephone* business. He learns by listening.

ME Listening to clients?

MY AGENT No, listening to *me*.

ME Oh, see, I thought–

MY AGENT You've got a meeting at [*my agent mentions a big network*] next week.

ME But I don't think–

MY AGENT Sorry, it's all set up.

ME Oh. Okay.

MY AGENT Did you see how I did that?

ME Did what?

MY AGENT I wasn't talking to you.

CUT TO:

We are at a professional crossroads. Our past series were entirely self-generated. That is to say, we sat in a room and stared at each other long enough until we had an idea and a script. The more popular and savvy approach is first to *ask* the networks what they might be interested in, and especially, which actors they have already put under a contract called a 'holding deal'.

235

You're then doing something called *developing for talent,* which means, simply, that you're coming up with a show for an actor who the network not only likes but is paying to sit around and be *available.* The word *talent* in this context simply means *actor and/ or actress.* It doesn't mean *talented.* It's just a noun, interchangeable with the word *mammal.*

The problem with developing for talent is that it's not quite as soul-satisfying as creating from whole cloth. And the truth is, somewhere between coming in to the office at eleven, and leaving at three, we kind of have a tiny little kernel of an idea that we'd like to flesh out. If it were up to us, we'd just write the thing like we always have.

CUT TO:

INT. CAMPANILE RESTAURANT – DAY

LUNCH WITH A COUPLE OF NETWORK EXECUTIVES.

EXECUTIVE #1   So . . . are you guys going to write another pilot or . . .

EXECUTIVE #2   . . . you know, we've got some great talent at the network . . .

EXECUTIVE #1   . . . some *terrific* talent . . .

EXECUTIVE #2   . . . some talent with actual *talent.*

ME   Well, obviously, we're not ruling anything out.

EXECUTIVE #1   Of course.

ME   I mean, we're *available.*

EXECUTIVE #2   Gotcha.

EXECUTIVE #1   So you're willing to develop for talent?

ME   Of course.

Executive #2 reaches across the table and grabs my arm.

EXECUTIVE #2 (*deeply, with great feeling*)   I applaud you.

CUT TO:

When they say *I applaud you* they mean *not so stuck up now, you arrogant shithead fuckfaces, are you?*

CUT TO:

INT. MY OFFICE – DAY

Later. The phone rings.

MY AGENT   Hi!

ME   Hi. And hi to your assistant.

MY AGENT   You're spoiling him! Look, I just got off the phone with the network. I don't know what you said at that lunch, but they're in love with you.

ME   Yeah, well, about that . . .

MY AGENT   You've been thinking, right?

ME   Right.

MY AGENT   You're not sure you want to develop for talent anymore, right?

ME   Right.

MY AGENT   So?

ME   Well, how do we get out of it?

MY AGENT   Get out of it? Why would you want to get out of it? Look, they'll send over some tapes, you watch them, if you like someone, great, if you don't, too bad.

ME   But what if we don't like any of them? What if the talent they've got holding deals with sucks?

MY AGENT   In other words, what if the earth is round and the sun is bright orange?

ME   Basically.

MY AGENT   Then I tell them that you're *available but not interested.*

ME   What happens then?

MY AGENT   Usually, they go nuts and offer you double the money.

ME   Oh.

MY AGENT   Why do you worry so much?

ME   Well, it's just that we actually do have kind of an idea for a show . . .

MY AGENT   What? *What?* When did this happen?

ME   Well, we've been sitting around thinking, and there's an idea we've been kicking around about a guy–

MY AGENT   A *young* guy, yeah . . .

ME   A guy who suddenly discovers that his dad–

MY AGENT   His *young* dad, yeah . . .

ME   Do you want to hear this or not?

MY AGENT   I do, I do. Really. Pitch away.

ME   You know what? Forget it. We'll just write the thing and send it to you.

MY AGENT   And you'll watch the tapes, right?

ME   No way.

MY AGENT   Be realistic.

ME   No.

MY AGENT   You only have nine months left on your deal.

ME   Then I have nine months to keep being unrealistic, right?

MY AGENT   That wasn't where I was going with that.

ME   Look, give us a month or two to write this one. Let's just see how it goes. If it works, and they buy it, then fine. If not . . .

MY AGENT   Then you'll watch the tapes?

ME   Yes. Then we'll watch the tapes.

MY AGENT   I applaud you.

CUT TO:

Of course, there's talent and there's talent. And no one around here is claiming to be above a little schmooze now and then.

For instance:

For many years, I have spent the Christmas holidays with family and friends on a tiny island in the Caribbean. The resort is a fairly low-key affair, but there are a few movie actors, a television star, a famous journalist, and a few politicians among the annual visitors. We all ignore each other cheerfully.

One year, however, a studio executive I know comes with his wife. He wants to know why I haven't taken advantage of our island setting (no quick escapes; no place to hide) to buttonhole one of the actors and convince him to do a television series. One in particular is said to be considering a return to television. All that remains, according to the studio executive, is someone to 'reel him in'. When I explained the logic underlying the concept of 'vacation', he stared at me uncomprehendingly.

'I'm not here to do deals,' I said, looking away imperiously. 'This isn't that kind of place.'

'I know,' he said, nodding vigorously, 'that's what makes it such a great place to do a deal. You know, you have the place to your-self. *No one else is going to poach that guy.*'

One morning, at breakfast, certain events beyond my control (newspaper, sudden gust of wind) caused me and the actor to exchange 'hellos'. And not just hellos, but handshakes and friends-in-common and, ultimately, some cups of coffee, a chat about 'The Business', some discussion of what television needs today, and finally a promise to have lunch next month in Los Angeles. In short, I schmoozed. I would like to deny it, but I can't. I schmoozed, and worse, while I schmoozed, all I could think about was, 'So this guy wants to do a television show, huh?'

239

The next afternoon, while I was sitting by the dock waiting for the evening boat to arrive, the television executive catches up to me. He sits down in the chair next to mine, takes a sip of his rum punch, and shuffles around a bit.

I don't turn around. I know what he is doing. He has seen me talking to the actor, and he is grinning triumphantly. His is grinning, if it's possible, audibly.

'Nice work today,' he says, devil-in-my-ear.

'I'm sure I don't know what you mean,' I huff.

'C'mon,' he drawls, taking the pineapple slice out of the drink and biting it right to the peel. 'You cornered the guy,' he says, lips smacking around the pineapple, 'and you did the deed.'

'Oh, *that*,' I say, with a dishonest shrug, 'I was just saying *hello*. We have *friends in common*, you see. It wasn't *business*! It was just a friendly *hello*.'

'Yeah. Right.'

'Look, I'm on vacation, okay? What kind of loser schmoozes people on *vacation*?'

'No, no, I'm not criticizing,' he says. 'I was impressed. It was pretty slick.'

'Well,' I say, chilly and offended, 'I don't come all the way out here to do *business*, okay? If I wanted to do that, I'd be in Hawaii.'

A moment passes. We sip our drinks.

'It *was* pretty slick,' I say.

'Absolutely,' he says, raising his glass. 'Happy New Year.'

One more story to prove that we're not inflexible artistes:

A few years back, a local television station broadcast an exposé of some popular local restaurants. With hidden cameras and undercover reporting, they revealed that some of the most popular Los Angeles restaurants are guilty of some of the most unsanitary practices.

Waiters were secretly filmed licking their fingers and nibbling from plates that were about to be served. Salad tossers were caught

240

sneezing into their hands and then tearing lettuce. Chefs were taped inadvertently knocking cigarette ash into stockpots.

The town was transfixed. In a city as scattered and scatter-brained as this one, few events manage to capture the collective attention. Fires, floods, riots and earthquakes are the usual unifiers. Now we can add *E. coli in your tagliatelle al formaggio* to the list.

'People are going nuts over this thing,' an agent friend of mine said. I was sitting in his glass-lined office waiting to go to a Dodgers game and the conversation turned, as it did everywhere in Los Angeles that month, to the restaurant exposé. 'I've eaten in a bunch of those restaurants. And you know what? The food was good. I say, if you enjoy it, that should be enough. Some things you don't want to see being put together. Some things you're better off not knowing.'

I looked out of his silent glass office, on to the great bullpen of the agency. It was a scene out of a Bosch painting: assistants were scurrying around, agents paced wildly, screaming into headset telephones. The whole office was in the throes of its normal, everyday panic attack.

'Sort of like, you should just enjoy the movie or the television show. But no one should ever see how one is prepared,' I said, gesturing to the chaos beyond.

He stared out into the bullpen. 'Christ, yeah,' he said. 'If people only knew what we have to do to put a project together, they'd throw up and never stop.'

In the wake of the exposé, the local health board swung into action. All over town, restaurants began sporting large plastic cards in their windows, official issue of the health board, with a letter grade in bright blue. The grades go from an 'A' (which, presumably, means that you have the guarantee of the County of Los Angeles that no matter what you order, you won't get dysentery) to 'C' (roughly, 'You eats here, you takes your chances').

For a few tense weeks, everyone in town was doing the same thing: we'd cruise slowly by our favorite restaurants, praying for an 'A' in the window. Or, at the very least, a respectable maybe-it's-just-a-case-of-a-slightly-not-cold-enough-refrigerator 'B'. In a city obsessed with rankings and ratings, with who's-in-who's-out, the plastic cards with the big blue letters cut right to the heart of things.

'But last week,' the agent says, 'my wife and I went to a local sushi restaurant. We'd gone there a million times. Didn't think anything of it. We go, sit down, have some hamachi, some neguro, you know. *Sushi*, right? Then, we're leaving, I look down, and against the window, *way down there*, is the Board of Health grade. Guess what it was?'

'B'? I guess.

'Nope. It was a "C". I'm like, "Holy crap, my wife and I just ate 'C' sushi." I mean, "C" pizza, *okay*, *maybe*, it's hot, you know, and heat kills everything. But "C" sushi?'

'Yeah, I'm not sure about "C" sushi.'

'So my wife and I spent the night making each other vomit.'

'Wow. Really? How? Did you watch the *Something's Gotta Give* DVD?'

'No, we–' He stops himself, then laughs mirthlessly. 'Funny. Our feeling was, better safe than sorry. But the upshot is, from now on, we're strictly "A" restaurants. For *everything*. Actually, I think they should rate food shops, too. And shoe stores, you know? All that trying-on-and-off and other people's feet all over the place. And gyms. I mean, you're naked in those places with *other people*.'

It's time to get to Dodger Stadium. It is axiomatic in Holly-wood that anything really important can only be discussed at the very last minute. It's the same principle which dictates that contract negotiations will break down irretrievably at six o'clock Friday afternoon, only to be revived an hour later, when everyone is hungry and cranky enough to settle. It is also what leads people to begin to reveal incredibly crucial bits of information just as the parking valet pulls up with their car, or, worse, while on the car phone, to say, 'The most important thing to bear in mind is . . .' or 'They're offering you the sum of . . .' just as they head into a canyon where cell coverage is spotty.

'Look, we represent a piece of talent that's got a network relationship.'

What he means is, a network has just signed a giant deal with a certain actress to star in her own half-hour comedy show.

'Who?' I ask.

He tells me the name of an actress who has recently declared during a television interview that she communicates with creatures from outer space. She has also, according to certain press reports, been in and out of drug rehabilitation several times. These things, though, don't really matter. Only one thing does.

'Is she funny?' I ask.

He shrugs. 'Not really. I mean, I don't think she's ever done comedy.'

'So she's crazy and she's not funny.'

'Right.'

I think about this for a minute.

'But she's got a deal,' he says. 'So are you interested? Please say "yes", because I already told them you'd take a meeting.'

'Not interested,' I say without pausing.

'She's A-list, I'm telling you.' He leans in, intensely.

I immediately picture this actress standing outside the studio gates, eyes drooping in drunken half-sleep, wearing a bright blue 'A' around her neck.

'Sorry,' I say, 'But A-list isn't what it used to be.'

Of course, we don't always say 'no' to those kinds of things. When you're applauded as much as we've been, you learn that taking a meeting with a *piece of talent* is the easiest part of development.

A few years ago, at the studio's behest, we met a very talented actor who was interested in doing a half-hour television show.

He's a funny guy: nimble, smart, with a hugely expressive face, and not too handsome – not handsome at all, really, which is perfect for comedy. Good looks tend to let the air out of any comic situation. Comedy relies on a certain amount of dire jeopardy for the main character, and if you're beautiful, how much trouble can you really be in? Because even after slipping on the banana peel, or waking up in a hotel room up next to a hooker with your wife on her way up from the lobby, or losing the suitcase full of cash for your boss's bail, if you've got great teeth and terrific breasts and cheekbones like tiny moons you're not really in much of a jam. You're beautiful. You'll figure it out.

Well, this actor wasn't beautiful, which made us interested in him in the first place. So after an hour or two of shooting the breeze and getting to know each other, *establishing a relationship* – you're hip to the lingo by now, right? – the three of us shook hands and parted, the actor back to his movie set, and the two of us back to our office to decide if we wanted to think up a series for him.

An hour later, the phone rang. It was the actor's manager. He wanted to know if we had any objection to having another guy, a friend of the actor's, coming on board as a producer.

'A producer of what?' I asked.

'Of the show. We want to attach him as a producer.'

'*Attach* him to whom?'

'To *you*. To the *show*.'

'We'd be happy to consider him for our writing staff. Send us his material.'

'But he can't write. He's not a writer.'

'Then what is he?'

'He's a producer. He *puts things together*. He *arranges elements*.'

'Still don't get what he does,' I said.

'He *facilitates*.'

'We don't need a facilitator. I mean, we write it. Your client acts it out. We get somebody to film it. What else is there?'

244

'This guy is real creative, I'm telling you. He's a terrifically creative person.'

'Can he write?'

'He's not a writer.'

'Then what is he?'

'He's a producer. He's attached and he's a producer.'

Let me tell you a story that I heard a few weeks ago:

A big television network signs a major Broadway star to do a series. This happens quite often, actually: the rigors of stage work – and the ability to charm an audience – are ideal training for a star of a half-hour comedy. So with the star suitably dazzled by flattery and woozy with gold fever, the network searches around for a writer.

They're looking for *auspices*, to use the industry term, which, like most industry terms, is neither accurate nor wholly literate. *Auspices*, around here, means not just a writer, but an über-writer – a guy, in other words, who will not only create a series and write the pilot episode, but who will also executive produce the resulting – one hopes – enormously enriching hit.

Hollywood almost always has two or three ways of describing the same job, each imprinted with its own little status DNA. There's no real difference, for instance, between a *cinematographer* and a *director of photography*, except that the former probably gets paid more money. Actors can be described as a *wonderful piece of talent*, an *element*, and, at the very top, *a creative force*. And a television writer is sometimes a *unique comic voice* then, if lucky, becomes a *writer/producer*, which, if everything works out, evolves into *showrunner*, until, finally, the six-figure *auspices*, as in: *We will pay a lot for a show produced under that writer's auspices.*

To be at the *auspices* stage of a career, for a television writer, is a little like being a 'made guy' in the mob: you're trustworthy, you're solid, and you have blood on your hands. 'What we need to find for you,' agents will tell a hot actor client who is considering a gig in series television, 'are the appropriate *auspices* to best serve your wonderful *creative force*.'

On with the story:

So the network finds some pretty impressive auspices – a guy with a hit show already on the air – and sets up the deal. The actor is thrilled (the guy writing his show – excuse me, under whose auspices the show will be produced – is the network's prize guy) and the writer, who is already rich, is on the brink of becoming *seriously* rich. Jerry *Seinfeld* rich.

Unfortunately, he can't write. He's awful. His scripts are unfunny, childish stacks of paper, with stories so conventional they're almost confusing, and jokes so flat you almost can't distinguish them from the stage directions. How this tiny talent of a man came to such worldly success is an example of the efficiency of the Hollywood economic model. You can get anybody to rewrite anything. Or, as the network executives like to say, 'We can always get somebody to make it *good*. What we need is somebody to *make* it.' A few years ago, this guy wrote a lousy, though professionally competent, script. All of the hackneyed elements were in place: setting, female lead character, pseudo-sexual tension – right out of the software program, SitCom 1.0. Not a lick of it was funny, of course, but that didn't bother the network. 'We can get somebody to plug the funny in,' they said.

So the show limps on to the network's schedule in the winter, sticks around until the following autumn, gets a few additions to the cast ('We can always plug some funny person into the cast,' I can hear them saying) and emerges as a late-blooming hit.

But the guy still can't write. But with a hit on the air and millions of dollars in the bank, he's forgotten that. All he knows is, 'Hey, look at me! I'm not just a writer! I'm auspices!'

So, over the holiday weekend, the guy writes the script for the Broadway actor. Early the next week, he gives it to a writer friend of his, to whom he has promised a staff-writing job.

'What do you think?' the writer asks his friend.

His friend has a choice: if he tells the truth, the writer may be so furious that he takes back the job offer on the spot; if he opts for mindless flattery, the writer may actually give the script to the Broadway actor *as is*, queering the deal, also resulting in his friend's unemployment. It's a classic Hollywood ethical dilemma: either choice ends up in a job search. The friend chooses the middle path, the typical Hollywood way – he tells the writer a half-truth.

'It's pretty good,' he says, slowly, hoping to be let off the hook. 'I mean, it's a first draft, right?'

'Nope. It's fine the way it is. At least, I think so. Don't *you*?'

'Oh, yeah. Yeah,' says the friend, mindful of his house payments. 'It's just that, I mean, shouldn't the network see it first? Maybe give it a second pass or something? You know? Like a polish or something? Just tweak it a little? Here and there? You know?'

The writer does not give the script to the network first. And he does not 'tweak' or 'polish' it at all. Instead, he flies to New York, presents the whole muddled, jarring, monotonous raft of drek to the Broadway actor, in his dressing room, between the matinee and the evening performance.

By the time his plane has landed at Los Angeles airport, the Broadway actor has read the script, called his agent, pulled out of the deal, and issued a press release announcing his decision to 'concentrate on the arena of feature films.'

'The dumb ass showed him the script,' the network executive fumed. 'He actually thinks he's a good writer. I tried to tell him, "You're not a good writer." I said, "You don't *have* to be a good writer. We can *get* somebody to be a good writer for you." And the guy says to me, "Then why have me do the show at all? If you can get somebody to write it, what do you need me for?" So I told him, "We like your auspices."'

Which, when you think about it, makes a certain kind of sense.

★

247

It used to be that television was the movie actor's boneyard. If you were getting old, hadn't had a decent movie part in a while, but drank too much or gambled too much or maybe just had to put some kids through college, you were what people around town would call 'ready for television'. As in: 'Is so-and-so ready for television?' 'Yes, but he doesn't know it yet.'

These days, with many actors on television commanding salaries in excess of $500,000 per episode – for, if we all don't have enough resentment stored up against them, a paltry twenty-two episodes per year – and even then, some of them get something called a 'producer credit', which is a license for mischief, well, it isn't a question anymore of being 'ready for television'. Some of the biggest names in Hollywood are raring for television. Some of them, in fact, are circling the studio in makeup.

That's the cynical reason why so many actors are 'ready for television'. The other reason is less colorful, but equally true. Most of the feature films being made these days are insufferable, ghastly little pieces of retreaded crap, with funny dialogue so unfunny, and scary dialogue so unscary, that television actually benefits from the comparison. So when an actor weighs the higher salary and the better material against the small step down in prestige . . . you see where I'm going with this.

A few years ago, when we were casting a television series, the network wanted us to meet with an aging movie star with an eye toward casting him in the lead role.

This happens quite often in television. Movie stars, especially *former* movie stars, regularly become 'available' for television shows, usually around tax time. It's an alluring gig for an actor: a steady paycheck, six months off, short work days . . . and still in the public eye.

The actor that we met with, though, wasn't your regular long-in-the-tooth, graceful-exit type. He was one of the biggest movie stars of all time. Twenty years ago, he was, in fact, the biggest box-office attraction in the world. Now, he was broke and in our

248

office trying to pretend that he wasn't broke and he wasn't asking for a job.

How he got broke was a simple case of making a gajillion dollars a year, but spending a gajillion and one. It's a remarkable sight, watching an actor spend money. They don't so much *spend* it as *fling it in all directions*. It cascades out of every orifice, to the assistants and the nannies and the household staff and the lawyers and the guy who helps you charter a plane. Get divorced, and the cost of everything doubles. Get divorced again, and you'll discover what ancient Chinese mathematicians called the 'ruinous curve.'

The meeting was heartbreaking. As much as we wanted to give him the job, we knew we couldn't. The few people who had worked with him in the intervening swan-dive years all gave us the same advice: run. He's crazy, they said. He refuses to work for days. He's late. He's impossible. He argues with the director. He re-blocks the cameras. He'll accuse you of trying to murder him. And worst of all, he punches people. Writers especially.

'If you cast him, you'll have to get a *side agreement*,' my agent said.

'What's a side agreement?' I asked.

'It's an understanding. A legal understanding between you and the studio. It means that if the guy hits you and you don't want to come to work anymore, they can't sue you for breach of contract.'

'Do you think he'll really hit us?'

'You're a writer, aren't you?'

'Then forget it,' I said. 'Who needs this kind of aggravation?'

There was a pause on the line.

'Well,' my agent began, slowly, 'before we get all "forget it" about this, let's remember that the guy is a *huge* star. A *gigantic* star. He's not just a piece of casting. He's a piece of business. He's an *element* to the show.'

'Meaning?'

'A star like that could make your show a hit. Do you really want to say "no" to that kind of opportunity?'

'Well . . .' I said, wavering.

'Look,' my agent said, 'what's so great about being easy to work with? I'm *horrible* to work with, and I'm doing okay. Everything has its drawbacks. Some stars make you hire their idiot friends on the writing staff, some insist you donate to their crackpot charities, some drink, some bang underage kids, and some . . .' My agent paused, winding up, '. . . and some even want to *write*. So in the grand scheme of things, what's a couple of swings from a former box-office sensation and star of your *hit* television show?'

I think about this for a moment.

'He can't hurt us, though, right?' I ask. 'What are we talking about? A black eye? Swollen lip?'

'Honestly? As your agent and legally enfranchised representative, I'm ethically bound to inform you that the guy was, in fact, an amateur boxer. What we are talking about is something on the order of a broken jaw or burst ear drum.'

In the end, we passed. The actor was charming in the meeting, but then, he was an actor. He's *supposed* to be charming in the meeting. A television show, even a hit television show, isn't worth having your teeth knocked out.

'You're crazy,' my agent said. 'You'd have a hit on your hands.'

'Sorry,' I said. 'I like my teeth and my jaw and my ear drums.'

'You still don't get this business, do you?'

We don't. So we start writing.

BEGIN AWFUL, CLICHÈD MONTAGE:

(MUSIC UP: AN UP-TEMPO HIT)

1. We're hard at work, staring at a large bulletin board on the wall . . .

2. Our assistant takes shorthand as we pace and gesticulate wildly . . .

3. The printer spits out pages and pages of dialogue . . .

4. We sit at a table, marking up a script with red pens . . .

5.   Silence. Lost in thought. Then, one of us says something, and the other bursts out laughing . . .

6.   Moonrise over Los Angeles . . .

7.   A darkened studio lot . . . PUSH IN TO REVEAL: One office light flickering . . . PUSH IN TO REVEAL: A finished script in the copying machine . . .

(MUSIC CROSSFADES OUT; SFX: COPYING MACHINE CROSSFADES IN)

END AWFUL, CLICHÈD MONTAGE

FADE OUT.

Another phone call, Monday, 2:36 p.m.

'*Are we all on the line?*'

  '*You've got Josh.*'

  '*Delia here.*'

  '*Jamal here.*'

  '*Trish.*'

  '*Eli.*'

  '*Hi, it's Beth.*'

  '*Okay then, I'll put Josh on the line.*'

  '*Hi, everyone.*'

  '*Hi Josh!*'

  '*How's Montreal?*'

  '*Great! Some really great new comic voices.*'

  '*That's great, Josh.*'

  '*Josh, hi, it's Delia. I'm new here, so I may be breaking the whole "protocol thing", but I've seen some of the tapes we've been getting from Aspen and Montreal and I really think there's something in the new wave of ironic man-boy comics reflecting on childhood. And I think we should be developing some kind of project along those lines.*'

  '*That's a good point, Delia.*'

  '*Thanks, Josh.*'

  '*Okay, so what are we doing here?*'

  '*Did you get a chance to see the material we sent you?*'

  '*Yeah.*'

  '*Well, we've put a call into him to give him some notes and feedback . . .*'

'Okay.'

'. . . And we wanted to get your thoughts first.'

'Okay.'

'Okay.'

'My feedback is I don't get it.'

'. . . "don't get it," okay . . .'

'I mean it's like stories and gossip and I don't know what else. Is it darkly comic and I just don't know it?'

'I think that's a fair response, Josh.'

'What do you think, Josh?'

'I guess my concern is that we may be dealing with some form of satire.'

'Yeah.'

'Yeah.'

'And that really is not going to work for us.'

'And what's the jeopardy here for this guy? Does anybody really care if he gets his hit show on the air? Is anyone in America going to root for this guy? It just seems elitist and pointless and . . . just a second, I've got the room service guy here . . . hey, I wanted the glass bottle of Evian, not the large plastic one.'

'?Que?'

'The GLASS bottle. Not the PLASTIC bottle. The PLASTIC gives you cancer.'

'Josh?'

'Yeah?'

'Do you think we should just shut this project down?'

'No, no. Wait a sec. Right! Glass! Right! No, no, we shouldn't shut it down. Just make the guy more like someone who people might like and respond to. Not so many stories. More jeopardy. More sex, maybe.'

'There's no sex in it at all, Josh.'

'Good point, Delia.'

'But don't you think we should focus our notes on the main character?'

'Yeah. Focus on making him a more believable, likable, heroic . . .'

'. . . passionately committed to his art and craft . . .'

'. . . striving . . .'

'. . . attractive . . .'

'. . . everyman.'

'Right.'

'Right.'

'Right.'

'That's him on the other line right now. Should we all get on, or . . .'

'Delia?'

'Yes?'

'Do you want to take this by yourself?'

'Sure!'

'Okay, he's all yours. 'Bye.'

''Bye.'

''Bye.'

''Bye.'

'You've got Delia. Go ahead.'

'Hello?'

'Hi!'

'Hi.'

'Thanks so much for getting back to us so quickly. First, I just want to introduce myself. I'm Delia and I'm sort of taking over for Beth and Eli and helping out while Josh is in Montreal.'

'Are you Trish's replacement?'

'No, actually, the whole team has been reorganized, and we're now broken up into "pods" that cover the various projects we have in development.'

'I'm in your pod?'

'Right!'

'Okay.'

'So first, let me just say, "Welcome to my pod!" No, seriously, I'm just so happy to be working with you. Anyway, I know how you writers all hate the whole "getting notes" thing and I totally agree with you. It's the worst part of my job. What I want to do is work with writers and *just kind of brainstorm and be creative and really contribute to the process. You should know that I'm really picky about the projects that I work on and when I work on something, I'm totally about that one project and just, like, so fucking passionate about it it's scary.'*

'Okay.'

'Great. So really our one basic note is, can the whole story start faster?'

'I'm sorry?'

'And is there some way to make one of the characters a little more reflective of the ironic man-boy voice?'

'I beg your pardon?'

'Let me send you some tape on that.'

WINTER: 'HAPPY HOLIDAYS'

At Christmas time Hollywood denizens suspend their usual adult-sized greed for the simpler, more innocent greed of a child.

Hollywood – climate and religious diversity notwithstanding – is a Christmas kind of place. And if one doesn't send out hundreds of Christmas cards (sample message: 'May the Joy of the Season Warm You and Your Family. A donation in your name has been made to an Important-Sounding-Charity.'); send gift baskets of tiny, inedible muffins; and in general behave as if one day's generosity can somehow mitigate 364 days of cruelty and selfishness; well then, just how does one expect to succeed in this town?

In what I now realize were the Fat Years – years, that is, when we had a television series in production – my office was a Christmas Wonderland. Baskets and baskets of fruit and whiskey and horrible-tasting Italian cookies jostled for space among the flowers and useless crystal items. The office reception area was thronged with messengers and delivery men bearing gifts. One year, a large television network sent out large red footlockers filled with candles and doodads and, oddly, a terrycloth bathrobe. (The robe I gave to my assistant: the thought of emerging from the shower, naked and dewy moist, and wrapping myself in something that came from the president of a television network was just too creepy.)

In fact, most of the gifts end up with the assistants. Hollywood, after all, is a truly Christmas kind of place. Here, it's the thought that counts. We don't care if the baked goods are stale, if the wine is obscure, if the bathrobe is creepy, or if the last thing we want is a weird crystal toe-shaped thing with the Time Warner logo on it – we just want it, wrapped and delivered. We just want to know that we're loved, even if only by a corporation's computer-generated people-we're-doing-business-with-this-year list.

So when Christmas rolls around, we celebrate in two distinct ways.

The first way, as I've mentioned, is by sending elaborate gifts to people who do not need them. Every agent, studio executive, network president, and entertainment lawyer sends every writer, actor, agent, studio executive, and network president they're in business with (or *want* to be in business with) some kind of gift – food is popular, as are small electronics.

The second way is by firing all of the low-level employees, forcing them off the payroll and on to state-sponsored unemployment benefits for the *two weeks* between Christmas and New Year's Day, and then promising to rehire them the first Monday in January. A hugely profitable television production company did just that last year, claiming that they needed to 'make economies to compensate for our increased level of executive gift-giving'.

In other words: we're doing so much business that we can barely afford to send everyone presents. See you in January.

My partner and I have always given out Christmas bonuses to our employees. Cash bonuses, by the way, and fairly generous ones, we thought.

In the years that we have a series in production, the bonus pool gets quite large – split unevenly among six or seven office assistants. In the years that we're developing a new series, the office is quite small: just us and our colorful-but-surly assistant.

Earlier this month, our assistant made it subtly clear that his annual bonus was too small. He made a few veiled comments like:

'My annual bonus is too small,' and, 'If it's going to be that small again this year, please just don't bother with it at all. It's too humiliating to take it to the bank.'

Stung, we had a conference. Our assistant, though cranky and reflexively disrespectful, is in fact an excellent assistant: his typing skills are impeccable, his shorthand is efficient and complete, and when we're in production, he runs a flawless team of sub-assistants. He is, in short, a valuable employee.

And at Christmas time, when our offices overflow with ridiculously extravagant food baskets and disconcertingly personal gift items, it seems churlish not to spread the largesse around a bit. My partner suggests a healthy increase in our assistant's annual bonus.

'But I gave him my massage oil,' I whine.

Still. Maybe a cash increase. We've been very busy these past months writing two scripts, each one of them requiring long days of fast typing.

'And I also gave him the lavender eye mask we got from the guy who fixes the fax machine,' I say, holding out.

In the end we decide to give our assistant what is known in Hollywood as a 'bump'. As in: 'We're bumping up your bonus.'

On bonus day, we handed the envelope to our assistant, who instantly put it aside and continued typing the script.

'Aren't you going to open it?' I asked.

'After I finish this,' he said airily. 'I don't want to lose my motivation to do a good job.'

'Open it,' I said in a low, irritated voice.

'After I finish typing–'

'Open it!' I barked.

He opened the envelope. The Christmas bonus check – now adjusted north by a zero – tumbled out.

He looked at the check. Barely a flicker crossed his face.

'What happened?' he asked. 'Did you get visited by three ghosts last night?'

'It's in recognition of all that you do,' I said, with distinct irony.

'Well,' he grumbled. 'Thanks, I guess.'

'You're welcome,' I snapped.

'Merry Christmas,' he sneered.

'Happy New Year,' I snarled. 'And hurry up with that goddam typing.'

The Christmas spirit, when it comes, always has a dollar sign attached.

DISSOLVE TO:

INT. MY OFFICE – DAY

I'm sitting at my desk, looking out the window. A large truck has just driven up outside, laden with enormous-looking wrapped gifts.

A delivery man hoists one or two on to his shoulders, and heads for our office door. He leans in.

DELIVERY MAN   Is this the *Frasier* office?

MY ASSISTANT   That's next door.

DELIVERY MAN   Thanks.

The door slams shut. The phone rings.

MY AGENT   Hi. Happy Holidays.

ME   Merry Christmas.

MY AGENT   That's like your subtle way of saying 'I'm not Jewish,' isn't it?

ME   No. A lot of my Jewish friends say 'Merry Christmas.'

MY AGENT   That's like your subtle way of saying 'A lot of Jewish people like to pretend that they're not around Christmas time,' right?

ME   Are you calling me anti-Semitic?

MY AGENT   Of course not. Of course not. You're just defensive. Your problem is that you only hear what you *want* to hear.

ME   Actually, my problem is that I *never* hear what I want to hear, even when what I want to hear is being said.

MY AGENT   Listen, I'm not your shrink. I just called to say that I'm heading out for the . . . *holidays* . . . and that I'm sending you a little something.

ME   Gosh, thanks.

MY AGENT   Simmer down. It's not a gift.

ME   Oh. What is it?

MY AGENT   It's the comprehensive list of all of the half-hour series that all of the networks are developing for next fall.

ME   Why on earth would I want to look at such a thing?

MY AGENT   Find out what you're up against for the fall. See what the competition is. You know, *info*.

ME   It sounds depressing.

MY AGENT   You know what's more depressing? Ending up next May with no shows on any network. I suspect then that you'll look back on the time you spent perusing the development list with a warm fuzzy feeling.

CUT TO:

My agent, as always, is right. The development list arrives, it is sixty-three pages long, and it is depressing. As I read it, Bob Cratchit-style, I see more vans pull up outside my door, all laden with gifts, all going to other people, people with shows on the air. A production facility I have never used, in a part of the San Fernando Valley I have never visited, inexplicably sends me a cardboard desk calendar. I give it to my assistant, who receives it with what looks like pity in his eyes.

The development list is a purely-Hollywood document: the list is based on unequal parts rumor, lies, and incontrovertible fact. No network wants its competitors to know its precise plans for the following year, so the list takes on the complexity of a

Le Carré novel. Some projects are clearly lies told by the network ('Harrison Ford Sitcom Project'); some are lies told by a studio ('One of seven thirteen-episode commitments'); some are last year's projects that no one knows the status of ('Writer doing feature film; may be avail. '06'); and some are outright ludicrous ('our little production company – twenty-two episode commitment').

Still, if only one-half of each network's development slate is factual, the news is very grim indeed. Each network, by my count, is actively developing fifteen or so series. And each network, by my count, only needs four.

CUT TO:

INT. MY OFFICE – DAY

We are sitting around watching CNBC, the financial news channel, to see if anyone is trying to purchase the studio where we work, or the network we want to order our show. Outside, the steady parade of gifts to other producers continues.

SFX: phone rings.

MY AGENT   Did you get the list?

ME   I did, thanks.

MY AGENT   And?

ME   It looks bad.

MY AGENT   Why?

ME   Look at all of the stuff they're developing. It's going to be hard for our script to cut through all of that, don't you think?

MY AGENT   Actually, I don't think it will be. I sent your script out last week and they bought it this morning. You're making a pilot.

ME   What? *What?*

MY AGENT   I thought to myself, 'Hey, should I tell him ahead of time, or should I just send it out and tell him later?' Isn't that what I said?

MY AGENT'S ASSISTANT   That's what you said.

MY AGENT   Ultimately, it was an easy decision to make. I mean, there's so much about this business that you can't handle, I thought I'd spare you the *agita*.

ME   Well, thanks. But then why did you send over the development lists?

MY AGENT   Because even now that you're making a pilot, you're still a long shot for a series order. And if you get to make twenty-two episodes, you're still likely to–

ME   Get cancelled in May. Got it. Thanks for the lesson.

MY AGENT   *That*, my friend, is my *Christmas* present to you. Merry Christmas.

ME   Happy holidays.

CUT TO:

I am meeting a woman for dinner at a local restaurant. I arrive a bit early, take a seat at the bar, and order a drink. Two seats down, also waiting for his date, is an actor I know vaguely. We wave to each other and strike up a conversation.

'How are you doing?' I ask.

'Pretty well,' he says. 'How about yourself?'

I tell him that my writing partner and I have just had our pilot picked up by the network. I tell him that we're happy to be casting and producing, because sitting around thinking all day is a difficult process. We throw out a lot of ideas, we sit in silence a great deal, and ultimately, we miss the structured day and organized existence that having a series in production provides.

He nods sympathetically.

'Well,' he says, 'I haven't worked in about a year. And at first, all that unstructured time kind of drove me nuts. All of those empty, aimless days spent waiting for auditions. The isolation. The sitting around. I really thought I was going to go insane. But lately, I've come to enjoy it.'

'Really?' I ask. 'How are you keeping busy?'

'I've been doing a lot of research lately,' he tells me. 'On the internet.'

'About what?' I ask.

He takes a sip of his beer, and then says, matter-of-factly: 'About the healthful effects of drinking your own urine.'

I'm a writer, obviously, and not a scientist. I can't speak for the healthful effects of anything, much less my acquaintance's new beverage choice. But I can say, without hesitation, that in all the times I've felt bored or out of sorts, had a show cancelled, been stymied for ideas, felt useless and without direction – felt, in other words, the way a writer in Hollywood feels when he's not asleep, I've never been tempted to, shall we say, sample my own wares.

'Hollywood,' someone once told me, 'is divided into two camps. In one camp are the people you have to wait for, the people who come up with the ideas and write the scripts. The writers, in other words. They're the "wait-fors". Nothing can happen and no one gets hired until they write the script. And in the other camp are the people who wait for the writers. Those people are actors. Also known as "waiters".'

The irony, of course, is that while they're waiting for a part to come along, most actors work as waiters. And while we're waiting for inspiration to strike, most writers are eating in restaurants. I like to think that if most actors were better waiters, we writers would get our food faster and get back to work sooner. And no one would be doing 'research' on the internet.

CUT TO:

INT. OFFICE – DAY

We are sitting with our casting director, who has brought a long list of actors who might be right for our show.

266

ME (*pointing to a name*)   What about him? How old is he?

CASTING DIRECTOR   His agent tells me that he's a very fit sixty. But I did a little checking and discovered that he was a contract player at MGM in the fifties, which makes him–

ME   Ninety. He's ninety.

CASTING DIRECTOR   His agent swears to me that he's a fit sixty.

ME   How old is his agent?

CASTING DIRECTOR   Twenty-seven.

ME   Next name.

We go to the next name, a big star.

CASTING DIRECTOR   This guy is perfect for you. He's funny, he's the right age, he's available and interested in television. He'd be a home run.

ME   Great. Let's bring him in to read for us.

CASTING DIRECTOR (*chuckling*)   Oh, he won't *read*. He's too big. He'll *meet*. He'll come in and *meet*.

ME   Umm, okay. Then why don't we get him a script and see if he's interested in the part, and if he is, then let's meet.

CASTING DIRECTOR   Are you offering him the part?

ME   How can we offer him the part if we haven't even met him yet?

CASTING DIRECTOR   Well, he won't read the script unless it comes with an offer.

ME   But how can we offer him a role unless we at least meet the man?

CASTING DIRECTOR (*in a bored monotone*)   He won't meet unless he reads and he won't read unless you offer it to him first. He's *offer only*.

ME   What about some guys who aren't *offer only*?

CASTING DIRECTOR   You don't want them. Trust me. Anyone worth casting won't read the script, won't audition, and probably isn't interested.

CUT TO:

It turns out, our casting director is telling the truth. The few agents who call to tell us that their clients have read our script, love it, and want nothing more than to audition for us this afternoon do their clients no service. We are instantly suspicious, and by the same stupid reasoning that leads you to reject a romantic partner who likes and respects you for one who lives to make you unhappy, we too reject the willing, easy, professional actor for the unattainable, super-sexy *offer only*.

The problem, as always, is money. Ordinarily, the studio fronts the money to pay the entire production tariff. In the local patois, they 'deficit' the production, meaning that they agree to lose tens of millions of dollars up front, in exchange for the potential bonanza that exists if the show lasts long enough to go into reruns. 'Long enough' is currently defined as roughly five years.

It's in the long-term interests of the studio to keep costs – and the financial risk – down. But since it's in their short-term interest, unfortunately, to supply the buying network with a dazzling product, it's a good idea to cast big stars in the show. Big, expensive stars.

Occasionally, for a big star – or what we call *a major piece of talent* – the network will agree to kick in a little money. But only as a last resort. And they'll never tell you until the very last minute.

The result is something out of Pinter: two cheapskates trying to avoid picking up the tab for dinner.

CUT TO:

INT. NETWORK PRESIDENT'S OFFICE – DAY

There are eight of us in the room. We are all reviewing the casting possibilities for our show.

NETWORK PRESIDENT   I like a lot of these names.

ME   Me too. Especially . . .

I name one of the actors on the list.

NETWORK PRESIDENT   I like him a lot.

ME   Me too.

CASTING DIRECTOR   Me too.

NETWORK VICE PRESIDENT   Me too.

STUDIO PRESIDENT   But he's expensive.

STUDIO VICE PRESIDENT   Very expensive.

NETWORK PRESIDENT   Is that a problem?

STUDIO PRESIDENT   I don't know. Is it?

NETWORK VICE PRESIDENT   For an important project like this, we should be prepared to pay top dollar, right?

STUDIO VICE PRESIDENT   We?

NETWORK PRESIDENT   Whoever.

STUDIO PRESIDENT   The point is, can we afford him?

NETWORK PRESIDENT   I don't know. Can we?

STUDIO PRESIDENT   I don't know. Can we?

CUT TO:

INT. OFFICE – FOUR DAYS LATER

The phone rings.

MY AGENT   Hi. I just got off the phone with the network. They're not so pleased with the way the studio has handled the casting. The word they used was *obstructionist.*

ME   Well, we've been going after some pretty expensive names.

MY AGENT   I know. Listen, everyone wants big names, no one wants to pay big money. It's the same everywhere. I want Armani Le Collezione; I'll pay for Armani Exchange.

ME   It's the *offer onlys* that have hurt us.

MY AGENT   Why are you bothering with *offer onlys*? C'mon! Do you have any idea how many great actors there are living in seedy apartments in the Valley, making their way from urine-smelling passageways to late-model Chevrolets for a drive to the day-old bakery on Magnolia and Burbank?

ME   What?

MY AGENT   Like it? I'm taking a creative writing class at UCLA Extension.

ME   Great.

MY AGENT   Relax. You'll find somebody. And it'll be somebody affordable.

ME   What if we don't?

MY AGENT   Then we tell everyone that the studio was obstructionist and you leave in a huff.

ME   Can we afford to leave?

MY AGENT   I don't know. Can you?

ME   I don't know. Can I?

MY AGENT   What?

ME   I mean, didn't you tell me that there were no more deals anywhere?

MY AGENT   I don't know. Did I?

Pause.

MY AGENT   Look, do you want to take some meetings around town at different studios? Just kind of a meet-'n'-greet situation? In case there's some money for deals next year?

ME   No. I want offers. No meetings. I'm *offer only*.

MY AGENT (*chuckling*)   You kill me. You really had me going there. Bye-bye.

270

ME   I'm serious.

MY AGENT   Bye-bye.

ME   I mean it. I'm totally–

SFX: Click. Dial tone.

   CUT TO:

About ten years ago, on a Hollywood soundstage, an actor threw such a tantrum that the next day he felt compelled to apologize to an assembly of the cast and crew. This is not as rare as it sounds: most actors, after a big meltdown scene, like to follow it up with a big apology scene. In this case, the actor made a tearful show of it, abjectly throwing himself on the mercy of a group of people who owed him their livelihood. (Surprise! They forgave him!)

   But he wound up his speech this way: You gotta understand, he said, what I've been through this month. A friend of mine has cancer, my girlfriend and I are having problems, and *I've been through an earthquake.*

   He was referring, of course, to the Northridge quake, which devastated parts of the San Fernando Valley, felled a freeway overpass, and killed over fifty people. But to this actor – and I suspect he's not the only actor who felt this way, nor, for that matter, the only person in the entertainment industry who felt this way – everything is a personal thing. Earthquake? *My* earthquake. Holocaust? *My* holocaust. As Daffy Duck once shouted to Elmer Fudd, trying to keep him from pulling the trigger, 'I'm different! Pain hurts *me*!'

   CUT TO:

INT. MY CAR – DAY

SFX: phone beeps. I answer.

MY AGENT   Hellloo.

ME   Hi.

MY AGENT   Congratulations! I hear you have an excellent cast!

ME   Thanks. We're pretty happy with the way it turned out.

MY AGENT   See? What did I tell you? It's impossible, it's too expensive, it can't be done, and then, suddenly, it's done.

ME   That's certainly how this turned out.

MY AGENT   I have a thought for the title of your show.

ME   We have a title.

MY AGENT   I mean a better title.

ME   What is it?

MY AGENT   Call it 'Here They Come!'

ME   I don't get it.

MY AGENT   It's about a young guy and his dad, right? Who are also friends? Get it? Growing up I had a friend and we were inseparable. And when people saw us coming, they'd say, 'Here they come!'

ME   I'm not sure America will get it.

MY AGENT   But *I'll* get it.

CUT TO:

We have employed the same assistant for several years. Besides being lightning fast with shorthand, he's also a devoted student of astrology, and he has acquainted us with the astrological concept of the 'void'.

Simply put, a *void* occurs during the absence of any astrological force. It means, essentially, that you are free floating. A void, by its very definition, is indifferent – the stars are neutral for however long the void lasts, which can be a few minutes or a couple of days.

After my partner and I spend a desultory afternoon of smoking and gossiping and staring at each other, we look forward to our assistant's ability to explain our laziness away with an astrological alibi: my trine is in his house, he's in retrograde, or (my personal favorite) something called *moon wobble*. The point is, it's not our fault.

'How're we doing?' one of us will ask. 'Are we in a void?'

And he will fix us with a withering gaze and answer, 'No we are not. Astrologically speaking, you *should* be working efficiently. And anyway, a void is what you bring to it.'

From the Hollywood perspective, a void is the worst possible situation. The heavens arrayed against you is preferable to their indifference. It is better to be on the top of everyone's enemies list – they know who you are! They can spell your name! At lunch they all talk about how awful you are! – than to be unknown, undespised, unspecial.

'I truly believe,' an agent told me once, 'that my grandparents were spared the horrors of Nazi Germany because God wanted me to revolutionize the talent representation business.'

Now *that's* special.

Worse, because 'a void is what you bring to it,' there are no tricks or blessings you can rely on to get you out of trouble, and no negative heavenly force you can use as an excuse when you fail. A void is the astrological version of having a script with no actor or director attached, of having a show with no big-name star or network commitment, of having to rely, at the end of the day, on the merits of the material. Nothing could be more terrifying.

CUT TO:

INT. MY OFFICE – DAY

We are having a cup of coffee. In less than an hour, we're holding the first reading of our pilot script. This is the event that sets the tone for the rest of the production week. The stage will be filled with executives from the network and the studio, with the actors and their agents, with various other personnel, and, finally, with us.

ME (*to my assistant*) How're we doing?

MY ASSISTANT (*quietly*) We're doing very well.

ME What does that mean?

MY ASSISTANT It means that halfway through the reading, we'll be void.

ME No!

MY ASSISTANT Remember: a void is what you bring to it.

ME That's what I'm afraid of.

MY ASSISTANT (*encouragingly*) And you're bringing a great script and a terrific cast. You'll be fine.

ME I guess so. Besides, just for a little extra good karma, as I turned left on Crenshaw Boulevard this morning, I gave the homeless guy who hangs out there five bucks.

MY PARTNER You did? Uh oh.

ME Uh oh what?

MY PARTNER I gave him twenty. You know what you have to do now, don't you?

I nod. I dash out to my car and zoom down Crenshaw Boulevard waving fifteen dollars out the window. Karma? My karma.

FADE OUT.

A 'Concept Meeting', Tuesday, 2:45 p.m.

'Should we wait for Josh?'

'I'm Josh.'

'No, I mean the other Josh. The head of the division.'

'Oh.'

'Oh, right.'

'Oh. Well, I think that Josh isn't going to be at this meeting. This is just a concept-y kind of meeting.'

'Concept-y?'

'I think what Delia means is that we're just going to give our feedback on the pages up to now, and maybe think of ways to platform some of the moments better.'

'Just a chance to take a beat.'

'Right. Take a beat.'

'Just to take a beat.'

'Thanks, Eli.'

'First, let me just say that everyone in the pod is thrilled with this project. Really.'

'It's my favorite project of the entire pod. And that includes drama hours and some reality business, too.'

'Gosh, thanks.'

'No, thank you. For bringing us this really edgy project.'

'You know, we're always saying that we want more edgy stuff, more stuff that's challenging to our audience, and this certainly is it!'

'Well, thank you.'

'And I think what we like the most about it is that it's dark and kind of inaccessible.'

'Inaccessible?'

'You know what I love about it? I love the whole "aging failure scrambling for money" aspect.'

'I like that part too, Delia.'

'Me too.'

'Me too.'

'That's still there? Because I was trying to . . .'

'I guess I want it to get even darker.'

'Darker?'

'Yeah. I mean, I'm getting the idea that you're holding back a little, you know . . .'

'Well, I'm trying to keep it likable.'

'Don't!'

'Don't?'

'No! Go for it! Get as dark and as edgy and as unlikable as you want. Really. That's what's working for me.'

'I agree with Delia.'

'I agree with Josh about agreeing with Delia.'

'Delia?'

'Yes, Eli?'

'Is there a sense – and I'm just throwing out an idea here – is there a sense that some of this could be even more dark, and more edgy?'

'I think I agree with you, Eli.'

'Because he could really push it, and we could easily dial it back if it gets too far.'

'Of course.'

'Of course.'

'Of course.'

'So . . . you want me to be even sharper?'

'Yes.'

'We're saying that we love the area you're in, in terms of tone.'

'Tonally, we love it.'

'Love it.'

'So don't worry about being likable?'

'But don't tell anyone I said so! They'll take my executive's license away!'

'Hahahahahahahaha.'

'Hahahahahahahaha.'

'Hahahahahahahaha.'

'You know, I don't even think of myself as an executive. I think of myself as a writer, but . . . you know . . .'

'A writer who runs a pod?'

'Right.'

SPRING: 'THE MIDDLE DISTANCE'

Fade in:

One of the more comforting aspects of Hollywood is how dependably it lives up to its clichés. You are, in fact, only as good as your last picture. You will, in the end, learn that you've been fired from the parking lot attendant. And it is, despite sprawling over two mountain ranges, a freshwater river, miles of coastline, three telephone area codes and a knot of concrete freeway, a very small town.

A friend of mine filmed a television pilot recently, and he and his partner, the director, take it to one of the market research facilities here in town to be focus-grouped. Thirty or forty scientifically assembled participants (culled from the local tourist traps) wait in the broiling sun for an hour or two until they are led into a dark room with a one-way mirror and told to watch the pilot, after which they will be asked for their responses, and after that presented with a crisp twenty-dollar bill. These drowsy, hungry, grouchy folks with a lifetime of unfulfilled longings hold the future of a million-dollar piece of film in their mitts. I often wonder why they always give them the money *after* the session, and not before, to cheer them up a bit, but this is the way they've always done it so this is the way they do it still.

The testing goes quite well. We call it 'testing' the pilot around here because of the grim clinical connotations of the word. In my friend's case, the focus group enjoyed the show, giving it a 'will watch' designation, which is about the highest possible rank. They were unanimously negative, however, on one point: a particular actress they all despised with equally high intensity. In the guided discussion that followed the screening and the questionnaires they filled out, the participants, to a person, remarked on the general badness of this particular actress. They all hated her. They hated her face. They hated her voice. They hated her body. They hated her totality. At one point in the show she is standing next to a box of newborn puppies. They decided that they also hated the puppies, which was a market-testing first: puppies, kittens, and children in wheelchairs always test very well.

The problem was that the actress was married to the director. And the director was behind the one-way mirror, listening to America tell him how repellent his wife was. Also behind the mirror were representatives from the studio that produced the pilot, the network that bought the pilot, and the writer, none of whom had the courage to so much as steal a sidelong glance at the director, who, presumably, stared straight ahead into the middle distance, with that vague, abstracted smile people get on their faces when they don't know what else to do.

CUT TO:

INT. MY OFFICE – DAY
The phone rings.

MY AGENT   Congratulations!

ME   For what?

MY AGENT   Just congratulations. Are you excited?

ME   About what? Congratulations for what?

MY AGENT   You shot a fabulous pilot that the whole town is talking about.

ME   We did?

MY AGENT   Don't you hear the buzz?

ME   We're too busy for buzz.

MY AGENT   Well then, let me clue you in. The buzz is very

good on your show. And you know what they say about the buzz.

ME   What do they say about it?

MY AGENT   The buzz is never wrong.

ME   Sure it is. I can't tell you the number of times I've heard great things about a show only to have it flop terribly.

MY AGENT   You're a nervous person. You're a doomsayer. Do you have TMJ?

ME   What's that?

MY AGENT   It's a muscular disease you get in the jaw from clenching it too much during bouts of stress. I'll bet you have it.

ME   (*unclenching jaw*)   Do not.

MY AGENT   It's sad, really. You're on the cusp of a big success. The buzz doesn't lie. The buzz is never wrong.

ME   What about shows that have great buzz around town, but then nobody in America watches?

MY AGENT   Usually by then the buzz has changed, only nobody noticed.

ME   Oh.

MY AGENT   Of course, I notice everything.

ME   Oh.

MY AGENT   I'll call you if the buzz changes.

CUT TO:

The story of the director and his actress wife was told to me at lunch one day. Our bored, apathetic waiter overheard the story and identified himself as one of the participants in the focus group. It seems that he and his other flat broke actor friends hang out at the Farmer's Market, a local tourist attraction, waiting to get

283

picked for focus groups. Whoever gets picked buys two pitchers of beer with the $20.

I ask our waiter about the actress that his group loathed with such certainty. He tells me that he actually thought she was pretty good, but that he had once taken an acting class with her and she had been a 'total bitch', so he turned the group against her. I ask him if he doesn't feel a little bit guilty, since the network, following the focus group, insisted that she be recast and the pilot re-shot without her. He shrugs. 'I dunno,' he says, 'I figured it was okay since the show sucked so bad. I mean, I knew it was never going to last more than six episodes.' I ask him how he knew that. 'The buzz, man,' he says, shrugging for the ninety-seventh time, 'the buzz on that show just totally *bit.*'

This is a small town. No matter where you are, you can hear the buzz.

CUT TO:

INT. MY OFFICE – DAY

The phone rings.

MY AGENT   Hi hi.

ME   Hi.

MY AGENT   I just thought you'd like to know that [my agent
    mentions the name of an actor who's in a new half-hour
    television pilot] just flipped his car and has checked himself
    into rehab.

ME   Ouch.

MY AGENT   Ouch and not ouch. Production has been postponed
    for six months, which means he's out of consideration for the
    fall. Which means that there's another slot available for a new
    show.

ME   Oh.

A pause.

MY AGENT   Like yours.

ME   Did we get an order?

MY AGENT   You didn't get one this morning? Wow. I was pretty sure you'd have one by now.

ME   Why?

MY AGENT   Because I have a dear friend – someone I've known a long time – someone I *go back with*, you know? And, his show has been scuttled.

ME   Why?

MY AGENT   They hated the pilot. What can I say? He's a dear, dear friend. A close personal friend. He's like a brother to me. But he can't write for shit.

ME   Oh.

MY AGENT   I mean, the man gives you *nothing. Nothing on the page*. And for some reason it's hard to really see that until you actually make the pilot.

ME   Well, since we're exchanging gossip, I hear that [I mention the name of another project] has hit the wall too. Apparently the pilot tested terribly.

MY AGENT   Not true. Not true at all.

ME   No?

MY AGENT   No. You know what that is? That's a vicious lie, that's what that is. Jesus, this town is sick.

ME   Gee, sorry.

MY AGENT   In the first place, the script was moving, passionate, and, may I say, magisterial.

ME   *Okay.*

MY AGENT   And in the second place, the network loved it. They're in love with it. And it tested fine, for your information. There were some concerns with male audience appeal, of course – there always are. And some of the female demos didn't really respond to the arena, but you know what? They hated *Seinfeld*, too. And *Friends*. Both shows tested for shit.

ME   Okay. Okay. *Okay.*

MY AGENT   So stop spreading lies. Stop smearing your filth all over town.

ME   I'm *sorry*. Okay? Man, what is it? Are you friends with the guy?

MY AGENT   He's a client.

ME   Oh.

MY AGENT   What? You thought you were my only client?

CUT TO:

INT. HAVANA ROOM – NIGHT

I'm drinking with a friend. He has a show on the air and is waiting to hear if the network is going to cancel it. I am suddenly struck by the thought that one year ago, I was in his shoes. And now, one year later, I'm the one with a hot pilot, warming up on the sidelines, ready to go.

That afternoon, he got a call from his network's president. It was intimated, but not said outright, that his show is about to be cancelled.

Because our pilot is for another network and because the failure of his show can in no way – even in the remotest possible sense – help our show, and because I was at his wedding, and because in the past, when I've been depressed about something or needed someone to talk to he has always been available and ready to take me out for a drink or snap me out of it, when I put my hand on his shoulder and say You got screwed, my friend, it was a good show you did and it deserved better, *what I actually mean is* You got screwed, my friend, it was a good show you did and it deserved better, *rather than what I*

286

usually mean, which is Does this event help me in some way? I need to think about this for a moment.

Of course, he cannot claim to be shocked. In the previous week, my friend's show had drawn what is known as a 'nine share,' which means that nine per cent of all television sets in use at the time were tuned to his show. As I'm writing, that's a bad number. You strive for double-digits at the very least.

MY FRIEND   I don't get it. We were doing so *goddam well.*

ME (*gently*)   But last week you pulled a 'nine.'

MY FRIEND   I know. That's what I mean. We were doing so *fuckin' well.*

ME (*tough-love style*)   C'mon, buddy. You got a 'nine.' That's . . . well, I'll be honest, that's a shit number. You're lucky they didn't yank the show in the middle of the broadcast.

MY FRIEND   Yeah, except every week they've been calling and telling us how much they love the show, and how happy they are with the numbers. Last week, when we bagged an eight share, they sent us all fruit baskets.

CUT TO:

My friend had committed a classic Hollywood error. He had received a fruit basket without grasping its subtext. To him, the gift card that read, 'Congratulations! We're thrilled with the ratings!' meant, roughly, 'Congratulations! We're thrilled with the ratings!' What it really meant was something closer to, 'You got a nine! Pack your things!'

He can be forgiven his confusion. With the explosion of new networks and the proliferation of cable stations, the expectations for network ratings have diminished considerably. Fifteen years ago, a twenty or twenty-five share would have indicated a moderate-to-low success. Today, that same number connotes a huge runaway hit.

287

Expectations, however, have not diminished so much that a nine means anything other than pretty instantaneous cancellation. In general, I've found, the problem with diminished expectations is that they never seem diminished enough.

The network management, though, will be relentlessly cheerful and encouraging right up until the moment that they cancel you. And it's almost impossible – or, more truthfully, it's almost impossible *for me* – to tell the difference between a genuine fruit basket and an impostor fruit basket.

The strange thing about the American television ratings is that for all of the attention paid to the *national* ratings, it's the *local* ratings that really count for big money. There are roughly one hundred and fifty television markets in the US – that is, regions that have three or more local network television affiliates. And because the major national networks only provide about nine hours of programming a day (two in the morning, one in the afternoon, four at night, and one or two during late night), that leaves a juicy fifteen hours for the local stations to fill with reruns, old movies, used-car ads, and general crap.

All of this is pretty irrelevant background information, frankly, but it does illustrate the hardiest of entertainment industry truths: the really big money is found in the most unglamorous places. In the feature film business, a Julia Roberts movie is great to have in your production pipeline, but its real value comes when you make every theater that wants to book it (or every international distributor that wants to sell it overseas) buy a couple of duds along with it. And in the television business, the primetime network shows are the loss-leading window-dressing baubles that attract the eyeballs that stick around for the reruns, old movies, used-car ads, and general crap.

But as much as I would like to have offered sympathy to my friend, I have a pilot in contention for the fall, and I am too wrapped up in my own numbers anxiety (not to mention daydreams of plush, early retirement) to offer much except to buy his drinks.

Besides, he's hard to feel too sorry for. He's a friend, of course, but friends are the people you see most clearly. And according to him, the network complained early on that his show wasn't funny enough and he rather arrogantly ignored them.

'So I told them,' he said to me over lunch one day, 'that I think jokes are *easy*. It's *easy* to be funny.'

'Really?' I asked him. 'It's always been kind of hard for me.'

'That's because your shows are *supposed* to be funny. They're like the filler between the good shows that are supposed to mean something.'

I would have felt insulted had I not been flattered. I have worked very hard to make our shows funny while avoiding 'meaning' anything. That, actually, is my working definition of 'entertainment'.

'Still,' I said, 'you could put in a few more jokes, right?'

'Aren't we all just *bored* of jokes?'

'I'm sorry?'

'What's so great about being funny? What is this obsession with funny funny funny all the time?'

'I wouldn't call it an *obsession*, really.'

'It's all just "set up, joke, set up, joke". I mean, just a string of hilarious one-liners? How easy is *that*?'

'Easy?'

My friend went on. 'I said to them, "Don't you want something different? Something that really breaks the cookie-cutter mold? Something *edgy*?" '

'What did they say?'

'They said they had that already. What they wanted was *funny*. And I told them that I don't do *funny*. I do *edge*. I do *meaningful television*.'

'And then what did they say?'

'They didn't say anything.'

'Oh.'

'I think I won them over.'

But of course, he didn't win them over. When they don't say anything, what they're saying is '*You're cancelled.*' But my friend didn't know that yet. He still thought he was doing fine. He's like a lot of people in Hollywood: they all want to do the marquee products; they all want to do the Julia Roberts movie; they all want to make the loss-leader. No one wants to do the filler. No one wants to be simply *funny*.

Except me. I know that it's the filler that pays the bills and buys the yachts and builds the houses by the sea.

CUT TO:

INT. MY CAR – DAY

I am driving to work. My car phone rings.

MY AGENT   Hi. Have you heard anything from the network? What have they said about your pilot?

ME   They called this morning. They said they're thrilled with it. They said it's a lock for the fall schedule.

MY AGENT   Oh no.

ME   I'm kidding. They didn't call.

MY AGENT   Don't do that to me. I'm plotzing here.

ME   It was a joke. Sorry.

MY AGENT   Okay. Fine. Look, as long as they don't send you any fruit baskets, you're still in contention.

CUT TO:

INT. OUR OFFICE – DAY

A messenger appears at our door, burdened by three large fruit baskets from our network. We panic.

I call my agent.

ME   We're dead! They sent us fruit baskets!

MY AGENT   What?

290

ME   We're dead!

MY AGENT   I'll call you right back.

SFX: hang up.

Moments pass. The phone rings.

MY AGENT   I just spoke with the VP over at the network. He assures me that the network is truly happy with the pilot, and that the fruit baskets are actual fruit baskets.

ME   They're really happy? Are you sure?

MY AGENT   I'm sure. Enjoy the fruit.

CUT TO:

On the way home, I give the fruit basket to the homeless man who hangs out by the freeway entrance. This time, I think to myself, the fruit baskets were sent without subtext. But next week? And the week after?

'Thank you, mister,' the homeless man says to me.

'Get used to it,' I mutter grimly.

The next day, my friend calls me up.

'It's official,' he says. 'We're cancelled.'

'Sorry to hear that,' I say.

'You know how it went down? This is classic. Get this: they call me up on Monday and tell me that they want to have a meeting this morning to discuss the creative direction and development of the show. For next season. And I said to them, "Does this mean there's going to be a creative direction and development of the show next season? Because I've been getting some pretty strong signals that we're about to be cancelled." And they're, like, "Are you kidding, we love the show, blah, blah, blah." So I'm thinking, okay, we're going to get to do a few more of these at least. So this morning I'm in my car, driving to the meeting–'

'The one they called, right?' I ask, just for clarification.

'Right. Right. The meeting *they* called. And my car phone rings.

It's the network. Calling to cancel the meeting. Because they're cancelling the show.'

'What about the meeting?'

'Right! What *about* the meeting? What *about* the *fucking* meeting?'

'That they called.'

'Right! That *they* called.'

'Did you ask them?'

'Oh yeah. And do you know what they said? They said that on *Monday* they didn't think they were going to be cancelling the show, but that *today*, this *morning*, they changed their minds.'

'Today is Wednesday.'

'Right. *Right!*'

'What happened between Monday and this morning?'

'I *asked* them that. And do you know what they said? They said that the research numbers hadn't been fully crunched on Monday because the guy who crunches them was at his kids' soccer game or spelling bee or tonsillectomy or whatever-the-fuck, and when he got back the next day, he discovered that, statistically, we could never be more than a nine-share show. And he sent the network president an email that night – last night – to that effect, but that the network president left early that day to go to some fucking charity bullshit thing – what's the thing where your skin gets all hard and your face turns into a big toenail?'

'Scleroderma?'

'Whatever the fuck. Anyway, he's there until late, doesn't check his email until this morning, by which time I'm on the fucking 134 heading to his fucking office.'

'Wow.'

'Wow is right.'

A moment passes. I can hear my friend slowly calming down.

'Do you know who I blame?' he asks, quietly.

'The network?' I ask helpfully.

'No. Not the network. Those guys are just doing their jobs. No, who I really blame is *America*. I blame them.'

'You're mad at America?'

'Damn right. I gave them a meaningful, nuanced half-hour show and they just ignored it. Just goddam *ignored* it. Well, you know what? Screw them.'

'Screw America?'

'Damn right. From now on, I'm only going to do *funny* shows. You know, like the kind you do. I mean, *fuck* it. From now on it's just *set up, joke, set up, joke.*'

Which, again, I know he means as an insult. But I also know that he's a friend, and in Hollywood, you're not obligated to be happy for your friends' successes, or be disappointed in their failures, or even think they're very good at their jobs. In Hollywood, to be a friend, your basic job is to sit there, listen to their bitter complaints, and agree with them that *yes, everyone at the network is a fucking moron* and *yes, everyone at the studio is a cowardly bureaucrat* and *yes, your stuff is so much better than anything out there.*

Jerry Lewis, the Ur-Jim Carrey, once bid farewell to a nightclub audience with this heartfelt prayer: 'May all of your friends,' he intoned, 'be show business people.'

What he meant, I guess, is that show business people – or, in the earlier jargon, 'show people' and in the earliest jargon, 'carnival people' – have uniquely deep and satisfying friendships. As Frank Sinatra was once overheard saying to a close friend, 'I wish that someone would hurt your family so that I could find that person and hurt them back.'

A few years ago, when we were shooting the pilot episode of a new series, we asked a veteran comedy writer to help us out for a day. The term is 'punch up': you invite an experienced vet to come to a run-through of your new show, then over a nice dinner and a good bottle of wine, hope that he pitches a dozen or so killer jokes and 'punches up' the script.

Although it may not seem like it to read this book, television writers form a loose but comprehensive web of friendships, and older writers, who are rich and bored and eager to help out, are sometimes the difference between a lackluster pilot that never becomes a series, and a hilarious pilot that makes it to air. This guy was one of the best, and we were excited to have him agree to help out.

'One question,' he said, 'before I get there.'

'Ask away,' I said.

'Who else will be working that day?'

I named a few of the junior-level writers. Then I named an older writer, a guy who's been around.

'Him?'

'Do you know him?' I ask.

'*Know* him? Yeah, I *know* him. I *hate* him. I *know* him and I *hate* him.'

'Oh. Will that be a problem?' I asked.

'Not for me,' the vet replied, ''cause I won't be there. Call me later, when he's gone.'

'But what did he do?' I asked, frantic. 'Why do you hate him?'

There was a long pause on the telephone line.

'Truth? I'm not sure. I can't remember.'

The only thing he remembered, naturally, was that he hated the guy. The other guy couldn't remember ever working with the old vet, and was completely bewildered by the feud.

Bewildered but philosophical: 'If the guy hates me, then he hates me. I never met him before in my life, but it takes a lot of integrity and discipline to hate a guy you've never met or worked with,' he said. 'And you gotta respect that.'

I am out having a drink with my best friend, an actor. He is telling me about the past television season, and how impossible it had been for him to get hired on a certain network.

'I couldn't figure it out for the longest time,' he says. 'I'd go on lots of auditions, have tons of call-backs, but in the end, they never hired me.'

I give him the it's-a-crazy-fuckin'-business shrug.

'But then I realized,' he went on, 'that it was always one particular network. Like I was being blackballed by someone in the casting department.'

'C'mon. You're being paranoid.'

'I'm serious. But not just *blackballed*. Blackballed with *extreme prejudice*, 'cause they'd call me in, then call me back, get my hopes up, and then bang, they'd pass on me. It was like someone out there really hated me.'

'Of course someone hated you. You're an actor.'

'Not just hated. *Hated* hated.'

I give him the it's-a-crazy-fuckin'-business-someone-always-hates-you-but-what-can-you-do-about-it shrug, which is similar to the basic it's-a-crazy-fuckin'-business shrug, except that it's delivered with a sad shake of the head.

'So I do a little research,' he tells me. 'I find out that the vice president of casting is a guy who was best friends with that girl I was living with when I . . . you know . . . *met my wife.*'

Met my wife is a sophisticated umbrella euphemism for a story that you can probably figure out yourself, in that it involves a guy, his girlfriend, and the woman who later became his wife. The story turns, as all love stories do, on issues of timing: when did *she* find out about *her*?

It turns out that the girl he was living with when he . . . you know . . . *met his wife* . . . had lots of friends in low-level jobs in the entertainment industry, friends who, in the intervening years, have acquired high-level jobs in the entertainment industry, and in one particular case, a high-level job in network television casting. And that guy, out of perverse and long-lived loyalty, is torturing my best friend.

'Wow,' I say. 'What are you going to do?'

295

'What can I do? I'm just going to wait it out, hope he gets bored, or hope that he suddenly realizes how bizarre it is to punish me for something that happened years ago.'

'Hmm. I guess that's all you can do.'

'Well,' he says, 'what did *you* do when you found out how much they hated you at the network?'

I look up from my drink. 'What network?'

My friend names the highest-rated network in American television.

'They hate me?' I ask.

'You didn't know?'

'*They* hate *me*?'

'You didn't know?'

'What did I ever do to them?' I ask in a tiny, childish voice.

'Maybe it's those stupid books you write, about how dumb they are. Where you write down all the stupid stuff they say.'

'But I make most of that up,' I shout. 'They *know* that, right?'

'Then maybe it's because you never listen to their notes. Who knows?' he says.

'But I can't believe you didn't know that they hate you. It's kind of a famous feud.'

'It's *famous*?'

'Well, isn't it obvious? They never buy any of your shows. I can't believe this is news to you.'

'I've never been hated before. I've always been the *hater*, not the *hatee*.'

He gives me a it's-a-crazy-fuckin'-business-someone-always-hates
-you-you-pathetic-out-of-touch-loser-I-can't-believe-you-didn't-
know shrug, which is similar to the basic it's-a-crazy-fuckin'
-business shrug except that in addition to the sad shake of the head, his eyes are closed.

CUT TO:

INT. MEN'S LOCKER ROOM AT THE SPORTS CLUB LA – DAY

The Sports Club LA is one of the more glamorous Industry gyms. It also has two of the dozen-or-so squash courts in town, which is why I'm there.

I am dressing. A well-toned man with the locker next to mine has just come from the shower. He sees another friend a few lockers down. His friend is portly and balding.

MAN Hey! How are you?

HIS FRIEND I'm okay. You?

MAN Not bad.

The man stares at his friend.

MAN (*cont'd*) Jesus, you've gained weight.

HIS FRIEND (*ruefully*)
Yeah, yeah. I know.

MAN No, I mean it. Like, what? Thirty pounds?

HIS FRIEND (*slightly defensive*) Twenty-five.

MAN Still.

HIS FRIEND I had cancer. Didn't exercise for a while.

MAN Oh.

HIS FRIEND (*moving off to the showers*) Nice to see you again.

MAN You too. Let's have lunch sometime.

HIS FRIEND I'll call you.

They wave. His friend moves off.

MAN (*muttering to no one in particular*) He didn't have cancer.

CUT TO:

For all I know, of course, the guy really *didn't* have cancer. Maybe he just ate too much pizza. Still, his friend felt under no obligation to a) believe him, b) pretend to believe him, or c) simply ignore the extra thirty pounds. He did, though, feel obliged to arrange a friendly lunch.

Charitable organizations capitalize on this weird kind of friendship. Every two weeks or so, an invitation will come to the office to a dinner in honor of some Industry heavyweight. The strategy is simple: The Center for Unhappy and Misshapen Children will decide to honor the newly-installed chairman of a studio, not because the chairman has ever expressed the slightest interest or concern for the Unhappy and Misshapen, but because there are enormous numbers of people in town who are willing, for the price of a piece of leathery chicken and a pale yellow carrot (roughly $1,500 per person), to publicly express their friendship with the new studio chief. Or, failing that, there are larger numbers of people who are willing, for the price of a single-page ad in the dinner's program, to express their friendship and admiration for the boss ($2,000 for a black-and-white ad, $4,000 for color, $20,000 for the back cover). These ads almost always have identical copy – something like: 'To New Studio Head, Your passion and caring inspire us all, with much love, Person You've Met Only Once.'

We got suckered into this recently. We shelled out $1,000 each to place a similar ad in the dinner program for a charity dinner in honor of the CEO of the conglomerate that owns the studio where we work. 'Best wishes,' we wished the guy. It wasn't necessary to append the phrase, 'From Two Guys You've Never Met or Laid Eyes On.' That was implied.

What *wasn't* implied was the news, one week after the dinner, that the CEO had left the conglomerate that owns our studio for another conglomerate that owns another studio. So we were out two grand for kissing the wrong guy's ass.

Let me tell you a story:

Recently, the president of a large division of a large studio was given his walking papers. Nothing personal, of course – the guy was good at his job (or, more accurately, as good as anyone else would be tasked with the same pointless responsibilities) – but the chairman of the studio had just installed a new president of the division under which the fired guy's division nested, and the new guy wanted to bring in fresh blood.

Usually, the new guy runs a bony finger down the organization chart and silently ticks off the names of everyone senior enough to gun for his job and fires them, thus ensuring that the new team running the studio has one powerful captain surrounded by terrified eunuchs. But firing people costs money – there are contracts, you see, and stock options – so the new guy has to be very careful to fire only those employees who pose an actual threat, by dint of their intelligence or courage or originality or some other personality defect, and not waste money on the drones.

So the old guy is out and he knows it. He's not bitter at all. Being fired, obviously, is proof of his value – if he wasn't good at his job, they would have promoted him. But he is more than a little broke. He has a house in the Riviera section of the Palisades (the best address in town, trust me on this one), a vacation place in Telluride, two kids at the Crossroads School, and a wife who has confused 'having a job' with 'writing a novel'. He needs a steady, fat stream of cash coming in to match the steady, slightly fatter stream of money flowing out, mostly to the American Express corporation and a mortgage banker specializing in something called 'jumbo financing'.

The financial ace up his tattered sleeve is a bushel of stock options that are, in our bubble-economy parlance, 'in the money'. So right after he gets his walking papers he calls up his old friend, the corporate treasurer, in New York. 'Hey, buddy,' he probably put it, 'you and I go way back, we're pals, our wives and kids know each other . . . I've got these options I want to cash in. I know you can't legally tell me exactly what to do, but I'd appreciate it, since we've been friends for so long, if you'd indicate to me if I should exercise them now, or if the rumors I hear are true and there's going to be a buyout of the studio, thus increasing their value tenfold, and making me a very rich man. A rich, retired man. What do you say, pal 'o mine?'

The story goes that there was a long pause on the line. And then the corporate treasurer said, 'My friend, I shouldn't tell you this, but just because you're you, I'll tell you unequivocally, that it doesn't matter at all.'

'So I should exercise the options today?'

'I'm telling you that it won't matter one way or the other.'

So the guy exercises his options. And it did matter one way or the other. The following Monday, a large media conglomerate announced a buyout of the studio, increasing the share price by a factor of ten, then, a few months later, by a factor of fifteen. Personally, I like to think that the corporate treasurer had the buyout agreement documents on his desk while he was telling his old friend, three thousand miles away, that it 'won't matter one way or the other.'

That's the way we operate out here. We're cruel, sure. But we're subtle.

So why didn't the treasurer tell his friend to hold on to his options? One possible explanation: it would be illegal to do so and corporate treasurers are notoriously honest.

Done laughing? Good. Let's get to the real reason he didn't.

He's mean. He's a mean, jealous guy and he didn't want his 'best friend' to be too much richer than he. A little richer, okay. A lot richer – and we're apparently talking in the tens of millions here – not okay.

Also, he knows that in Hollywood behavior of this kind has no consequences. Those two guys, it should be noted, are still close friends. Sure, they might have hit a rough patch around, say, the time the stock price hit $108 per share (up from its quaintly respectable option price of $6) but they've worked through it, see. The definition of 'friend' is so elastic in Hollywood that it includes the definition of 'enemy'. This town is so small that everyone eventually brutalizes everyone else. We're like rats in a coffee can: nowhere to go but at each other.

Last month, for instance, the president of one of the top-rated large television networks was unceremoniously booted from his job. It was long in coming, we all thought. The network was starting to lose its luster: the old hits were running out of gas and the new season had been a tire-screeching car wreck of failures. Worse, his past success had made him arrogant and impossible to deal with, and at least two writers I know had named characters after him: in one cop show, his namesake was a gay cannibal serial killer; in another, he was a severely retarded little boy.

Still, when he was booted, they gave him something called a *golden parachute*, which means, roughly, that he has been paid handsomely to get out and get out quick. He got some cash and a production deal at the network, the standard industry goodbye for a worn-out executive. (If you grasp the logic underlying the decision to reward an executive who can't come up with any more hits with a high-priced production deal so he can try to come up with some more hits, then by all means come to Hollywood and seek your fortune. If not, stay put.)

But even with his savings and his parachute, we all knew that the guy's got a big house to pay for and expensive tastes. Worse, he has ambition. So instead of retiring quietly (and cheaply) out-of-state, he decided to try to make a go of it on his own, you know, to *put things together.* To *brainstorm creatively with the writers.* To *serve as a catalyst for disparate elements.* He's always thought of himself as *creative* and *not just one of those uptight executives.* So, he decided, *I'm going to be a producer.*

Before that could happen, though, he needed to mend some fences. You don't spend as many years in the big boy chair as he did and not piss a lot of people off. So he had to spend six days driving around town visiting the various writers who despise him, tearfully attempting to make amends. He is a smart guy, this former network president. He will have to attach himself to something. And somewhere in Hollywood there is a writer who has

301

both forgiveness in his heart and a project that needs a guy who *facilitates.*

Mending fences isn't easy. It takes a certain talent. A couple of years ago, a young, aggressive talent agent – there are no other kinds, of course, but around here we still use the formal honorific – devised a brilliant trick to solve a thorny problem.

The ordinary back-and-forth efficiency of commerce in Hollywood is often blocked by pride. It's hard to believe, I know – the people who made *Boat Trip* have pride? The guys behind *America's Most Talented Kids* have pride? – but it's nevertheless true. We've all got a little place in this sticky spider's web, and it's important to keep up appearances. Small issues like 'who called whom first' and 'let's meet in *my* office; no, let's meet in *my* office' often sink entire deals. And because film and television projects always include three distinct and prideful elements (the star, the director, the studio, the network, the writer – pick any three) most of the time the business resembles a huge costume ball where everyone wants to dance, but no one wants to have to ask.

Which is where agents come in. This particular young, aggressive talent agent had figured out that if you place a call to one party, announce yourself as someone else – someone, say, that the person you're calling has a stalled, bogged-down deal with – then, while you're waiting to be put through, call the *other* guy, announce yourself as the first guy, then link the two calls using the conference button on the phone, you can easily get two people who weren't going to call each other (unless the *other* guy made the first move) to talk, to discuss, and to eventually make a deal, preferably on a project that one of your clients has an interest in.

This trick only works because no one in Hollywood places his own phone calls.

What happens is this: Important Person tells Important Person's Assistant to call Down To Earth Me. My phone rings. My Down To Earth Assistant answers (not even the Down To Earth answer their own phones, of course) and is told that Important Person wants to talk to Down To Earth Me. I pick up my phone and say a cheery 'Hello, Important Person!' at which point Important Person's Assistant says, in a voice both bemused and pitiful, 'Just a moment. I'll put Important Person on the line.'

You can see, then, how easy it is to call someone on the phone and still make it seem as if they've called you. Because in Hollywood – and I'm not sure Hollywood is all that different from the rest of the world in this respect – it is far better to be called than to be calling.

The scariest words in the English language are, 'You don't remember me, do you?'

Well, maybe not the scariest. The *actual* scariest words are probably, 'The chef doesn't believe in printed menus, so I'll just describe what we're offering tonight,' but 'You don't remember me, do you?' is right up there.

I heard those words at a meeting with the president of one of the biggest studios in Hollywood. I had been presented the customary bottle of water, guided to the plush suede sofa, and just at the moment that the small talk puttered to a stop, he fixed me with a half-smile and dropped the bomb.

I didn't remember him. At all. But we're roughly the same age, so our paths could have crossed and double-crossed lots of times: school, college, film school, the early days of our careers – really, when you think of it, the past is filled with dozens (maybe even hundreds) of moments in which one is, to say the least, not at one's best. And those moments are preserved in *someone's* memory, like tiny buried stink bombs, ready to be dug up and exploded with a simple 'You don't remember me, do you?'

Think of the terrible possibilities: I'm the guy you threw up on in college. I'm the guy who was up for the job you eventually got. I was the guy answering the phones the day you decided to let the first guy who answered the phone have it. I was your waiter. Or, worst of all for someone who has worked in Hollywood for four-teen years, I was your assistant.

This story, though, has a happy ending.

About a dozen years ago, when I was a just-hired young televi-sion writer and he was a just-arrived aspiring studio executive, his mom and my mom somehow met, and mothers being mothers, a couple of hours of my time was pledged to help the new kid figure out the town. Which I did, apparently. We had breakfast together, apparently. Advice was given, a bagel was toasted and buttered, and I, according to him, was nice and encouraging.

Lucky for me I was, because now the guy is a pretty successful and powerful studio executive, the maker of the very crucial funds disbursement decisions that I, as a writer and producer, like to be on the receiving end of. Which just goes to reinforce the only rule in Hollywood worth remembering: be nice to *everybody*. Because you never know.

The good news is the standard of good behavior in Hollywood is so low that to be known as a nice guy is really more a matter of *not* being known as a *not* nice guy.

I recently heard a story about a hot young producer and her assistant. Stuck on a story pitch, the producer decamped to a swank Las Vegas hotel, bringing along her assistant for some pool-side brainstorming. As she floated, blissfully, in the hotel pool, her hapless assistant, clicking away on her laptop, sweltered in the desert sun. As the summer heat approached 105 degrees, the producer looked up at her sweat-drenched, fainting assistant and said, airily, 'You know, if you like, you can dangle your toes in the water. Just don't get the keyboard wet.'

There's a lot about the universe that's unknowable, of course, but there are three absolute certainties. One, there will come a time when that assistant, motivated by memories of heatstroke and a thirst for revenge, will have risen to a high and powerful post; two, there will come a time when that producer will be temporarily down on her luck and in need of a friend in high places; and three, the two will meet over a couple of bottles of water around a suede sofa. And by then it will be too late.

Be nice to *everybody*. Or at least, in Hollywood, don't be *not* nice to anybody. Because you never know.

And the truth is, success in Hollywood is often just a matter of hanging around here long enough and not taking 'no' for an answer. California has always attracted that kind of zealous operator. When you pick up the east side of the country and tilt things down to our way, what shakes loose are the kind of people who aren't very tethered to begin with. And those of us who have come here, to make it big in pictures, or grapes, or lettuce, or software, or real estate often forget that this nutty, loosely woven state has been a magnet for dreamers and no-accounts for a long time. Hollywood natives like to set themselves apart from the *arriviste* horde, but if you go back far enough – and sometimes, not really far back at all – every industry character shares a certain kind of seedy heritage with the earliest California Gold Rush newcomers. We all came, whether to pan for gold or to develop television sitcoms, to enjoy a dollop of prosperous counter-culture rootlessness. California's most exemplary citizens, in other words, have had two things in common since 1849: blue jeans and greed.

We all came out to LA in waves, and those who came out at roughly the same time ended up knowing each other – like me and the now-studio-chief – and in some cases, became friends. It's like we were all part of the same freshman class, matriculates to the University of the Entertainment Industry, and so we either knew each other, from film school or threadbare parties or friend-of-a-friend-who's-an-assistant-to-somebody connections, or knew *of* each other.

I had a friend named Paul who came out to Hollywood a little bit after I did. We knew each other before – we went to the same high school – so when he came out, he gave me a call and we rekindled our friendship. He worked as a production assistant on a lot of movies and was often away on location. He and I would get together occasionally and drink beer and complain to each other about things that I'm sure were important then, but that have since slipped my mind. This was about six or seven years ago, and the things that concerned me around the time I turned thirty are vastly different from the things that concern me now, as I'm staring forty in the immediate distance.

One day, Paul called me up during a frantic production week and asked me out for a drink. He had been fired, he said. At the time, he was a young development executive at a busy and successful film production company. Getting fired from that kind of job was a rite of passage in a young executive's life, it seemed to me. We met that night, talked, drank a few beers, and said good night.

The next day, he shot himself.

This was my eulogy at his memorial service:

For Paul

The first time I saw Paul was 1981, or maybe 1982. We were in high school and Paul was my Cluster president. The school is divided into residential areas, clusters, and because it's a fancy boarding school and kids need things to put on their college applications, each cluster has a president. Paul was mine, which made sense, because Paul in high school was a lot like Paul later: charming, laughing, smiling. Same reassuring watery voice. If you were me in 1981 and you met Paul in 1981, you'd look up to him.

The last time I saw Paul was Monday, December 1st. He called me at work and asked if I was around later to get a beer. He was having a career crisis, he told me, and would fill me in later. We met at my house, walked to the Firehouse on Rose, had a few beers, and Paul told me that he had been fired. We talked for a long time about next steps, possibilities, things like that. We talked in that zig-zag fashion men use when they're circling around a big subject – switching from career and future to whether it would be fun to run a restaurant, to whether either one of us was going to

306

go to our fifteenth high-school reunion. When you go to high school with someone, you've got a million and one things to talk about to keep you from talking about what's really important. We decided that we would both tell everyone we were going and pay the fee, but when the weekend came, we wouldn't show up. That way, we could avoid entreating phone calls from our Class Agent, not have to show up, and still get the T-shirt. They called Last Call, we finished our beers, walked back to my place, talked a bit more, then Paul drove home. A day later, he was dead.

The minute something like this happens, people tell you not to blame yourself. 'You couldn't know,' they say. 'People hide things.' A colleague of mine grabbed me a few minutes after I heard the news and said, in a low voice: 'This happened to me in 1967. Know this before you begin: you will never know why he did this.' What did we talk about that night? Why didn't we get right into it? Why didn't he just tell me how hopeless and broken down he felt, how inconsolable. But if he had, what would I have done? What would I have said? Why didn't I tell him that night that he was a good friend to me – and he was: he would get me out of the house when I was going stir crazy, he would drag me to parties because he knew that if he didn't, I'd stay at home and play with the dog – are we flattering ourselves to think that if Paul had known, in those last awful lonely hours, how much the small things he did meant to us, that he wouldn't have done this? 'People hide things,' I know. Paul hid his sadness. But I hid my affection.

This terrible thing happened to Paul. But it also happened to us. He's not here to answer our questions, and if somehow he was, we still wouldn't understand. Paul was fighting a war against sadness. And he thought he was fighting it alone. How wrong he was.

A week after Paul's death, I wrote three letters to friends who have been good to me, who are important to me, but who I have never told. They were embarrassing letters to write, and the minute I dropped them in the mailbox, I regretted it. But they were sent.

I did these things in honor of Paul. My good friend Paul. A person I never knew.

It went over pretty well. The writer's ego in me is impossible to smother, so I was gratified when people came up to me later, after the service, to thank me for my words, and to ask for copies. But a true writer is more than an egomaniac. He's also a pathological liar. And in my eulogy, I hadn't told the truth.

'What did we talk about that night?' Well, actually, I remembered what we talked about that night. Paul asked me for a job. I told him that I couldn't give him one.

He didn't seem desperate to me – he asked me in an offhand, joking, unserious way that I didn't know at the time – but have discovered since – is the tone some people use when they really are desperate, and not joking, and serious. So when he asked me, with a half-laugh and a shrug, I returned the favor. I pretended it was a joke, clapped him on the back and said something like, 'Hey man, anything I could get for you would be beneath you anyway.' And something empty like, 'This is an opportunity to be more entrepreneurial and independent, to strike out on your own, no one ever makes his mark in one of those small production boutiques, you hated it anyway, you were born for hands-on producing not idiotic office politics.' Or something.

And the truth is, I really couldn't have offered him a job anyway – though I was the executive producer of a – in the end, not very – successful half-hour television comedy, and in Paul's eyes seemed probably a lot more powerful than I was, or than I felt I was. Had the show been a hit, maybe I could have thrown my weight around and found something for him, anything. And then even if he went ahead and shot himself anyway, I wouldn't have felt like I felt when I heard the news two days later. Because what I felt then wasn't really surprise or shock, but a blast of recognition. *Oh*, I thought to myself, *that's what we were talking about. That's why the whole conversation felt so weird and awkward. That's why he said goodbye so formally. I knew something was different, I just didn't know what. And I didn't ask.* And then, *What kind of miserable shit am I, anyway?*

Because for me it was an act of indecency not to do what I could for my hurting friend, not to bend a few rules and stick my neck out. I failed the central and elemental test of friendship and loyalty. We had been in the same class, he and I – both literally and in the Hollywood sense – and I let him down.

What I should have said to Paul, when he was really down and, I found out later, suicidal, was 'Thanks for dragging me out to parties, and introducing me to pretty girls, and getting me out of the house, and not letting me talk to the same girl at the party all night and inviting me to have dinner with you and twenty-five of your awful, ghastly, chattering studio-executive friends, because, though I pretended to have a rotten time, I actually had a great time, and thanks.'

I mean, he probably would have shot himself anyway – I've read enough of the literature now to know that suicides aren't averted by friendly testimonials and do-nothing jobs – but at least he wouldn't have felt . . . I don't know . . . unimportant. Unappreciated. Unremembered. Whatever.

FADE OUT.

Meeting in an editing room, Thursday, 12:45 p.m.

'See? Right there! Right there!'

'What about it?'

'Can we just freeze for a moment on that frame?'

'Here?'

'Right. Right. See, this is sort of what we've been talking about during this process. I mean, it's a terrific act break, really. Just very strong and I think we get a sense of the guy, you know. What makes him tick and stuff. But something about it . . .'

'Do you not want to go to Paul's memorial service? Is it too heavy? I'm just trying to tell that part of the story with as much dignity as I can.'

'Oh, God, yeah, dignity. Of course. No, we think it's great, really. Just great.'

'Josh, can I chime in here?'

'Of course, Delia.'

'It's just that, one of the things we've been struggling with in this piece is the sense that people might feel that, in a sense, that during the process you're describing – the story you're telling, there's a feeling of a sense that you may not be likable. That people may not like you very much. At all.'

'You guys have mentioned that, yeah.'

'So . . . ?'

'But I thought you wanted it edgy. I mean, wasn't that the sense of the–'

'Yeah, yeah. No. Right. Yeah.'

'Yeah, no, right. Right.'

'Right, yeah, yeah. No. Right. Yeah.'

'So I guess what I was doing was trying to push it a bit. Even if that means I come off unlikable.'

'Not you, of course. I mean, your character. It's just that, when your friend asks you for a job—'

'Paul. His name is Paul.'

'Right. I mean, when Paul asks you for a job . . .'

'And you say . . . no . . .'

'It's just like all of a sudden, I'm thinking . . .'

'We don't like this guy very much.'

'Right, Josh. That was what I was trying to say. And then he commits suicide and we're sort of left with the feeling that . . .'

'Well, that you're responsible.'

'A little.'

'Well, more than a little.'

'Oh. So it comes off as my fault? Because I didn't give him a job?'

'A teeny skosh, yes.'

'I thought it was clear that I didn't really have a job to give him. And that, in the end, it wouldn't have made a difference.'

'I think what Josh is getting at is that for the purposes of the story, what if you did offer him a job?'

'So he wouldn't kill himself? Are you saying we should cut the whole section?'

'No, no, no, no. We really like that he kills himself.'

'We love that he kills himself.'

'Killing himself is great! Just great!'

'It's just that this way, you get to offer him a job like a good, likable person would, and he kills himself anyway, and you come off as a good guy.'

'What do you think of that? Remember, we're just tossing out ideas, here.'

'Well . . . I guess . . . I mean, what makes this difficult is that it really happened to me this way. And what I was going for – and I'm

312

not saying it's successfully done, I'm just saying what I was going for – is some kind of telling of the story in a truthful way. I guess what I'm saying is that while I'd like to be more likable, I also have to be honest. At least when I'm telling this part of the story.'

'Well, no one wants you to change anything you don't feel comfortable changing.'

'This is your vision. Totally.'

'Totally.'

'Totally.'

'Keep it edgy!'

'Oh, yeah, right. Right. Yeah.'

'Yeah, no. No, keep it edgy, yeah.'

'Yeah. No.'

'Well, thanks.'

'Josh, can I chime in here a moment?'

'Sure, Delia.'

'What about the possibility that he offers Paul the job and Paul takes the job and then Paul doesn't commit suicide? Just a thought.'

'I like that a lot.'

'Me too.'

'Me too.'

'Me too.'

'And you know something? It really isn't all that much of a change.'

'Right, no, yeah, yeah, yeah, yeah, right, no, no.'

'Right, no, yeah, yeah, yeah, yeah, right, no, no.'

'Right, no, yeah, yeah, yeah, yeah, right, no, no.'

MAY: 'RERUN'

Fade in:

INT. REGENCY HOTEL BAR – MANHATTAN – NIGHT

I am sitting at the bar waiting to meet a friend. I know personally, or have worked with, or know people who have worked with, every single person in the bar.

I was here – right here, in this exact spot – one year ago tonight.

An agent slaps me on the back. His eyes are red and his tie is askew.

AGENT Hey man.

ME Hi.

AGENT Let me buy you a drink.

ME Thanks, but I'm on my way out.

AGENT Then let me give you two tickets to the Hillary Clinton thing.

ME Gee, that's very generous of you. But, really, I'm heading out.

AGENT Hey, but, let me just say, dude, that it's awesome about your show, man. Awesome. *Awesome.*

ME Thanks. Really.

AGENT Fuckin' great pilot. Totally great.

ME Thanks. Really.

AGENT So how many writers do you think you're going to be hiring? Because we've got some incredible guys who are just off deals, you know . . .

ME   Not sure, really. Maybe when we get back to LA we'll get into it.

AGENT   I'm telling you, it's a bloodbath out there. I've got clients out of work, no deals, it's like . . . it's like . . . and I'm here just workin' it for them . . .

ME   Yeah, hey, we're all in the same boat. Our deal is up in a month and . . .

AGENT   You guys have a show on the air! It's fuckin' awesome! You're going to be fine!

ME   Well, the ratings have to be good when we première, and . . .

AGENT   Well, listen, I shouldn't be pitching my clients to you right now, when I'm so . . . so . . .
The agent begins staring at an attractive young woman who has just entered the bar.

ME   So . . . wasted?

THE AGENT MOVES OFF.

AGENT (*to attractive woman*)   Would you like to meet Hillary Clinton?

CUT TO:

INT. HOTEL ELEVATOR – NIGHT

An executive from another studio steps into the elevator after me.

EXECUTIVE   Hi!

ME   Hi.

EXECUTIVE   I'm off to see Hillary.

ME   Great.

EXECUTIVE   By the way, love the pilot, man. Just great. Congratulations. Gonna be a great series.

ME   Thanks.

EXECUTIVE   And I'm not just blowing smoke up your ass.

ME   I appreciate your saying that.

EXECUTIVE   I'm serious. If I had any money I'd be offering you a deal.

The elevator door opens. The executive steps out.

EXECUTIVE (*cont'd*)   But I don't.

The doors close.

FADE OUT.

A market research testing facility in Burbank,
California, Friday, 4:30 p.m.

'Okay, could everyone take their seats, please?'
  'How do these paddles work, dude?'
  'Okay, those are dials, and please take your seat, sir.'
  'I was told there would be pizza.'
  'Okay, pizza will be served – can we all sit down, please? – pizza
will be served at the conclusion of the test screening.'
  'Are these the only seats?'
  'Can we all take a seat, please? And yes, ma'am, all the seats are the
same. If you feel that you need a . . . more ample . . . size seat, perhaps
we can find something . . .'
  'No, I can squeeze in.'
  'Wonderful.'
  'How do these paddle things go?'
  'Okay, those are dials and . . .'
  'Do the paddles, like, stick on to our chests or whatever for . . .'
  'Okay, please, everyone, take a seat. No, the dials – they're dials,
not paddles – are there for you to hold during the screening.'
  'I don't have no paddles.'
  'I got two paddles.'
  'Okay, sir, please hand one of your dials – they're dials, not paddles
– to the gentleman sitting next to you.'
  'Mine's plugged in. Are the paddles supposed to be plugged in?'
  'Yes, the dials – they're dials, not paddles – are each connected to a

computer, which will record your reaction to the show we're about to screen.'

'*Mine don't click or nothing.'*

'*I was told there would be pizza.'*

'*Mine don't work either.'*

'*My paddle is busted, dude.'*

'*Okay, the dials – they're dials, not paddles – don't click or anything. You just twist the knob to the right when you're enjoying the program, and then, if you find you're not enjoying it or are bored, just turn the knob back to the left.'*

'*I got a question.'*

'*Yes?'*

'*My paddle thingy isn't clicking.'*

'*Okay, the dials – they're dials, not paddles – don't click. They turn. To the right indicates that you're enjoying the screening. To the left indicates that you aren't. Your responses are sent to the computer through the wire attached to the handset, and the producers of the program can get a sense of how much you as an audience have enjoyed their program. Okay? Are we ready to go?'*

'*I'm concerned about my privacy.'*

'*I'm concerned about the pizza.'*

'*Okay, pizza will be served after the screening. And your privacy is protected every step of the way, ma'am. No one in the testing facility has your name or address. If you still feel concerned about privacy, you may excuse yourself from this screening.'*

'*Do I still get the pizza?'*

'*No, ma'am.'*

'*I'll stay.'*

'*Okay, I think we're ready to begin the screening. Please, everyone, turn your dials to the center to begin. Make sure the red lines on the dial match the red line on the handset. Okay? Is everyone ready?'*

'*My paddles don't click.'*

'*Can we move the dial a little bit to the right if we're enjoying this part of the screening, too? I mean, if we're enjoying you?'*

322

'Okay, the dials don't click – they're paddles, not dials – they turn. And we'd like everyone to center their dials so the red lines match up, okay? Okay, ready? Ready? Let's begin.'

SUMMER: 'KEEP IT SHUT'

Fade in:

Television comedy isn't really 'written' in the traditional sense. It's quilted. The first draft of any episode, of course, has a single author. But after the first 'table reading', which kicks off the production week, the script goes through several revisions. The entire writing staff gathers in one room, what has come to be called *The Room* in Industry parlance, and performs a collective rewrite. Whatever didn't work at that day's run-through is massaged and rewritten by a team of competitive, caustic comedy writers.

A full season's worth of episodes – about twenty-two in all – is an almost impossible task for one writer, or even two working as a team. Production itself requires so many other duties – casting, editing, listening to the network, working with actors, coming up with future episodes, rewriting scripts – that it's not realistic to write every episode yourself. So writers have to do something that is a real challenge for them: they have to work together politely. The protocol of *The Room* is as complicated and subtle as kabuki theater.

A rewrite session is like getting paid to undergo unpleasant group therapy. The writer sits in a room with the rest of the writers and someone called the 'writer's assistant' (who isn't a bottle of whiskey but is someone with lightning fast shorthand skills) and pitches new jokes as the group moves through the script. Every writer pretends to remember his first successful pitch, but it's unlikely to be the case. The whole thing is so nerve-shattering that your first week on a staff is spent sitting in cold sweaty clothes and seeing through a red fog. The rules are, as follows: 1. Never pitch a joke twice; if it doesn't get a laugh the first time, you lose. 2. Never pitch a problem in a script, especially a logic problem, something like 'Why wouldn't Sam just *call* Diane?' That's like pulling a loose thread in a cheap sweater, and you will be mercilessly abused by your colleagues for the rest of your career, which promises to be deadly and short. For to be branded 'bad in *the room*' around town is a sure way to get kicked out of the system.

A friend of mine told me that a certain legendary television writer/producer once dispensed this bit of wisdom, which for my money is the single best piece of advice I've ever heard: as my friend walked nervously into the room on his very first day in the television business, the old pro took him aside, and said to him in a gravelly murmur, 'Keep it shut.'

Once, to test his advice, I spent a week early in my career saying absolutely nothing in the room – just sitting quietly with a pleasant smile on my face. I was rewarded, on Friday afternoon, as I was walking to my car, with the current executive producer sidling up next to me, putting his arm around my shoulder, and saying, 'Great work this week. Really great.'

I'm not sure if he was kidding or not, and truth be told, it didn't really matter. What he meant was, I had been deemed 'good in the room'.

CUT TO:

INT. MY OFFICE – DAY

We are hiring writers for the staff of our new series. The phone rings continuously with agents pitching their clients to us. I am on the phone with a particularly aggressive one.

AGENT   Let me tell you, this guy is great. He's – and I'm
  running out of superlatives here – great. Great with story.
  Great with jokes.

ME   Fine. Send a script.

AGENT   Okay. Great.

ME   Thanks. 'Bye.

AGENT   One sec. There's just one thing you need to know.

ME   What?

AGENT   He can't be in *The Room*.

ME   What?

AGENT   He can't be in the room. He just can't.

ME   Why?

AGENT   The last show he was on, they were very cruel. There was a lot of . . . psychological . . . stuff going on.

ME   Like what?

AGENT   Like some of the younger writers would snigger at some of his joke pitches. Say things like 'I think I saw that on an old *I Love Lucy*.' When he didn't get one of their pitches, they'd say it was a 'generational misunderstanding'. During late rewrites, they kept ordering spicy food that didn't agree with him. That sort of thing.

ME   Oh.

AGENT   He's still a little shell-shocked. So instead of actually being in the room, he's at home on speakerphone.

ME   He's home?

AGENT   In his tub.

ME   He's in the bath?

AGENT   He finds the warm water very soothing.

ME   Hmmmm.

AGENT   Look, he's really been through the wringer. And let's be honest, you guys need some old timers on your staff.

ME   How old is he?

AGENT   Actually, federal law prohibits the asking of that question.

ME   Sorry.

AGENT   He's forty-two. But he thinks young.

CUT TO:

To be described, at forty-two years old, as a *young thinker*, is just one of the reasons that writers have it worse than actors.

Writers, though, in theory anyway, make their own breaks. To succeed as an actor, you need the right part and the right look. To succeed as a television writer, all you need to do is master the technology of the pencil. But success means working, anonymously, with other writers who probably hate you, or would if they knew how much you hate them. It means always trying to be funnier than the writer just below you in the hierarchy. It means that no matter how much everyone seems to get along, or how many times your bosses, the executive producers, tell you that you're doing a great job, you still take your career temperature every night on the way home. You still replay the day over and over in your head, asking yourself why you didn't think of the show-saving pitch, or the killer button to the last scene, and why the new kid, who looks twelve, did.

An actor friend of mine tells this story:

He is on an audition for a small part on a top-rated comedy series. He is, by way of background, a nice-looking guy and not untalented. He has, as we say around here, 'comedy chops', which means, as we say around here, 'that he knows his way around a joke'. He can be funny, in other words. Halfway through his audition, while he is still speaking, the producer of the show turns to the casting director and says, in a loud voice, 'I told you to bring me some *good* looking people!'

The audition is over; my friend slinks out.

330

He told me this story over too many beers one night, and after listening to several hours of writers-get-no-respect and Hollywood-is-a-tough-place-for-a-writer from me. What could I do after hearing a story like that but mumble a few supportive comments and pick up the check?

Still, actors *ask* for that kind of abuse, and for all of their pretensions to 'the work' or 'the craft', or, even more ludicrously, 'the art', let's face it – it's still about 'everybody pay attention to me.' Writers, on the other hand, linger in the shadows and corrode quietly. I have seen actors waiting to audition for the same role genuinely wish each other well. 'Break a leg, man,' they'll say to each other, and you know they mean it because they're wearing that mentally-exhausted expression actors wear when they've said something unscripted.

Writers, of course, loathe each other. Writers, especially television writers (and even more especially, *bad* television writers) are enemies-list makers and gossip-spreaders, score-settlers and secret drinkers.

In fact, the only thing more bitter and furious than a roomful of writers is a convention hall full of writers, which unfortunately describes a meeting of the Writers Guild of America, West.

Every few years, the WGA – the putative screenwriters' trade union – suffers an institutional nervous breakdown as its members, made up entirely of writers and therefore unable to agree on anything, attempts to agree on the terms of a new contract with the studios.

The sticking point invariably centers at some new profit source exploited by the studios – DVD sales, say, or pay-per-view satellite broadcasts – that they have neglected to pass on to the writer. The working writers – and that number is somewhat smaller than 100 per cent of the membership of the WGA West – tend to be philosophical about these issues. Sure, we get angry and bitter. But we're writers. We were angry and bitter *before* we got into this business. In some cases I could mention, anger and bitterness were the primary inspiration for a particular writer to saddle up and move to Los Angeles. I know one guy who became a television writer simply because it afforded him the opportunity to write on a cop show and name all the strippers, whores and girl junkies after his mother.

The non-working writers are a more querulous lot. Freed from the burden of actually having to show up to a job every day, they look to the occasional WGA strike to round out their social calendar, to catch up with old friends on the picket line. And since all writers crave excuses for not writing, what better excuse for being unproductive than a strike. Writing? Not me. I'm *honoring my brother and sister scribes!* I'm *taking part in the labor movement!* Lazy? Untalented? Nope. Just committed to social justice. Rarely has sitting on your ass outside the studio gates, carrying a picket sign while eating a ham sandwich ever seemed so glamorous.

So the working writers – especially the young ones – hate strike talk. And the non-working writers see a strike as a great way to get out of the house. The remaining group – the rich writers who are not working by choice – form a kind of swing vote. They all meet at the WGA Membership meeting, an event so chaotic and anger-charged that it's hard to believe it's taking place in Southern California. It seems almost Bosnian in the intensity of its bitterness.

CUT TO:

INT. SANTA MONICA CONVENTION CENTER – NIGHT

I am milling around the lobby of the convention center, waiting to get a cup of coffee. Behind me, in the auditorium, I can hear the speaker, a WGA board member, in mid-reminiscence.

BOARD MEMBER (O.S.)   . . . and it was here, in this convention center, that I was privileged, in nineteen hundred and seventy-two, to hear the very moving words of Krisnamurti

332

Singthongpet, a very wise man who was instrumental in getting my then-wife to agree to an 'open marriage,' which, at the time . . .

I move a few writers closer to the coffee urn. I see an acquaintance of mine, a man I know for a fact to be worth serious coin – in the tens of millions of dollars – stuff sugar packets into his jacket pockets.

Back in the auditorium, I hear the meeting get underway. A member is using his 'free speech' time to rail against the perpetual WGA meeting topic, the Hollywood Blacklist of the 1950s. The Blacklist was, essentially, a list of writers who, because of their affiliation with the Communist Party, were unemployable by the major studios. It now functions as a handy excuse for older writers who, because of their incredible lack of talent, were unemployable by the major studios.

ELDERLY VOICE (O.S.) (SHOUTING EVERY FEW WORDS)   . . . and I am SO ANGRY! The blacklist DESTROYED this town! It RAPED this industry! And it IMPOVERISHED our culture! I was CHEATED out of credit for pictures that I WROTE! I never saw my OWN goddam NAME on ANY of my BEST work. *The Cannibal Fixers* – NO CREDIT! *Bongo Beauties* – NO CREDIT!

I move two science fiction writers and one children's cartoon writer closer to the coffee. An older writer sidles up next to me.

OLDER WRITER   Hey. I know you.

ME   Hi.

OLDER WRITER   You spoke on a panel discussion I went to.

ME   Hi.

OLDER WRITER   So, do you ever hire older writers on those TV shows of yours?

This is an inevitable question, and a touchy one. Older writers often feel pushed aside by younger ones, and resent the richer deals of

333

today's business. 'Ageism' is what they call it, with a writer's tin ear for self-irony.

ME   Oh, by all means. We like to work with writers who have more experience. In fact, we work regularly with two or three writers in their sixties.

I mention their names. The older writer shrugs.

OLDER WRITER   Oh, those guys. I know those guys. They're good writers. But I don't mean them. I mean, do you ever hire just *ordinary* older writers?

CUT TO:

The great benefit of the Writers Guild of America, West is its rich and full health plan. Everything is covered, including thirty days every five years at the Betty Ford Clinic, which seems generous to the point of encouragement. In a town like this one, filled with vegetarians, exercise addicts, healthy livers and hypochondriacs – and these groups intersect in a big way – handing someone a medical care blank check is like handing someone a hobby.

And let's face it: the bulk of the WGA membership is made up of hard-working, fairly successful retired writers who are looking for something to do. I'd rather they spend their days at the gastroenterologist than walking the picket line.

Years ago, a few months after landing my first writing job in Hollywood, the membership of the WGA was seriously considering a strike. After a long, screaming membership meeting (try to imagine a dysfunctional family of 300 sitting down to Christmas dinner and you'll get the picture) they – we, I should say – decided, in true writers' form, to postpone any decision for a month or two.

I walked out to my car with another writer, about twenty years my senior.

'I'm worried about a strike,' I said.

'A strike is what we need around here,' he muttered bitterly.

'But I'll be broke in a month. I need to work,' I said.

'You'll be better off in the long run,' the older writer replied, patting me reassuringly on the shoulder. 'Did I ever tell you about how we won the thirty days in Betty Ford? We did it by walking out! By sticking together!'

'But don't you think the studios have a point?' I asked. 'After all, they take all the risk.'

'To hell with them!' he shouted. 'Fuck management! Fuck the power structure! Fuck those fucking fuckers!'

And with that, he sped off in his BMW 750il.

The Betty Ford Center treats many addictions, though not, thankfully, the addictions to inappropriate rage and luxury automobiles. It leaves these uncured, giving the Hollywood writer a reason to get out of bed.

A few years ago, a network television executive was asked to describe his ideal audience. He was looking for 'voracious consumers of free television,' he said, people who couldn't afford cable services, didn't have jobs during the day or reasons to go to bed early, and who were easily overwhelmed by programming choices and so preferred to stick with one channel throughout the day.

His ideal audience, in other words, was the very young, the very old, and the very sick.

Today, the target audience has shifted a bit. The very old and the very sick are on their own. The desirable demographics that all the major networks battle over are the very young, the somewhat young, and the under-thirty. That's the main reason network television has an eerie *Lord of the Flies* vibe to it: almost every show features, exclusively, characters without a trace of the tiny lines and wrinkles that begin to appear around, say, the age of thirty-two.

Television advertisers want young audiences, it seems, so programs that skew young command higher advertising rates. The theory goes something like this: old people read magazines and newspapers, they watch the news channels and listen to the radio – that makes finding them a lot easier and therefore cheaper.

Young people, on the other hand, spend a great deal of time listening to depressing music and doing alarming things to their hair, not reading magazines and definitely not bothering with the newspaper, so when you get one trapped in front of a television set, grab him. Their feckless indolence makes them worth more, perversely. The poor over-forty set, with their good jobs and sense of civic responsibility, are a dime a dozen.

Perhaps more importantly, old people – again, I'm using the Standard Industry Definition of *old people*, which is anyone over forty – have already decided so many things about their lives – what foods they like to eat, which soft drinks they prefer, how they like to cure their headaches and their stuffy noses, things like that. Young people – untrustworthy, promiscuous, persuadable – tend not to have settled on a few key brands, and can thus be persuaded that doctors have indeed recently created an ointment that makes pimples disappear, that switching soft drink preferences increases opportunities for casual sex, and that certain fast-food restaurants are merry places filled with attractive, laughing young people.

A few years ago, we produced a series in which the two main characters, in an act of purely contrarian bloody-mindedness, were in their sixties. In other words, the combined age of our two lead actors was roughly that of all six *Friends* combined. Our audience was respectably large, but unrespectably old. The people who watched our show all had jobs and mortgages and expenses – in other words, useless scum.

'Hey, you guys were cancelled?' People older than forty would ask that question, and I always dreaded giving the answer. 'But why?' they would ask. 'I *loved* that show.'

And I would say, 'Well, the audience demographic wasn't in the desirable range for network television.'

And they would look confused.

And then I would be forced to say that while we had a great many viewers, their average age was forty-plus, which made them unimportant to advertisers and, consequently, to network executives. And then the color would drain out of the face of the person I was talking to, and he would stammer and cough in the half-rage half-sadness appropriate to someone who has just been told that his *entire life*, its needs, triumphs, accomplishments, and meaning, is *undesirable*, and that America's vast army of consumer product manufacturers and advertisers wouldn't care if he and his contemporaries dropped dead on the spot. Eventually, his eyes would dilate and fix themselves on the middle distance.

And I'd be glad to still be in my thirties. Barely.

CUT TO:

I am out having a beer with my plastic surgeon friend. He has a booming Beverly Hills practice and always has great stories, mostly about liposuction and breast augmentation. Most of his patients are involved in the entertainment industry, and come to him for simple nips and tucks here and there – to be, what he calls, 'refreshed'. He is talking about one of his new patients, a well-known young actress. He won't tell me her name.

'She is absolutely beautiful,' he says. 'She has a *perfect* body.'

'Who is it?' I want to know.

He shakes his head. 'Can't say. Patient confidentiality.'

'What does she want done?'

'Her neck,' he answers. 'Every other part of her is perfect.'

'Her *neck*? What was wrong with her neck?'

'Nothing, really. A little loose. Some diminished tautness. Nothing major,' he says. 'But the neck is tricky. You can't really wait until it sags and completely loses its elasticity. You have to adjust it a little bit every year or so. Take it in an inch now and then. You can't put the neck off, like the chin or the forehead. Gotta start early.'

'How old is she?'

'That's the problem. She's twenty-eight. She waited *way* too long. Should've come to me four years ago.'

I laugh and shake my head. To be twenty-eight and worried about your neck! I take a sip of my beer and look at my reflection in the mirror at the back of the bar. I think I look okay. Not great, but okay. I lift my chin and tilt my head back to get a good look at my neck. My friend watches me do this.

He clears his throat. 'You know,' he says, 'you'd be surprised how many of my patients are men. It's considered totally acceptable for a guy to want to get a little work done.'

I scoff.

'I'm serious,' he says. He mentions the name of a young actor in a hugely-popular sitcom. 'He came to me for a simple nose job, and left with a chin implant, an ear bob, and a male breast aug.'

'You gave him breasts?' I ask, laughing.

'I gave him *pectorals*,' he says. 'I turned him into a romantic lead. Before me, he was strictly character roles.'

'Forget it,' I say. 'I'm not an actor and I'm not paying you $25,000 to stretch my neck.'

'Don't flatter yourself. The neck is the least of your problems. For you, I'd recommend an eye tuck, a forehead lift, a chin implant, a jaw shape, and some lipo around the jowls *before* we even think about the neck.'

'Forget it,' I say. 'I'm going to let myself deteriorate naturally.'

'Try this,' he says.

He puts my hands together, as if in prayer. He tucks my thumbs under my chin, and places my two index fingers against my nose.

'Now,' he says, 'leaving your thumbs touching, open your hands up, like you're trying to smooth out your face. Pull back gently.'

I do it.

'Now, hold,' he says. 'And look in the mirror.'

I do. I see a tight, wrinkle-free face. I see a pronounced jawline. I see the familiar facelift perpetual smile. I see myself, refreshed.

'Forget it,' I say, still holding back my face.

'Suit yourself,' he says, finishing the rest of his beer.

I drop my face and do the same. We pay for our drinks and walk to our cars.

'Tonight,' he says, ominously, 'you'll brush your teeth and look at yourself in the mirror, and you'll think, "hey, I don't look bad." And later this week, maybe in the morning after you've shaved, you'll chuckle to yourself and do the thumbs-under-the-chin trick, just for a laugh. But you'll start to notice all the little droops and sags. The folds of skin that suddenly appear. The creases where nothing should crease. And then maybe you'll hear about a couple of young writers, guys in their early twenties, who are suddenly hot. And the years will start running together in your memory and teenaged boys will start calling you "sir" and the grey hairs will start sprouting and every single morning you'll tuck your thumbs under your chin, "just to see," you'll tell yourself. And then one day you'll be in my office.'

I stare into the night, car keys still dangling in my hand.

'Who are you?' I ask. 'The devil?'

My friend laughs. 'Nope. Just a plastic surgeon in Beverly Hills.'

He gets into his new Mercedes and speeds away. How many 'breast augs' does it take to buy that car? How many chin lifts for the Chevy Blazer, his other car? How many 'refreshers' for the two weeks in Vail, Colorado? I'll let myself turn into a raisin before I'll give him one penny, I think to myself. Nobody is retiring on *my* neck.

But then I remembered:

A year or two ago, during a casting session, I ran into a former high-school classmate. I had just stepped out to refill my coffee, and there she was: still ravishing, sitting with a dozen or so other actresses, ready to audition for me, my producing partner, and our casting staff.

'Hey!' I shouted.

'Hey!' she shouted back.

We gave each other a little squeeze and a peck on the cheek. I remembered her as a beautiful girl, and here she was, in my office, a beautiful woman.

'How long has it been?' I asked, and as I started to mentally calculate the intervening years, I felt her hand close tightly around my wrist.

'Do you have a sec?' she asked.

I walked with her to the coffee machine. She whispered frantically. 'See, I play twenty-three, twenty-four, okay?'

'Excuse me?'

'I'm twenty-four. Twenty-five at the max.'

'But we were in the same high-school class,' I said, still not getting it. She looked at me for a moment, eyes wide and fierce, like she was trying to drill her meaning into my head.

'Oh,' I said, finally getting it. '*Oh.*'

'It's just, you know, the *business*,' she said.

'Should I pretend not to know you?'

She put her hand on my shoulder and shook her head in pity.

'No,' she said, 'you can say you know me. But I'd appreciate it if you said that you were *better* friends with my *older* sister.'

I didn't even have time to spin some filthy casting-couch fantasies. I was shunted off into an undesirable demographic. I'm too old, even for people my own age.

CUT TO:

INT. MY CAR – DAY

I'm on the phone. An agent is pitching another client.

ME   Sorry, we're all staffed up.

AGENT   Really?

ME   Really.

AGENT   No, really?

ME   Yes, really.

AGENT   So who did you hire?

ME   Well, I'd rather not say right now. We're still waiting to close a few deals.

340

AGENT   Oh, okay. I understand. So who did you hire?

ME   I can't say. We're waiting to close a few deals.

AGENT   Yeah, but can I just know?

ME   No.

AGENT   C'mon. They think I'm too old over here at the agency. They're sending out signals around here that they're thinking about firing me, and it'll really help if I had some titbit to show how plugged in and on top of things I am.

ME   What kind of signals?

AGENT   Things like, one of the younger partners took me aside Monday morning and said, 'We're thinking about firing you.' And then one of the twenty-something assistants mentioned casually that everyone here hates me. Subtle stuff.

CUT TO:

One of the pleasures of having a television show in production is hanging out with the other writers on the staff while eating junk food, gossiping, telling filthy jokes, and complaining. Writers, in general, tend to do these things anyway – at any lunch spot in Hollywood, at any time, there will almost always be a table of writers where the phrases 'stingy rat bastards' and 'smug network eunuch punks' can be overheard – but somehow it means more when all of the writers are complaining about the same person while working on the same show.

The other pleasure is sharing particularly egregious agent stories.

When our pilot was ordered for the fall schedule, we hired a small staff of very talented writers, with varying degrees of television writing experience. The least experienced writer, it turns out, was a real find: funny, polite, literate, and saddled with enough personal eccentricities to make talking behind his back interesting. He was good enough at his job, in fact, to have stirred our sympathies (first-time staff writers make very little money) so we raised his salary a pinch.

In Hollywood, of course, you don't just call the hireling into your office and bark at him, gruff-but-lovable-style: 'Hey, shitbird, you're doin' a great job. The pay packet's going to be heavier from here on out.' Instead, you must telephone a reedy-voiced bureaucrat who works at the studio in a department called, with ominous vagueness, 'Business Affairs', tell that person to call the writer's agent, have the writer's agent call the writer, and then, after the agent has called the writer with the news, drag the writer in your office before he can blurt out 'Thanks for the raise!' in front of the other writers on the staff who didn't get a raise and aren't getting a raise until their contracts specifically call for it, because, after all, you're not made of money, are you?

Here's what happened: the staff writer was at home, writing a draft. We placed a call to Business Affairs, and kicked off the dominoes. The next day the writer sauntered into work, full of praise for his agent, who, we were informed, had called the writer the day before to tell him that after some 'secret negotiations' and 'major arm-twisting', the agent had wrangled some extra money for the fledgling writer – 'We've sweetened the pot for you, kiddo,' the agent told the client, 'We went to the wall for you, and guess what? They blinked.'

CUT TO:

INT. HAVANA ROOM – DAY

A swank Hollywood cigar club. I am having lunch with an agent who is a partner in the agency that represents me. I have just told him the preceding story.

AGENT   Are you kidding me?

ME   Nope. Happened just like that.

AGENT   I think that's . . . that's . . . *immoral.* And I'm an agent.

I laugh.

342

AGENT *(cont'd)*   He cheated his client out of knowing that he was doing a good job. What a creep. The kid should dump that agent.

ME   I agree.

AGENT   So did you set the kid straight?

ME   You bet.

AGENT   Good. You know, the business, it's getting so sick. So cutthroat. Used to be, you wouldn't lie to a client and you wouldn't hit on someone else's client.

ME   'Hit on?'

AGENT   Yeah. Try to steal. You know, 'hit on', 'flirt with', 'seduce'.

ME   Interesting terminology.

AGENT   If someone else's client *called you first,* then you could go to bed with him. But only if the guy called *you.*

ME   'Go to bed with?'

AGENT   Sign as a client.

The agent waves to a few men in suits at another table.

AGENT *(cont'd)*   Look at this place. Filled with agents. It's a real pick-up place. You must get 'hit on' a lot.

ME   Well, yes.

AGENT   But you're happy with your representation, right?

ME   Yes, of course.

AGENT *(shrugging)*   If you weren't, you'd tell me.

A long pause.

AGENT *(cont'd)*   Right?

CUT TO:

343

INT. SOUNDSTAGE – NIGHT

We're shooting an episode of our series. As the cameras reload, the audience warm-up guy goes into his act. I'm standing on the stage floor. A young agent at the agency that represents me approaches.

YOUNG AGENT   Hey, man. How's it goin'?

All young agents speak fluent 'guy'.

ME   Fine. You?

YOUNG AGENT   Cool.

Because I don't speak fluent 'guy', the conversation falters. A long pause.

YOUNG AGENT (*cont'd*)   Heard about what that dude did to that dude you have on staff. That is totally messed up, man.

ME   Yes, I agree.

YOUNG AGENT (*Surveying the knot of writers hovering nearby*)
So which one is he?
I point him out.

YOUNG AGENT (*cont'd*)   'Scuse me.
He canters over to the writer.

DISSOLVE TO:

EXT. STUDIO PARKING LOT – LATER THAT NIGHT

We've wrapped. Another show in the can. I walk to my car. At the far end of the parking lot, through the gauzy evening mist, I can make out the twin silhouettes of the young agent and the staff writer.

The writer is standing by his open car door. The agent is leaning against it, talking with animated intensity. The writer is being 'hit on'.

It's like a Hopper painting: lonely, sad, funny, and a perfect snapshot of Hollywood. One guy wants to make a sale; the other guy just wants to go home.

CUT TO:

In the end, the writer left his agent for the young agent in the parking lot. It was a principled decision, of course – no one likes being lied to – but it was also an emotional one – everyone likes being hit on. To be worth a seduction scene (something along the lines of 'you're so talented' and 'you've got a huge future') just makes it sweeter. The truth, though, is that I have an iron-clad contract with the writer which gives me an option on his services for three years. So whoever he signs with – the old agent, the new agent, his mother, his priest – he's mine for three seasons at a previously agreed-upon price. He's young. He'll figure it out.

A writer friend of mine tells this story:

He is working on a television series with a predominantly black cast. It is early in the run of the series – early enough, in fact, for most of the cast to be driving the cars they drove before winning the part. (There is no sight more soothing to a writer than the sight of an actor driving a Subaru.)

The episode that they are rehearsing that week is a simple one: two of the male characters are supposed to take care of a third character's apartment. It is filled with expensive and fragile trinkets. Connect the dots: hijinks ensue.

The block comedy scene – industry lingo for the big scene in the second act when the hilarity kicks in – is a simple affair of two clumsy men, a bunch of breakable props, and a small fire.

After a decent run-through, one of the actors knocks on my friend's office door. He is angry. He launches into a speech. His voice is trembling with anger: he is humiliated by the script; he refuses to perform it again; it is a racist and vile depiction of his people, reinforcing the clumsy, slow-witted, trip-over-your-own-feet stereotype of yesteryear, and as a proud African-American male he will not demean himself or denigrate his race in such a grotesque manner.

345

My friend takes a deep breath. He nods sympathetically and shrugs. 'Consider it gone,' he says quietly. 'Though it's a shame. You really are a master of physical comedy.'

A long pause.

'I am?'

'Are you kidding? You're telling me you haven't had training?'

'Well, nothing formal.'

'What can I say? It's . . . Chaplinesque. But forget it. It's cut.'

Another long pause.

In the end, they did the scene as written. Flattery always, always, *always* works.

CUT TO:

INT. MY OFFICE – DAY

We have filmed the first few episodes of our series. Things are going well, so we go through the day uneasily. Every day without a disaster just makes the inevitable one that much more brutal. And the inevitable one takes place a week from now, when we have our broadcast première. Which means we'll get our first set of ratings.

It's a strange sort of lag, but familiar, too. We're deeply into the production process – characters have been defined, and in some cases redefined; story areas have been discovered and tossed out; the creaky ensemble of strangers has begun to click together. The show, in other words, is working.

Except that nobody has seen it yet. *We* think we're doing fine. *We* love the show. America, though, has yet to be consulted. And when that happens, when we have our opening night, all of the enthusiasm and humming energy and optimistic window-shopping will either seem brilliantly intuitive or hilariously delusional.

It's this way all over Hollywood. It takes a year, at least, for an actor's hard work, or a director's vision, to make it to a screen near you – and by that time, they've probably forgotten the tantrums and struggles and the certain knowledge that the picture they're working on is *just absolute crap*. Maybe, in the ensuing months, their memories have embroidered the experience into something good and auspicious. So later, when the movie comes out, and they're pushing it at press junkets worldwide, they have to relive the entire episode, and are humiliated a second time; and later still, when it comes out on DVD and there's another round of humiliations. And on. And on. The lag is a killer.

In television, if possible, it's worse. Because you're always about eight or ten episodes ahead of your air date, in the early stages you really have the sense that the show is getting better all the time. It's a foolish sense, though, because the audience is going to see them *in order*, bad ones first. And they may not stick around to watch a series get better.

Today, though, the universal symbol of series success has come over the transom in the form of a 'spec', or sample, script. In order to get a job writing for television, you must first complete a few sample scripts of some of the better shows on the air. The logic, I guess, is that if you can write a good episode of *Frasier*, then you'll be able to master the writing chores on the show about the zany family and their robot housekeeper.

You only write specs for shows that have an air of longevity. So it's with some excitement that I announce to my partner that some aspiring writer has penned his own script for our little show, and although studio policy, good sense, and much better things to do argue against it, I open the envelope and dig in. Oh, sure, there's a tiny voice in my head saying *Hey, wait a minute – the show hasn't even aired yet. Who could possibly have seen it? How did anyone know enough about it to write a spec episode?* But I hate that voice. It's an irritating voice. I prefer the voice that says *Wow, this is like some kind of sign from the heavens. The buzz must be great around this show! It's going to be a hit; no, wait, it IS a hit; no, wait, it's a MONSTER hit. It's the seventh arrondisse-ment, right? That's the really good one? Rue du Bac? Rue Jacob? Right? Right?*

347

The title of the episode is 'Joey Moves In,' which I find odd. There is, to my knowledge, no 'Joey' character on my series. I try to keep up on these things. But the name rings a faint bell.

INSERT SHOT: FLIPPING PAGES

Huge speeches for 'Joey.' Pages and pages of 'Joey' dialogue. 'Joey' this and 'Joey' that.

CUT TO:

Joey, it turns out, is technically a character on our series. He had one line, in episode two. He was a customer in a bookstore. The spec entitled, with alarming stupidity, 'Joey Moves In,' was penned by the actor who played the part. He has taken the bull by the horns. He has written himself a role as a series regular. He thinks, like most actors, that most writers are mildly mentally retarded and will not notice that the 'Joey' actor and the 'Joey Moves In' author are one and the same. Worse, he thinks I will finish his script. I don't.

Actors have a difficult life out here, of course. Many of the talented ones never make it. Some simply aren't lucky. And others, the really talented ones, aren't good-looking enough.

The actor who essayed the role of 'Joey,' (one tiny line: 'Did you like this book, man?') was handsome enough, and will probably eke out some sort of living. But like most actors in his position, he couldn't quite master the requirements of the role of 'Joey', which were, simply, to say his line in as neutral a tone as possible, and then to move quickly away. The first day of rehearsal he did it perfectly and we laughed, because, after all, we wrote it. The second day of rehearsal, emboldened by his triumph, 'Joey' put a little more spin on the ball and blew it. The third day, he really loaded up the attitude (*'Hey*, did you enjoy *this* book, man?!') and

348

it was time to have a little talk with him. 'Hey, man,' I said to him after the run-through, in my best actor-dude dialect, 'throw it away, okay?'

He looked at me blankly.

'Throw it away,' I said. 'Just say it. Just say the line straight.'

'Really?' he asked.

'Really,' I answered.

'But I'm trying to activate my choice.'

I looked at him blankly.

He clarified: 'I'm trying to give Joey a little texture.'

'Well, don't,' I said. 'Just throw it away.'

When we shot the episode two days later, he was a lot better. But still never as good as he was that first day, before he started acting.

CUT TO:

INT. MY OFFICE – DAY

I am on the phone with my agent, and I mention the spec script and the day player.

ME *(winding up)*   And that just proves what I've always said. Actors are crazy. Completely out of touch with reality. Easy to flatter, easy to manipulate, impossible to treat as equals.

MY AGENT *(laughing)*   I just had this exact conversation! I was just talking to the guy who runs your studio and he said the exact same thing to me, in the exact same words! Isn't that weird?

ME   That is odd. Which actor was he talking about?

MY AGENT   Oh, he wasn't talking about actors. He was talking about *writers*.

ME   Oh.

CUT TO:

When a writer gives you his script to read, he usually says something totally dishonest like, 'Hey, let me know what you *really* think, okay?' In other words, he wants you to be honest. He can take it, he says. 'I know there're some rough spots in the second act,' he may say, 'so just give me your honest opinion.'

There is, though, only one response that he will find acceptable. He wants you to read his script in a kind of rapture, laughing yourself in tears at the right spots, emitting low moans of pleasure or surprise here and there, until you finally wipe the mist from your eyes, hold the script to your breast, look at him with awe and gratitude and a dash of what-a-terrible-burden-such-insight-must-be pity, and say in a low, quavery voice, 'This is one of the greatest scripts I have ever read. It is absolutely perfect.'

Anything short of that – anything even a *fraction* short of that – will be a crushing disappointment. The writer will say something like, 'You hate it, don't you?' And you will say something like, 'No, no! I love it! But you're right about the second act. But I love it!'

The writer will respond with: 'You hate the second act? I thought that was the best part.'

And you will counter with: 'I *like* the second act. But it's just a little slow.'

Writer: 'Why are you trying to destroy me?'

You: 'I'm just being constructive.'

Writer: 'You call *that* constructive?'

You: 'What do you want me to say? That it was one of the greatest scripts I have ever read? That it's absolutely perfect?'

Writer: 'Yes!'

You: 'I thought you wanted my honest opinion.'

Writer: 'I want *that* to *be* your honest opinion.'

Which is why so many writers have been married so many times.

Having a show in production is like being in a continuous note session. Story ideas, scripts, run-throughs, rough-cuts – all of these phases require the input of the network and the studio. Mostly, these notes follow a simple pattern: everyone will read the

350

script, digest it, identify the one or two things about it which make it unique, and then ask us to remove those one or two things. Really talented executives know all the traps of giving a writer notes, so almost every note session begins with, 'This is the best script I have ever read. It is absolutely perfect.'

Followed by: 'But we have a few notes.'

Knowing how to make enormous changes sound like tiny 'adjustments' is, in fact, the only useful skill most studio types possess.

'Is there any way,' we were once asked by a studio executive, 'that you could show the main character *doing* something incredibly heroic and totally *saving* the day in a simple one-page scene we can slap on the top?'

We shook our heads.

'C'mon, guys,' the exec said, 'a simple one-pager. Boom, he does something heroic, everybody loves the guy, boom, back into the story.'

Hollywood is a collaborative place. Everyone has to work together in some kind of harmony, after all, with mutual respect and good manners intact for the next project – which is why, by the way, so many of those projects are so awful – so *getting* notes takes as much elaborate courtesy as *giving* them.

'Good idea,' we usually say after hearing a particularly asinine suggestion, 'we'll take a look at that.'

And we assiduously write down every idea, no matter how foolish or nutty or destructive.

Another trick we use is to lavish praise on the most innocuous note – can the main character have a dog, say, or can his bicycle be bright red? – something easy to change and totally irrelevant, which enables us to ignore several other stupid suggestions that *aren't* irrelevant and would *hurt* the script while still seeming like 'team players'.

Once, in a meeting with the studio, after they had just finished giving notes, the executive added, in a smooth manage-the-talent tone, 'Great script, guys.'

But I was unable to let him think he's managing me. I had to manage *him*.

'Great notes,' I replied.

He looked at me uneasily.

'Really?' he asked. 'You writers usually hate getting notes from the studio.'

'No, no,' I said. 'Well, not from *you*. Yours are particularly good.'

'Well, thank you.'

'Especially the one about the red bicycle. I think that will clarify the core conflict in that character's arc,' I blathered.

'You're full of shit,' he said. 'Now, please, just listen to the notes and see if you can't implement them without screwing up your . . . what do you writers call it? . . . your *vision*. Stop trying to manage me.'

I looked up from my paper, where I have been assiduously copying down everything he says.

'Good idea,' I said. 'We'll take a look at that.'

Back when I was an unemployed film student, I convinced myself that spending all day at the movies wasn't a sign of laziness, but of a deep commitment to my craft and an equally strong interest in what I pretty unironically called *the language of cinema*.

It also cost about eight dollars a day, at which point I realized that it was either *the language of cinema* or *the consumption of beer*, and, well, figure it out yourself.

The good news for anyone who wants to watch their movie and drink it too, however, is that at any given time in Hollywood, someone is holding a test screening of his most recent film. Sometimes these are held in large theaters – easy to slip into anonymously – and sometimes in plush, rented screening rooms with free snacks galore. And because the guest lists for these things are drawn up and supervised by the lowest ranking person around – the press assistant's assistant, the studio boss's water boy, the guy who underlines *Variety* for his boss the talent agent – it's easy to crash any screening with just a simple phone call.

Hollywood is a vast, rainless version of *Upstairs, Downstairs* – all the downstairs types know each other, hang out together, exchange gossip, and call each other on their bosses' cell phones. It's a class system organized by age: people in their early twenties tend to know everyone else in town that age, and the result is an invisible web that links the assistants, the young actors, the agents-in-training, and, lucky for me, the unemployed film students.

A free screening brings out the web in force. One assistant calls another, and before you know it, dozens of unemployed young lazybones are parking their rusted Subarus and smoking Hondas on side streets all over town (valet parking is five dollars, you see), donning their very best leather jackets, and heading into the VIP line.

After the screening, we'd walk out into the lobby, past the phalanx of studio executives and marketing gurus, past the actors and their cigarettes, and finally, past the nervous-looking director. I'd always make eye contact with the director, smile knowingly, then give him a thumbs-up sign, like I was a big shot who knew what was what, like I was an *important person* and not *an unemployed film student driving a Subaru.*

Once, sauntering out, I gave the half-smile/thumbs-up to the director – a particularly famous and powerful one this time – and was almost out the door when he called me back.

'Hey!' he shouted.

I stopped. Turned around. My stomach kept turning.

'Yeah?' I said, trying to act cool.

'Whadja think?' he asked, mistaking me for an *important person.*

I shrugged nonchalantly, though inside my leather jacket I was drenched in sweat.

'Could lose twelve minutes, easy.'

The director looked at me for a moment. Then nodded.

'Yeah,' he said. 'Faster is better.'

He started to say something else, but I didn't hear him. I was dashing out to my Subaru.

Last month, I was invited to a screening of a major picture with a November release date. The guy who invited me is the president of production at a large movie studio in town, though I remember him as the guy who used to underline *Variety* for his talent-agent boss back when I was an unemployed film student. This proves that if you stick around Hollywood long enough, good things happen.

The movie, though, was not a good thing. It was an awful thing. An awfully long thing.

Walking out of the screening – held in a plush, intimate screening room with free drinks and snacks, the kind of place where I used to eat enough for dinner and take enough for lunch the next day – my friend pulled me aside.

'What did you think?' he asked, worried.

I shrugged. 'It's not bad,' I lied. 'How close is it to being done?'

'How *close*?' he hollered in a whisper. 'That's our final cut. That's it.'

'Oh,' I said.

'So what do you think?'

I shrugged again. 'To tell you the truth,' I said, 'I think it could lose twelve minutes.'

I started to move away. He pulled me back.

'Twelve minutes? What the hell kind of crap answer is that?'

'Well . . .'

'I ask you here as a favor, and that's the best you can do? Twelve minutes? It can lose twelve minutes? We're talking about *my job* here, okay?'

He was upset and I had let him down. I suddenly felt guilty for all the invitations and free Xeroxing this guy had provided for me all those years ago. I could do better than 'twelve minutes,' I was pretty sure.

'Well,' I began, 'not this, but I think it could lose ten minutes in the first half if you just cut out the ex-wife character.'

His face lit up. 'Yes! Of course!'

'And then, I mean, not this, but you could just end it at the kiss in the airport.'

He nodded vigorously. 'I agree. Hey, man, thanks. I owe you, okay?'

He hugged me. I gave my ticket to the valet parking attendant and waited for my car. The truth is, it doesn't really matter where my friend found the twelve minutes to cut. Certain movies can't be too short.

CUT TO:

EXT. TERRORIST CAMP – DAY

Bearded evildoers sit in a circle. One of their number holds a large calendar aloft. A date is circled.

PUSH IN: He taps the calendar and points to the date.

EVILDOER   Thees, my friends, is the date of our next act of terror!

The group begins to chuckle.

PUSH IN DEEPER: On the calendar is written in spidery script: 'Première of that guy's new sitcom.'

EVILDOER (*cont'd*)   Eeet ees a most perfect date! We will not only bring the west to its knees, but we will make sure that the première of that annoying guy's new sitcom is disrupted by news coverage! That he never gets a clear shot at garnering an audience!

The group chuckle turns into a laugh, then a series of guffaws, then a crescendo of side-splitting laughter.

DISSOLVE TO:

INT. OVAL OFFICE – DAY

The president is at his desk, surrounded by advisors.

PRESIDENT   When am I scheduled to deliver my address to the nation, outlining my new economic and tax policy?

ADVISOR   We're thinking next Tuesday, sir?

PRESIDENT   But doesn't that guy's new sitcom première on Monday?

ADVISOR   I believe it might, sir.

PRESIDENT   So then how, exactly, am I going to disrupt things by pre-empting primetime programming on at least one of the coasts, resulting in a lopsided première and an unreliable set of initial ratings, thus crushing whatever momentum his show might have?

ADVISOR   Ummmm. Sir? I'm sorry. Is that one of our goals?

PRESIDENT   You're goddam right it is. Little shit keeps talking about moving to France? Not on *my* watch.

CUT TO:

INT. SOUNDSTAGE – NIGHT

A première party is in progress. The cast and crew are lounging around the set, drinking beer and eating pizza. We've all gathered together to watch the première episode together. It's been months since we shot it – back then, before we went to New York and got a series order, we didn't call it the 'première episode.' We just called it 'the pilot.' But now, barring some kind of terrorist attack or presidential meddling, it's about to be broadcast coast-to-coast in primetime.

In years past, we've thrown pretty lavish première parties at swank restaurants and private clubs. There were self-congratulatory speeches and champagne toasts and little gift bags and any other act of hubris we could think of to scuttle our own shaky good luck. This time, we're playing it cool. Pizza. Beer. A cake. Low key. Head down.

I'm holding a beer and staring out into the distance.

VOICE   Hey . . .

ME   Why does the president hate me?

356

Our casting director is standing next to me.

CASTING DIRECTOR   Excuse me?

I snap out of it.

ME   I'm sorry. I was just daydreaming. Is the show about to start?
Our casting director looks at me strangely.

CASTING DIRECTOR   It *did* start. It's over.

*I look around, and suddenly, the sound comes up. Laughter. The
theme music. And applause as the credits roll.*

ME   Great. So now all I have to do is wait for the ratings.

CASTING DIRECTOR   You don't really know how to enjoy a
moment, do you?

ME   I've always found 'enjoying the moment' to be some kind of
trick.

CASTING DIRECTOR   You're sort of a pessimist, aren't you?

ME   Give me a break. Is it quote pessimistic unquote to prepare
yourself for bad news? Bad news that you know is going to
come?

CASTING DIRECTOR   Um, yes.

ME   Will you excuse me? I'm going to get another beer. This
one is half-empty.

I cross away.

DISSOLVE TO:

INT. SOUNDSTAGE – LATER

*I am standing in a cluster that includes my agent and a network execu-
tive. I have been complaining that the network is ratings-obsessed, and
that if we don't do well tonight, we'll be cancelled quickly, without the
opportunity to build an audience. The network executive is trying to
reassure me that this is not the case.*

NETWORK EXECUTIVE   Don't focus so much on the ratings.

AGENT   That's what I've been trying to tell him.

NETWORK EXECUTIVE   We look at a lot of things. How much you retain of the previous show's audience, things like that.

ME   What else?

NETWORK EXECUTIVE   Oh, you know. It's not all about the numbers. It's about the rating *you* get, the rating the show *before* you gets, all sorts of stuff.

ME   Like what?

NETWORK EXECUTIVE   *Tons* of things. Like how many people watch your show as opposed to how many were watching *other* shows at the same time. And how that compares with the show that was on right before you. Really a whole number of factors.

ME   Such as?

NETWORK EXECUTIVE   Really just a whole *bunch* of things. We take *loads* of things into account. It's not just about the numbers. It's about *so many* things.

ME   For instance?

NETWORK EXECUTIVE   Well, there's the rating of the show on right before you . . .

DISSOLVE TO:

INT. SOUNDSTAGE – LATER

I am talking to one of the camera operators and his wife. He's been on the crew of the last four series we've done. His wife is telling me how much she likes our show.

ME   That's very nice of you to say. Thanks.

CAMERA OPERATOR   Really, she really does.

CAMERA OPERATOR'S WIFE   It's true. I remember coming to the pilot and laughing and laughing and telling him, *This one, honey, this one is going to be a big hit.*

ME Well, from your lips, huh?

CAMERA OPERATOR'S WIFE And I'm not just saying that. A lot of the shows he works on are just awful, aren't they honey?

The camera operator shifts uncomfortably. His wife charges on.

CAMERA OPERATOR'S WIFE (*cont'd*) He was on one show – which one was it, hon? – and we both just *hated* it, *hated hated* it. And I would tell him, *Honey, you'd better be lookin' for a job!* '*Cause this one stiiiiiiiiiiiiiinnnnnnnkkkkkkkksssssss!* What was the name of that one?

I silently count to ten, wondering when it will dawn on her that the show she hated so much was one of ours.

I get to three. Her eyes suddenly widen. She's about to say something when:

CAMERA OPERATOR Let's get some more pizza.

He leads her off.

DISSOLVE TO:

EXT. CITY STREETS – NIGHT

I'm driving home. On the hillsides, the lights of a hundred thousand houses glitter like tiny stars. If I look closely, within each twinkle is a flickering blue dot. Each blue dot is a TV. And on each TV is a show.

I wonder whose.

The fairy lights of the hillside are repeated in the windows of the houses I pass, and stacked in neat columns of the apartment buildings and high-rise condominiums that line the Santa Monica freeway.

Flickering dots of blue. Each one a show.

I wonder whose.

CUT TO:

INT. MY BEDROOM – MORNING

It is 5 a.m.. In one hour, the previous night's Nielsen Overnight Ratings are available.

The 'overnights' are the preliminary numbers culled from the thirty-three major urban television markets in the United States. They tell you how well your show did in the cities. Later in the day, by noon or so, those numbers will be adjusted to include the rural and suburban areas. Those are the 'nationals', upon which are based things like advertising rates, weekly rankings, and my salary.

The overnights and the nationals can differ widely. A show that appeals to a primarily urban audience might experience a two or three point drop when the nationals come out; likewise, a family-oriented show might pick up an extra point or two later in the day when the suburban markets are counted.

In fact, there's no real point to the overnights at all, except that when you have a show on the night before, and you're lying awake at 5 a.m., you'll take any information you can get.

And also: the first number sets a tone. If it's high, your day is made, a bullet is dodged. If it's low, you wait glumly for the network to send you a fruit basket, to express unconditional support, and then, a few weeks later, to yank you from the schedule. It doesn't really matter that this is just a snapshot. That the number may grow over time, as people find the series and become involved with the characters. That history is paved with the gold networks have earned by sticking with a show they liked despite a lackluster première. That the subsequent episodes are funnier, smarter, and more attractive. That this one *has* to work because you're not sure you've got another one in you. That you feel, after a bunch of years in this business and being nice to people and playing fair and doing your best that you're *due*. That you *get it, okay?* That this is a business of set-up-joke-set-up-joke, and this is where the joke comes in, but it would be nice, this time, if the joke *wasn't* on you. You've heard that one already. It's been done a couple of times and we've all had a good laugh but now, really, as you wait for the overnights to come in, you really have to *insist* that we try a *different* joke this time, that the joke be on, oh, you don't know, let's just say the waiter at La Palette, a nice little café on the Rue de Seine, who discovers that the American guy with the idiotic smile on his face is going to be coming in here *every day* from now on, because he lives around the corner and really doesn't have anything better to do than sit on the terrace, sipping a coffee or a *pamplemousse Schweppes* chuckling to himself about network notes, and casting sessions, and phone calls from his agent, and other artifacts of ancient history.

At 6 a.m. I begin calling the special network ratings phone line. Each network assigns some low-ranking serf to wake up early, collect the primetime ratings for the previous night, and then record them on to a telephone information line, in a voice as chipper as possible.

I call the number. The recording still has the numbers from two days before, which means the new numbers aren't available, or, worse, that the kid has overslept.

I call every five minutes until I hear a new recording.

RECORDED VOICE   The Nielsen Overnight Ratings for the
  thirty-three metered markets, for Monday, are as follows: at
  eight o'clock–

And I hang up, quickly. This is a fruitless exercise. The numbers that matter, the nationals, won't come out until lunch. The only reason to call in for the overnights is to have something to worry about for the next seven hours.

Whatever. I call the number again.

RECORDED VOICE   The Nielsen Overnight Ratings for the
  thirty-three metered markets, for Monday, are as follows: at
  eight o'clock–

And I hang up again. It suddenly occurs to me that this is going to be a long, long set up. I'd better settle in for the joke.

FADE OUT.

A market research testing facility in Burbank, California, Friday, 5:15 p.m.

'How'd we do?'

'Hard to say, Josh.'

'What are the overall numbers?'

'Okay with women eighteen to thirty-five. Better with men twenty-five to fifty.'

'Look, Delia's going to be calling me in fifteen minutes and I need to know . . .'

'Delia?'

'She's the new head of the division.'

'What happened to Josh?'

'I'm Josh.'

'I mean the other Josh. The head of the division.'

'Resigned.'

'Resigned?'

'Well, fired. Delia's the new head. Look, before we call the writer I need to top line Delia.'

'Okay. I'm crunching them as fast as I can. Overall score is not bad. But not much interest in the lead.'

'Damn! I knew it!'

'Some of the other characters are maybe breakouts. People like the agent – especially men eighteen to thirty-five – and they like the setting. Women eighteen to thirty-five like the setting. Older women twenty-five to fifty want more of an emotional story.'

'What about teens and tweens?'

'Not much support with the tweens. A little stronger with the teens. "Too much blah blah" is a typical teen comment from the questionnaires.'

'Okay. Bright spots?'

'Strongly favorable characters – the agent, the various friends – and real eighteen to thirty-five support for the tone and the milieu.'

'Okay. Good. Down sides?'

'Pretty much across the board they don't like the main guy. Teens found him "snotty and uptight." Women eighteen to thirty-five found him unappealing physically and emotionally. Women twenty-five to fifty felt that he needed to grow up. "This guy needs to get slapped" is a typical comment. Men across the board felt he was a complaining candy ass.'

'Okay. Not bad.'

'No, not bad at all. I think you've got yourself a hit. If you lose the guy.'

'Right. Lose the guy.'

'Lose the guy. Everybody wants you to lose the guy.'

'Trouble is, it's about him. I mean, he wrote it.'

'So? That doesn't mean you can't dump him.'

'I know.'

'I'm telling you, from these numbers, with him in it, you're dead. Lose him, and you've got a hit.'

'Okay. Okay. That's what I'll tell Delia.'

'Josh? Delia's on line one.'

'Hey! Great news . . . strongly positive. But they want us to lose the guy . . . right . . . just hate him . . . no, just him . . . that's what we're thinking . . . I mean, with him we're dead, without him . . . right . . . right . . . lose the guy, right . . . so do you want to call . . . or . . . yeah, if you think it should come from me . . . right . . . just lose the guy . . . right. Okay. Thanks, Delia. 'Bye.'

'How'd it go?'

'Great. I think she really trusts me with some of the big stuff.'

'So you get to call him and tell him that we're going forward with the project . . .'

'*Just not with him in it, yeah.*'

'*Is that going to be hard?*'

'*I don't think so. I'll just call him and tell him how the testing went. He'll figure it out.*'

'*So you're going to call him?*'

'*Yeah.*'

'*Do you have his home number?*'

'*Yeah.*'

'*So why aren't you calling him right now?*'

'*Because I think he's home right now. I'll call him later, when he's out.*'

ACKNOWLEDGEMENTS

Despite the message sent by the previous pages, I've been very lucky to have been represented by three smart, honest, terrific agents. The legendary Beth Uffner shaped and guided the first part of my career, and she was followed by Ted Chervin, one of the smartest agents ever, and who remains a friend. My current agent, Brett Loncar, has drawn up a legal document that attests that he in no way resembles the agent in these books. I will sign the document, with one amendment: like the agent in this book, he always tells the truth and gives excellent advice.

I was doubly lucky to have found – well, she found me – a patient and tireless literary agent, Felicity Rubinstein. She still thinks I'm about to deliver a novel.

Most of these books appeared in various shapes in various publications, and honesty compels me to admit that some parts of this book appeared more than once. Some of it appeared in print, in print again, and *then* on the radio during my weekly commentary on KCRW, the popular Los Angeles public radio station. This is called "repurposing content," but it's really just another form of laziness and/or fraud. My thanks to all of them – especially to Toby Young, the impresario and editor of the late, great *Modern Review* – for allowing me to work out what therapists might call my *life issues* in their pages and on their airwaves. Plus, they gave me money for it. Not great money, but still green and spendable.

The best years of my career were spent working with my writing partner, Dan Staley.

A NOTE ON THE AUTHOR

Rob Long is a writer and producer in Hollywood. He began his career writing on TV's long-running *Cheers*, and served as co-executive producer in its final season. He has co-written several feature film scripts, including *Just a Shot Away*, currently in pre-production with a France-based production company. He is a contributing editor of *National Review* and *Newsweek International*, and writes occasionally for the *Wall Street Journal*. His weekly radio commentary, 'Martini Shot', can be heard on Los Angeles-based public radio station KCRW, and on-line at kcrw.com. His recent book, *Conversations with My Agent*, chronicled his early career in television.

Rob Long graduated from Yale University in 1987, and spent two years at UCLA School of Film, Theater and Television, where he has also served as an Adjunct Professor of Screenwriting. He serves on the board of directors of My Friend's Place, an agency for homeless teens in Hollywood, and the American Cinema Foundation.

A NOTE ON THE TYPE

The text of this book is set in Linotype Sabon, named
after the type founder, Jacques Sabon. It was designed by
Jan Tschichold and jointly developed by Linotype, Mono-
type, and Stempel, in response to a need for a typeface to be
available in identical form for mechanical hot metal composition and hand composition using foundry type. Tschichold
based his design for Sabon roman on a font engraved by
Garamond, and Sabon italic on a font by Granjon.

It was first used in 1966 and has proved
an enduring modern classic.